# Socializing Identities through Speech Style

**SECOND LANGUAGE ACQUISITION**
**Series Editor:** Professor David Singleton, *Trinity College, Dublin, Ireland*

This series brings together titles dealing with a variety of aspects of language acquisition and processing in situations where a language or languages other than the native language is involved. Second language is thus interpreted in its broadest possible sense. The volumes included in the series all offer in their different ways, on the one hand, exposition and discussion of empirical findings and, on the other, some degree of theoretical reflection. In this latter connection, no particular theoretical stance is privileged in the series; nor is any relevant perspective – sociolinguistic, psycholinguistic, neurolinguistic, etc. – deemed out of place. The intended readership of the series includes final-year undergraduates working on second language acquisition projects, postgraduate students involved in second language acquisition research, and researchers and teachers in general whose interests include a second language acquisition component.

**Other Books in the Series**
Language Learners in Study Abroad Contexts
    *Margaret A. DuFon and Eton Churchill (eds)*
Motivation, Language Attitudes and Globalisation: A Hungarian Perspective
    *Zoltán Dörnyei, Kata Csizér and Nóra Németh*
Age and the Rate of Foreign Language Learning
    *Carmen Muñoz (ed.)*
Investigating Tasks in Formal Language Learning
    *María del Pilar García Mayo (ed.)*
Input for Instructed L2 Learners: The Relevance of Relevance
    *Anna Nizegorodcew*
Cross-linguistic Similarity in Foreign Language Learning
    *Håkan Ringbom*
Second Language Lexical Processes
    *Zsolt Lengyel and Judit Navracsics (eds)*
Third or Additional Language Acquisition
    *Gessica De Angelis*
Understanding Second Language Process
    *ZhaoHong Han (ed.)*
Japan's Built-in Lexicon of English-based Loanwords
    *Frank E. Daulton*
Vocabulary Learning Strategies and Foreign Language Acquisition
    *Višnja Pavičić Takač*
Foreign Language Input: Initial Processing
    *Rebekah Rast*
Morphosyntactic Issues in Second Language Acquisition
    *Danuta Gabryś-Barker(ed)*
Investigating Pragmatics in Foreign Language Learning, Teaching and Testing
    *Eva Alcón Soler and Alicia Martínez-Flor (eds)*
Language Learners with Special Needs: An International Perspective
    *Judit Kormos and Edit H. Kontra (eds)*
Language Learning Strategies in Independent Settings
    *Stella Hurd and Tim Lewis (eds)*

**For more details of these or any other of our publications, please contact:**
**Multilingual Matters, St Nicholas House, 31-34 High Street,**
**Bristol, BS1 2AW, England**
**http://www.multilingual-matters.com**

SECOND LANGUAGE ACQUISITION 32
*Series Editor*: David Singleton, *Trinity College, Dublin, Ireland*

# Socializing Identities through Speech Style

## Learners of Japanese as a Foreign Language

Haruko Minegishi Cook

**MULTILINGUAL MATTERS**
Bristol • Buffalo • Toronto

# For Ken

**Library of Congress Cataloging in Publication Data**
Cook, Haruko Minegishi.
Socializing Identities Through Speech Style:Learners of Japanese as a Foreign
Language/Haruko Minegishi Cook.
Second Language Acquisition: 32
Includes bibliographical references and indexes.
1. Japanese language–Social aspects. 2. Japanese language–Spoken Japanese. I. Title.
PL524.75.C65 2008
495.6'8007–dc22              2008012758

**British Library Cataloguing in Publication Data**
A catalogue entry for this book is available from the British Library.

ISBN-13: 978-1-84769-101-9 (hbk)
ISBN-13: 978-1-84769-100-2 (pbk)

**Multilingual Matters**
*UK*: St Nicholas House, 31-34 High Street, Bristol, BS1 2AW.
*USA*: UTP, 2250 Military Road, Tonawanda, NY 14150, USA.
*Canada*: UTP, 5201 Dufferin Street, North York, Ontario M3H 5T8, Canada.

The policy of Multilingual Matters/Channel View Publications is to use papers that
are natural, renewable and recyclable products, made from wood grown in
sustainable forests. In the manufacturing process of our books, and to further support
our policy, preference is given to printers that have FSC and PEFC Chain of Custody
certification. The FSC and/or PEFC logos will appear on those books where full
certification has been granted to the printer concerned.

Typeset by Datapage International Ltd.
Printed and bound in Great Britain by the Cromwell Press Ltd.

# Contents

Acknowledgements . . . . . . . . . . . . . . . . . . . . . . . . . . . . . .vii

1   Introduction: An Indexical Approach to Language and
    Language Socialization . . . . . . . . . . . . . . . . . . . . . . . . . . .1
        An Indexical Approach: Language as an Integral
        Part of the Social World . . . . . . . . . . . . . . . . . . . . . . . . . .2
        Language Socialization. . . . . . . . . . . . . . . . . . . . . . . . . . .3
        An Indexical Approach to the Japanese Addressee
        Honorific Form . . . . . . . . . . . . . . . . . . . . . . . . . 8
        Data and Methodology . . . . . . . . . . . . . . . . . . . . . . .9
        Plan of the Book. . . . . . . . . . . . . . . . . . . . . . . . .17

2   Social Meaning and Indexicality . . . . . . . . . . . . . . . . . . . .19
        Social Meaning. . . . . . . . . . . . . . . . . . . . . . . . . . .19
        Indexicality . . . . . . . . . . . . . . . . . . . . . . . . . .21
        The Creative Aspect of Indexicality . . . . . . . . . . . . . . . . .24
        Indexing Social Contexts: Linguistic Forms and
        Their Functions . . . . . . . . . . . . . . . . . . . . . . . . . . .26
        Linguistic Indexes of Affective and Epistemic Stances . . . . . . .29
        Markedness in Social Meaning. . . . . . . . . . . . . . . . . . . .32
        Conclusion. . . . . . . . . . . . . . . . . . . . . . . . . . . .33

3   Functions of the *Masu* Form . . . . . . . . . . . . . . . . . . . . . .35
        Previous Accounts of the *Masu* Form. . . . . . . . . . . . . . . . .35
        An Indexical Account of the *Masu* Form . . . . . . . . . . . . . . .45
        The Pattern of the *Masu* Form Usages in Japanese
        Family Conversation . . . . . . . . . . . . . . . . . . . . . . . . .49
        Normative Uses of the *Masu* Form in
        Family Conversation . . . . . . . . . . . . . . . . . . . . . . . . .62
        Conclusion. . . . . . . . . . . . . . . . . . . . . . . . . . . .64

4   Identity Construction Through Use of the *Masu* Form:
    JFL Learners and Host Families . . . . . . . . . . . . . . . . . . . . .66
        Previous Studies on JFL Learners' Acquisition
        of the *Masu* Form. . . . . . . . . . . . . . . . . . . . . . . . . .66
        Uses of the *Masu* Form in Dinnertime Talk:
        The Learners and the Host Families. . . . . . . . . . . . . . . . . .70

Indexing Social Identities Through the
Self-presentational Stance . . . . . . . . . . . . . . . . . . . . . . . . . . . . 76
Self-presentational Stance as an Individual Choice . . . . . . . . . 90
Direct Quotation: Voices of Society . . . . . . . . . . . . . . . . . . . . . 92
Conclusion . . . . . . . . . . . . . . . . . . . . . . . . . . . . . . . . . . . . . . 102

5   Marked and Unmarked Uses of the *Masu* Form
in the Homestay Context . . . . . . . . . . . . . . . . . . . . . . . . . . . . 107
*Masu* Form Uses that Index the *Soto* Context . . . . . . . . . . . . 108
Marked Uses of the *Masu* Form in the
Homestay Context . . . . . . . . . . . . . . . . . . . . . . . . . . . . . . . . 112
Socialization Effects on the Learners . . . . . . . . . . . . . . . . . . . 118
Variations of Interactional Styles Among
Host Families . . . . . . . . . . . . . . . . . . . . . . . . . . . . . . . . . . . . 123
Limits of Awareness of Speech Style . . . . . . . . . . . . . . . . . . . 142
Conclusion . . . . . . . . . . . . . . . . . . . . . . . . . . . . . . . . . . . . . . 145

6   Explicit Language Socialization: Socialization to
Use Polite Language . . . . . . . . . . . . . . . . . . . . . . . . . . . . . . . 150
Socialization to Speak in a Formal Setting . . . . . . . . . . . . . . . 151
Indexing the 'On-stage' Presentational Frame
Through the *Masu* Form . . . . . . . . . . . . . . . . . . . . . . . . . . . . 160
Explicit Accounts of Sociolinguistic Rules . . . . . . . . . . . . . . . 166
Conclusion . . . . . . . . . . . . . . . . . . . . . . . . . . . . . . . . . . . . . . 175

7   Implications of the Study for L2 Pragmatics
and Pedagogy . . . . . . . . . . . . . . . . . . . . . . . . . . . . . . . . . . . . 177
Contributions of Study Abroad Experiences to
Learners' Acquisition of Speech Styles . . . . . . . . . . . . . . . . . . 177
Descriptions of Speech Styles in Japanese
Language Textbooks . . . . . . . . . . . . . . . . . . . . . . . . . . . . . . . 185
An Indexical Approach to the Instruction
of the *Masu* Form . . . . . . . . . . . . . . . . . . . . . . . . . . . . . . . . . 192
The Importance of Analysis of Social Contexts . . . . . . . . . . . . 195
Conclusion . . . . . . . . . . . . . . . . . . . . . . . . . . . . . . . . . . . . . . 196

8   Conclusion . . . . . . . . . . . . . . . . . . . . . . . . . . . . . . . . . . . . . . 199
Summary of the Main Points . . . . . . . . . . . . . . . . . . . . . . . . . 199
Contributions of the Study and Directions
for Future Research . . . . . . . . . . . . . . . . . . . . . . . . . . . . . . . . 203

Appendix 1 . . . . . . . . . . . . . . . . . . . . . . . . . . . . . . . . . . . . . . . . . . 206
Appendix 2 . . . . . . . . . . . . . . . . . . . . . . . . . . . . . . . . . . . . . . . . . . 209
References . . . . . . . . . . . . . . . . . . . . . . . . . . . . . . . . . . . . . . . . . . 211
Index . . . . . . . . . . . . . . . . . . . . . . . . . . . . . . . . . . . . . . . . . . . . . . 224

# Acknowledgements

I am indebted to a number of people who have supported this work and assisted me in many ways. First, this book owes a great deal to the learners of Japanese and their Japanese host families who participated in my research project by video-recording their dinnertime conversations. Without their cooperation, this research would not have been possible. Furthermore, I am grateful for the help that the staff members of the Center for International Studies at Obirin University and those of the Center for International Education at Waseda University provided to me by finding learners of Japanese as well as Japanese host families for my research project. In particular, I would like to extend my special thanks to Michiko Otsuka of the Center for International Studies at Obirin University, who kindly assisted me by finding participants for my research project during her busy schedule. Unfortunately, she passed away in December 2007. I would like to express my deepest sympathy to her family. I also want to thank Michiko Sasaki, who initially introduced me to the Center for International Studies at Obirin University.

Furthermore, I would like to thank Takako Toth, Misato Sugawara and Rino Kawase, who spent many hours transcribing the recordings of the dinnertime conversation data, Hikari Nishida, who helped me compiling the index, and Yumiko Enyo, who helped by assessing the learners' oral proficiency level. My special thanks goes to Eton Churchill, who not only assisted me with the final preparation of the manuscript but also provided me with constructive comments on an earlier version of this manuscript.

Many other people contributed at different stages of my work. Amy Ohta inspired me to examine dinnertime conversations between JFL learners and their Japanese host families and discussed with me the initial idea of this book project. Gabriele Kasper gave me both academic and morale support. I would like to express my gratitude to her for her generous encouragement, in particular, at a time of difficulty I encountered while creating this book. I am also grateful for the insightful comments and criticisms many people gave me over the years on earlier versions of some chapters.

I would like to express my gratitude to David Singleton, the SLA series editor, and Marjukka Grover of Multilingual Matters for providing this opportunity to publish my research and for their speedy preparation of the manuscript.

The research reported in this book was supported by a University of Hawaii Japan Studies Endowment Special Project Award and a grant from the US Department of Education, which established the National Foreign Language Resource Center at the University of Hawaii at Manoa (CFDA 84.229, P229A020002). However, the contents do not necessarily represent the policy of the Department of Education, and one should not assume endorsement by the federal government.

# Chapter 1

# Introduction: An Indexical Approach to Language and Language Socialization

Taking an indexical approach, this book examines how learners of Japanese as a foreign language (henceforth JFL learners) and their host family members express their identities through uses of the so-called 'addressee honorific' *masu* form (verbal ending) during dinnertime conversation.[1] I define 'indexicality' as the function of language that points to an aspect of the social dimension in the immediate situation at hand. As the same linguistic form can be used in varied situations, an indexical approach takes the view that a linguistic form evokes multiple indexical (or social) meanings.[2] This book explores multiple social meanings of the *masu* form in Japanese.

This book differs from previous research on learners' acquisition of the honorifics in important ways. First, the focus of the book is not on the statistical analysis of learners' development of sociopragmatic competence (e.g. Rose & Ng Kwai-fun, 2001; Takahashi, 2001; Tateyama, 2001), but rather on ways in which the learners and their host family members use linguistic resources to construct their social identities in the daily routine of dinnertime talk. The pragmatic development of foreign language learners is intricately interwoven with their social identity in the target community (Kasper, 2001). In order to understand how foreign language learners acquire appropriate use of the *masu* form in interaction with host family members, 'it is critical to observe learners in social engagements and include the co-participants' situated actions in the analysis' (Kasper & Rose, 2002: 301). Secondly, this book questions the conventional and widely accepted meaning of the *masu* form as a marker of politeness or formality. It demonstrates that the *masu* form is not limited to politeness or formality but has multiple social meanings, and that these meanings are also fluid and context-dependent (cf. Cook, 1998). To approach the topic of how JFL learners are socialized to use the *masu* form, it is essential to analyze use of the form in interaction. This study examines use of the *masu* form under the assumption that it occurs in conversation among people in close relationships and plays an important role in socializing learners. Previous studies on JFL learners' pragmatic development assume that the *masu* form only occurs in talk with people in distant relationships (*soto* 'out-group/outside' context) and does not occur in conversation with people in close relationships (*uchi* 'in-group/inside' context). To date, studies that examine learners' use of the *masu* form in conversation with people in close relationships are scarce. Thirdly, this book is different from previous research on learners' acquisition of the *masu* form in that the data come from naturally occurring conversation outside of the classroom. Previous studies collected data from formal settings such as classroom interactions (Ishida, 2001) and interviews (Marriott, 1993, 1995). The significance of examining learners' use of the *masu* form in dinnertime talk with the host family is that this informal setting is paralleled by the context of family conversation in which L1 Japanese children first learn to use the *masu* form (Clancy, 1985; Cook, 1996a, 1997).

By going beyond the assumption that *masu* is uniquely a form related to honorifics, this book contributes to our knowledge of the nature of honorifics and their functions. This book draws on language socialization (Ochs, 1988, 1990, 1996; Ochs & Schieffelin, 1995; Schieffelin & Ochs, 1986, 1996) and a theory of indexicality (e.g. Hanks, 1990, 2000; Ochs, 1990; Silverstein, 1976), both of which are founded on the assumption that language is an integral part of the social world. This introduction briefly discusses the indexical approach and language socialization as they relate to the study of this book. It also summarizes the significance of an indexical approach in examining the so-called 'addressee honorific form' in Japanese.

## An Indexical Approach: Language as an Integral Part of the Social World

In an indexical approach, language is a socially organized phenomenon, and meaning is not a sole property of language but is situated and negotiated in social context (cf. Duranti & Goodwin, 1992; Gumperz & Levinson, 1996; Hanks, 1990, 2000). A linguistic form has the potential of taking on a variety of meanings. For example, the linguistic expression *here* points to a place closer to the speaker, which is the literal meaning of *here*. When this meaning is used in context, the indexical function of language can evoke multiple social meanings. If the speaker is standing by the table in the room *here* refers to the area where the table is located. If the speaker is standing by the door, *here* denotes the area where the door is located. If the speaker points to the window by her side and utters 'Here!', then this expression refers to the window. In each instance, the linguistic expression *here* indexes a different object in the immediate situation. This function of language has also been referred to as deictic function, and classic examples of deixis are person, place and time (cf. Levinson, 1983). The indexical function, however, is not limited to person, place or time deixis. For example, the utterance 'Can you hold this for me?' is usually understood as an indirect request in ordinary conversation, but may be understood in a clinical setting as a question asking the addressee's ability to use his or her arm (in particular, if the patient is asked this question by a nurse or a doctor). The fuzzy boundary between linguistic form and context indicates that all linguistic forms are potentially indexical, i.e. that the meaning of the linguistic form is relativized to social context.

The notion of 'context' needs some clarification. Duranti and Goodwin (1992: 3) define 'context' as 'a frame (Goffman, 1974) that surrounds the event being examined and provides resources for its appropriate interpretation'. The frame that surrounds the event is not merely the setting that statically surrounds an utterance but the social and psychological world in which the participants of a speech event interact at a given moment. In other words, context is comprised of the setting, participants, language ideology, activity type, the sequential organization of talk and the state of knowledge of the interlocutors in the social interaction. Throughout this book, the term 'context' is used in this sense. The complexity of context provides an ongoing interactive process. Within the social context, the participants act in habitual patterns including their ways of interpreting linguistic forms (cf. Hanks, 1996). Underspecified linguistic meaning is enriched by the interlocutors' habitual pattern of joint orientation to the linguistic form in the local context. Thus, although the ways in which interlocutors interpret verbal forms are not rule-governed, their joint achievement is based on habitual routine patterns. The interlocutors may deviate from the habitual routine. These deviations are not considered as violations of social rules but seen as a 'marked' pattern of behavior in contrast to the habitual or 'unmarked' pattern (Myers-Scotton, 1993).

The interdependency of language and social context set forth by an indexical perspective of language sees language as a tool to construct social situations (cf. Ochs, 1988). Just as we use various tools to create the physical environment, language is a tool available to us to express who we are, how we feel, what we know and what activity we are engaged in. In other words, we choose particular linguistic forms to accomplish the interactional goal at hand. Thus, more emphasis is placed on the 'agency' (cf. Duranti, 2006; Giddens, 1979) of the language user. I will return to the discussion of indexicality in Chapter 2.

## Language Socialization

From an indexical view of language, novices' acquisition of language is not simply seen as the development of grammatical competence (i.e. how novices acquire the tacit knowledge of abstract linguistic rules) but as a process of language socialization (i.e. the acquisition of linguistic and sociocultural knowledge in social context) (Ochs, 1988, 1990, 1996;

Ochs & Schieffelin, 1995; Schieffelin & Ochs, 1986, 1996). An indexical
approach entails that language acquisition is embedded in social context.
Ochs and Schieffelin (1995: 74) state, '...in every community, grammatical forms are inextricably tied to, and hence index, culturally organized
situations of use...' Thus, language socialization research contends that
acquiring language goes hand-in-hand with acquiring sociocultural
knowledge.

Language socialization draws on several research frameworks that
investigate the social organization of context. These research frameworks
include linguistic anthropology (e.g. Hymes, 1964), sociocultural theory
(Vygotsky, 1962, 1978; Leontyev, 1981a, 1981b) and the dialogic approach
to language (Bakhtin, 1981; Voloshinov, 1973[1929]), ethnomethodology
(e.g. Cicourel, 1973; Heritage, 1984), conversation analysis (e.g. Sacks
*et al.*, 1974; Schegloff, 1968), social psychology (e.g. Lave, 1988; Lave
& Wenger, 1991), semiotics (Silverstein, 1976) and social constructivism
(e.g. Bucholtz, 1999, Bucholtz & Hall, 2004; Holms & Myerhoff, 1999;
Rogoff, 1990). In this theoretical tradition, social context, including social
identities, are not given *a priori* but constructed in social interaction.
Human beings use language to build sociocultural worlds, and language
is an indexical tool to accomplish this end. Thus, language socialization
research considers language acquisition to be embedded in cultural
practice. It investigates how novices learn to become competent members
in a social group by participating in the daily routines. In this process,
novices are socialized through the use of language as well as socialized in
how to use language (Schieffelin & Ochs, 1986).

Language socialization can be either explicit or implicit. Explicit
socialization includes overt statements about social norms, values and
beliefs, as well as 'modeling', in which a member of the group models
linguistic expressions for a novice to repeat.[3] While explicit socialization
concerns the content of talk, implicit socialization can be achieved
through the use of grammatical structures such as Japanese sentence-
final particles (cf. Cook, 1990a) and interactional mechanisms such as
repairs (cf. He, 2004). Although explicit socialization is more salient,
implicit socialization is more pervasive. In Ochs' words (1990: 291), 'The
greatest part of sociocultural information is keyed *implicitly*, through
language use.' Implicit language socialization is a powerful socialization
process, in which indexicality creates a link between language and
sociocultural knowledge. While novices can resist the social norms
inherent in explicit socialization, it is not easy to reject the sociocultural
knowledge implicit in the use of grammatical structures or interactional
mechanisms.

Learning to understand the 'indexical potentials' of linguistic forms is
at the core of language socialization. Ochs states (1996: 414):

A novice's understanding of linguistic forms entails an understanding of their indexical potential (i.e. the situational constellations of by whom, for what, when, where and to what ends forms are conventionally employed) in co-ordination with co-occurring linguistic forms and other symbolic dimensions of the situation at hand.

Language socialization studies investigate how particular linguistic forms are used and interpreted in a local community, and how novices are guided by experts/members to learn the semiotic processes of indexes in the routine practices of everyday life.

Language socialization takes place not only during the early years of human life but also across our life spans (Schieffelin & Ochs, 1986). We experience language socialization in our daily routines, as well as when we acquire the communicative skills necessary for participating in a new social group or community. For example, to become a doctor, we need to learn how to speak and act as a doctor acts, and to become a lawyer, we need to learn how to speak and act as a lawyer acts. Obtaining a medical degree alone does not make one a doctor. A part of being a doctor is an appropriate display of the social identity of a doctor and ratified by patients, nurses, lab technicians and other doctors in social interaction.

## Identity in the language socialization paradigm

The notion of social identity is of relevance to the argument of this book, and can be defined as 'the linguistic construction' of group membership (Kroskrity, 2001: 106) within a particular context. As evidenced in the above example of the identity of a doctor, from the language socialization perspective, one's social identity is not *a priori* given but co-constructed in moment-by-moment social interaction by the use of particular languages or linguistic forms as resources. This does not mean that an individual does not have a social identity prior to interaction. For example, someone who has a medical degree is a medical doctor. Such an identity is referred to as a 'transportable identity' (Zimmerman, 1998). However, a medical doctor does not display this social identity all the time. In fact, he or she has multiple social identities, one of which is being a medical doctor. It is in interaction that he or she orients to a particular social identity. In this sense, identity is not treated as a static category but as a fluid and interactionally emerging process. The interlocutor's social identity may shift from turn to turn in order to achieve his or her interactional goals.

Language plays an important role in identity construction and some linguistic structures explicitly encode the speaker's identity. For example, the Japanese pronoun *boku*, meaning 'I', indexes that the identity of the speaker is a male. However, most linguistic structures do not directly index social identities. Ochs (1993: 289) states: 'the relation of language to social identity is not direct but rather *mediated* by the interlocutor's understandings of conventions for doing particular social acts and stances...' In other words, most identities do not have a one-to-one relationship with linguistic forms but are indirectly indexed by social acts and/or stances directly indexed by linguistic structures. A given linguistic form is mediated by the interlocutor's understanding of conventions and infers a certain social identity. For example, the identity of a teacher can be indirectly indexed by the speaker's use of a quiz question. The identity of a female in Japanese society may be indirectly indexed by soft-sounding sentence-final particles in Japanese. In Chapter 2, I will further discuss Ochs' two-step model of indexical relations, which concerns identity construction. In this book, the term 'identity' is used in the sense that it is constructed and continually emergent in moment-by-moment social interaction.

## L2 language socialization research

Language socialization research has largely focused on young children's first language socialization (cf. Ochs, 1988; Schieffelin, 1990; Schieffelin & Ochs, 1986). More recently scholars have expanded the scope of language socialization research to second language acquisition (SLA) (e.g. Bayley & Schecter, 2003; Watson-Gegeo, 2001; Watson-Gegeo & Nielsen, 2003; Zuengler & Cole, 2005). Assuming that language acquisition and acculturation are the same process, these scholars claim that L2 learners are novices in that they are in the process of acquiring a new language as well as relevant sociocultural knowledge. From the language socialization perspective, a second or foreign language is acquired as learners participate in daily routines with native speakers of the target language. Most L2 language socialization studies have examined educational settings, which include ESL classes (Duff, 2002; Duff & Early, 1999; Poole 1992), heritage language classes (He, 2000, 2003, 2004; Lo, 2004), foreign language classes (Ohta, 1999; Yoshimi, 1999) and study abroad contexts (DuFon & Churchill, 2006; Siegal, 1994, 1995, 1996). Only a few studies have investigated L2 socialization in the workplace (Duff *et al.*, 2000; Li, 2000). As L2 socialization research studies a wide range of educational institutions and workplaces, in which L2 learners of different age groups study or work with varied goals, the issues that L2 language socialization research deals with are much more complex. While L1 learners are young children expected to become competent members of the community in which they were born, L2 learners have a choice as to whether or not to become or act like a member of the community in which the target language is spoken. Thus, Zuengler and Cole (2005) raise a question concerning the basic tenets of

L1 language socialization, namely, the end point of language socialization and the categories of 'expert' and 'novice'. Zuengler and Cole state (2005: 314):

> ...we must question the assumption of a presumed end point of language socialization. An additional concern is the assumption of neatly-bounded categories of 'expert' and 'novice'.

The basic notions that have been assumed in L1 language socialization may not apply to L2 language socialization research.

The claim that L2 learners may not choose to be socialized into norms of the target language and culture is made mostly by studies that examine explicit socialization processes, in which the member/expert explicitly tells the novice sociocultural norms. As proposed by Ochs (1990), however, a powerful language socialization process is implicit socialization. By participating in routine activities conducted in the target language, learners acquire sociocultural information, which is implicitly encoded in linguistic structures or interactional mechanisms (He, 2000, 2003; Lo, 2004). Without access to conscious knowledge of the social meaning of a given linguistic structure or interactional mechanism, learners are not able to make a conscious choice to accept or reject the social identity indexed through the language in context. Thus, the end point of implicit language socialization for L2 learners cannot deviate much from the sociocultural norms of the target language.

Chapters 3, 4 and 5 of this book deal with a case of implicit language socialization, for there is a discrepancy between the host families' belief about the honorifics and their practice, and the host family members are not consciously aware of how they actually use the *masu* form. Therefore, they are not able to explicitly tell learners about their actual usages. Generally native speakers of Japanese believe that the *masu* form is not used in conversation among people in close relationships such as family members, and most Japanese language textbooks provide the same explanation about this form (see more discussion on this point in Chapter 7). This suggests that neither the Japanese host family members nor the learners are aware of the uses of the *masu* form in family conversation. In fact, none of the participants of this study indicated in a questionnaire that they were paying attention to the *masu* form in dinnertime conversation. Furthermore, as we shall see, for the most part, the *masu* form is not used in the prescribed fashion (i.e. as a marker of politeness or formality) in family conversation. Thus, as the nature of *masu* usages in this context is not overtly accessible to the participants, the *masu* form in this context serves as an ideal linguistic feature to study implicit language socialization.

## An Indexical Approach to the Japanese Addressee Honorific Form

This book describes how JFL learners and their host families express their identities during dinnertime conversation through style shifts as a linguistic resource. Style shifts between the addressee honorific *masu* form and its non-honorific counterpart, the plain form (e.g. *-ru* as in *taberu* 'to eat') are among the most salient features of Japanese that construct aspects of social context (e.g. social identity among others). A number of previous studies in Japanese linguistics and sociolinguistics analyzed the *masu* form from a structuralist perspective (e.g. Harada, 1976; Ide, 1982; Martin, 1964; Neustupny, 1978; Niyekawa, 1991). These studies, which largely proposed a one-to-one mapping between the linguistic form and an aspect of social context, present a somewhat static and deterministic view on the Japanese style shifts and honorific usages, for they do not always take the diversity of social contexts and participants into consideration. More recently, I have proposed (Cook, 1996a, 1997, 1998) that the *masu* form is an index that foregrounds the self-presentational stance of the speaker. As a result, use of the *masu* form evokes various social identities and activities in different social contexts. This proposal can account for its diverse uses in social interaction, which the previous accounts of the *masu* form as a politeness marker have failed to do. Several different social contexts such as family dinnertime conversation (Cook, 1996a, 1997), elementary school classrooms (Cook, 1996b, 1998), interviews and quarrels (Cook, 1998) and academic consultation sessions in universities (Cook, 2006a) have been investigated from the indexical perspective. These studies replace the received deterministic view and offer an account for the fluidity of social identities of the interactants.

The indexical approach, however, has not yet been adopted in studies of style shifts involving non-native speakers of Japanese. There have, however, been a few studies on the acquisition of the *masu* form by JFL learners in the classroom setting and in an interview situation (Cook, 2001, 2002a; Ishida, 2001; Marriott, 1993, 1995). Assuming that the *masu* form is a marker of formality or politeness, these studies investigated learners' uses of the *masu* form and concluded that it is extremely difficult for JFL learners to use the *masu* form appropriately. What is common among these studies is that they examined use of the *masu* form in formal social contexts (i.e. classrooms and interviews). The *masu* form is interpreted as a marker of politeness or formality as other aspects of the context index formality, and sustained displays of the self-presentational stance are expected. It is, however, important to investigate the *masu* form used in informal social contexts such as family conversation, because the ways in which the *masu* form is used in family conversation provide the basis from which other uses develop in social contexts outside the family. To date, however, how the *masu* form is used in homestay contexts has not been a focus of research. This is perhaps because in JFL classroom instruction the *masu* form is taught as a formal form, which is the explanation found in most Japanese textbooks (see Chapter 7), and the idea that the *masu* form occurs in informal family conversation has not been entertained by researchers.

In first language acquisition, family conversation is the locus of language socialization. Universally, in family conversation children first learn to speak their first language in a culturally appropriate manner. Similarly, for language learners in a study abroad context, interaction with the host family can be important to their linguistic and cultural development (Dewey, 2005). The inherently underspecified meaning of an index, with its broad range of social meaning, makes it difficult to teach in isolation; for example, through direct instruction in the foreign language classroom. Gumperz (1996: 329) asserts that indexes are learned only in natural settings:

> [Indexes] are acquired through primary socialization in family or friendship circles or intensive communicative co-operation in a finite range of institutionalized environments.

Adults are not experiencing their primary socialization when they learn a foreign language. However, the experience of staying and interacting with the host family in the country where the target language is spoken provides learners with an opportunity that somewhat resembles primary socialization. As Gumperz suggests, the best way to explore how learners are socialized to use indexes appropriately is to examine how they use indexes in interactions with native speakers of the target language. A few previous studies (Iino, 1996; Siegal, 1994) mention JFL learners' acquisition of the *masu* form in natural settings, but they do not focus on style shifts.

This book fills this gap and sheds new light on our understanding of the complex indexicality of the *masu* form and its acquisition during L2 language socialization.

## Data and Methodology

Sociolinguistic research concerning the complex indexicality of linguistic forms requires naturally occurring data that are rich in contextual information and a qualitative and microanalytic research method. Furthermore, to study learners' acquisition of indexes, it is important to include all the participants in the data, for the learner's competence is co-constructed with the participants in interaction (cf. Kasper & Rose, 2002). The present study uses as its main data dinnertime conversations between JFL learners and their Japanese host families. Family dinnertime conversation provides rich contextual information. Moreover, in many cultures, family dinnertime is one of the social contexts in which family members routinely gather together and spontaneously share their stories (Blum-Kulka, 1997; Heath, 1986; Ochs *et al.*, 1989, 1992).[4] It is bounded by the beginning and ending of the meal. Family dinners 'are an intergenerational, language rich activity type' (Blum-Kulka, 1997: 264) and are a locus for developing children's perspective-taking, metacognition, analytical/critical thinking and theory reconstruction (Ochs *et al.*, 1992). In many cultures, dinnertime conversation provides children with an opportunity to learn to express who they are, what they are doing, how they feel and how to talk in a culturally appropriate manner through 'guided participation' (Rogoff, 1990). Similarly, for foreign language learners, dinnertime conversation with the host family can be central to their development of the target language and of sociocultural knowledge through direct and indirect routine participation in talk (Knight & Schmidt-Rinehart, 2002).

Among the different activities learners engage in during their studying abroad experiences, dinnertime conversation with the host family is a significant experience for learners in terms of the length and intensity of interaction. Typically, in a year-long program, learners spend several hours a day speaking in Japanese with host family members for a period of eight or nine months. The literature on L2 pragmatics (Kasper & Rose, 2002; Klein *et al.*, 1995; Siegal, 1994) argues that it is not simply the learner's length of stay in the target community that promotes development of pragmatic ability. What matters most is 'the quality of nonnative speakers' exposure and social contacts' (Kasper & Rose, 2002: 196). Dinnertime conversation can provide learners with just such quality exposure and social contacts. The present data and those of other studies on study abroad programs (e.g. Cook, 2006a; DuFon, 2006; Iino, 1996, 2006; McMeekin, 2003, 2006; 2007) indicate that during dinnertime the learner is often the center of conversation and that topics revolve around the learner. McMeekin (2003), who compared negotiation strategies of JFL learners in two contexts – one in a Japanese language classroom and the other in conversation with the host family – demonstrates that in conversation with the host family, learners are given personal attention, and the topics of conversation concern the learners' personal life. In contrast, in the Japanese language classroom, the time each learner participates in talk is very limited.

A total of 25 dinnertime conversations (25 video- and 25 audio-taped simultaneously) of nine JFL learners and their Japanese host families were collected and transcribed. The transcribed data were analyzed qualitatively. In addition, two separate questionnaires – one for the JFL learners and the other for the host families – were distributed to the participants for supplementary data. The questionnaire for the JFL learners was written in English, and the one for the host family was written in Japanese. In all host families, the host mother filled out the questionnaire while the learners themselves completed theirs.[5]

## Participants

### The JFL learners

The nine learners consisted of four females and five males. Their Japanese proficiency level ranged from novice to advanced along the Oral Proficiency Interview (OPI) scale.[6] As the nature of the study is ethnographic, measuring the development of each learner's Japanese proficiency level is not an essential component of the study. The Japanese proficiency levels given in Table 1.1 are assessments made by a trained

**Table 1.1** JFL learners

| Name | Japanese proficiency level (OPI scale) | Japanese language learning experiences prior to arriving in Japan | Length of stay in Japan with the current host family |
|---|---|---|---|
| Alice | Novice | 2 years in university | 4 months |
| Tom | Novice | 5 semesters in university | 4 months |
| Kate | Novice/high | 2 years in university | 8 months |
| Rick | Intermediate/low | 3 years in university | 4 months |
| Greg | Intermediate | 4 years in university | 4 months |
| Skip | Advanced/low | 2 years in university | 9 months (stayed in Japan before for 2 months) |
| Pete | Advanced | 2 and a half years in university | 3 months (stayed in Japan before for 6 months) |
| Mary | Advanced | 1 year in university, mother is native speaker of Japanese | 12 months |
| Ellen | Advanced | 6 years in high school, 2 years in university, mother is native speaker of Japanese | 8 months (stayed in Japan before for 3 years) |

All the learners' names are pseudonyms.

OPI examiner based on the dinnertime conversational data. All learners are native speakers of English. Alice, Kate and Mary are British, and the rest are American. The learners are all college students who studied JFL at a university in their home country for two to four years prior to going to Japan. Both Mary and Ellen have a mother who is a native speaker of Japanese. They did not speak Japanese in the home as children but heard their mothers speak Japanese at times. Besides having a native speaker mother, Ellen also studied Japanese for six years in high school. She lived in Japan for three years between the ages of six and nine. The learners are all enrolled in a year-in-Japan program studying the Japanese language as well as subjects related to Japan in Japanese universities in the Tokyo area. During their stay in Japan, which is typically about nine months, they live with a Japanese host family. At the time of the data collection, Mary had lived in Japan with the host family for 12 months, Skip, for nine months, and Ellen and Kate, for eight months. Skip had previously stayed in Japan for two months during the summer. Pete had studied Japanese in Akita Prefecture (northern part of Honshu) for six months prior to this study abroad experience in the Tokyo area. The rest of the learners had lived in Japan with their host family for four months at the time of the data collection.

Table 1.2 shows the learners' reasons for studying Japanese in Japan. As shown in Table 1.2, the JFL learners' reasons for studying Japanese were mostly integrative (i.e. a general interest in Japanese culture). For most of the learners, the reason for participating in a year-long study abroad program was that they thought that the best way to learn Japanese is to study it where it is spoken. In the case of Kate and Mary, a year of study abroad is required for their degree program in their universities in England. Skip's participation in a six-week summer study program in Japan made him want to participate in a long-term program in Japan.

*The host families*

The host families are typical middle-class Japanese families in the Tokyo area, and they consist of speakers of Tokyo standard Japanese with one exception.[7] Table 1.3 shows who in each host family participated in the dinnertime talk with the learner.

In all segments of the dinnertime conversation data, the learner and the host mother are always present. Other participants in dinnertime conversation include the host father, host siblings and/or the host grandmother. Not all the host fathers participated in the dinners because of their work schedule. The host siblings were college-age or older except for Alice's host family, which had three small children. In two dinnertime conversations, guests were invited to the dinner. In one of the dinner conversations in Rick's host family, the host brother's college friend was

**Table 1.2** JFL learners' reasons for studying Japanese in Japan

| *Name* | *Reasons for studying Japanese* | *Reasons for studying in Japan* |
|---|---|---|
| Alice | Unknown | Unknown |
| Tom | Interests in Japanese culture, media, and business | To improve Japanese language skills |
| Kate | Interests in Japanese culture | As part of her degree course |
| Rick | Studied Japanese in high school and has become very interested in Japanese | Japan is the best place to study Japanese and learn about its patterns of life |
| Greg | General interests in languages as well as interests in Japanese video-games and animation | Japan is the best place to study Japanese |
| Skip | Interests in East Asian culture and ways of thinking | Six-week summer trip to Osaka during his sophomore year made him want to participate in a year-in-Japan program |
| Pete | To communicate in Japanese on a personal level | Immersion is the best possible way to acquire a higher level of proficiency |
| Mary | To improve communication with Japanese relatives | As part of her degree course |
| Ellen | To improve communication with Japanese relatives and to master a second language | To better her Japanese language ability and broaden her field of vision |

invited, and in one of the dinnertime conversations in Mary's host family, two of Mary's classmates from her university (American and Irish friends) were invited. Because outsiders are included in these conversations, they do not represent typical family conversations. When a guest is invited to the family, the frequency of the host family members' *masu* form often increases. For this reason, these segments were excluded from the calculation of frequency counts of the *masu* form. In all the host families, the host mother is the central figure. She talks most with the learner and takes care of him or her.

All but Kate's host family had had experience hosting foreign students in the past. The host families' reason for hosting a foreign student was mostly an interest in foreign culture. Skip and Mary's families volunteered to be host families because they wanted to reciprocate the

**Table 1.3** Host families

| Host family | Members who participated in dinnertime talk | Reason for hosting a learner |
|---|---|---|
| Alice's family | Host mother<br>Host brothers (ages 10 and 7)<br>Host sister (age 5) | Interest in foreign culture<br>Want foreigners to<br>understand Japan |
| Tom's family | Host mother and father<br>Host sister (age 19) | Interest in international<br>exchange |
| Kate' family | Host mother<br>Host brother (college age) | Both daughter and son lived<br>in a foreign country and<br>stayed with a host family. |
| Rick's family | Host mother and father<br>Host brother (age 24)<br>Host sister (age 30) | To get to know a foreigner<br>Good for the family members |
| Greg's family | Host mother | Desire to learn about foreign<br>culture |
| Skip's family | Host mother<br>Host sister (college age) | The daughter lived in a<br>foreign country and stayed<br>with a host family. |
| Pete's family | Host mother and father<br>Host grandmother | (does not state the reason) |
| Mary's family | Host mother and father<br>Host brother (college age) | The daughter lived in a<br>foreign country and stayed<br>with a host family. |
| Ellen's family | Host mother and father | The daughter wants to learn<br>English. |

kindness their daughters had received from their American host families when they studied in the USA. The host families spent about 1–3 hours at home with the learners on a daily basis. All but Tom's host family said in the questionnaire that the learners and the host family members spoke with each other in Japanese more than 90% of the time. Only Tom's host family reported that they spoke in Japanese with Tom more than two-thirds of the time, whereas about one-third of the time they spoke in English. The learners' reports concerning the percentage of time spent using the Japanese language with the host family are consistent with those of the host families, except for the reports given by Kate and Skip. Although Kate's and Skip's host families reported that they spoke in Japanese more than 90% of the time, Kate stated that she spoke in

Japanese with her host mother 100% but with her host brother only 50% of the time. Skip stated that he spoke in Japanese with his host family 80% of the time and in English 20% of the time. The recorded dinnertime conversation data that I collected indicate that the participants' reports more or less reflect their actual practice. For the most part, the dinnertime conversations in the data were carried out in Japanese. Only Tom and his host family once in a while switched to English, as his host father seemed to want to use English. For the most part, codeswitching to English is rare in the present data. The learners ate dinner with their host family members 3–6 times a week and talked, among other topics, about Japanese culture, cooking, their college life and current events.

## Data collection and analysis

In order to record the conversations, the researcher asked the learners to place a video camera on a tripod and a small audio-cassette recorder on the dinner table. Dinnertime conversations were recorded three times (three different evenings) by each learner with one exception. Skip recorded the conversation only once for 90 minutes. All recordings were made at the host family's house within a month. The learners and host families were asked to turn off the TV during dinner.[8] The length of each dinnertime conversation ranged from 30 to 90 minutes, averaging 52 minutes. The researcher was not present at the dinner in order to keep the conversation as natural as possible. After the recordings, to gather more information about the backgrounds of the learners and their host families, separate questionnaires were given to the learners and their host families.[9] The questionnaires are provided in Appendices 1 and 2. To ensure that the learners and host family members did not pay special attention to style shifts while the dinnertime conversations were recorded, I did not include questions specifically on speech styles in the questionnaire. The entire corpus was transcribed first by three trained assistants who were native speakers of Japanese and then checked by the researcher.

As the Japanese language is an agglutinative language, word boundaries are not always clear. Therefore, at times it is not easy to distinguish what is and what is not a word. However, for word frequency counts, it is necessary to use a systematic way to segment words. For this purpose, the data were transcribed according to the CHAT *wakachigaki* (word segmentation) system proposed for CHILD (MacWhinney & Oshima-Takane, 1998).

In order to compare the frequencies of the *masu* form use between the host families and the JFL learners, the utterances of the families and those of the learners were separated and the frequencies of the *masu* form were calculated for each group. The number of the *masu* forms was divided by the total number of words spoken in the corpus for each, which was then multiplied by 2000. This yielded a frequency index per 2000 words for both the host families and JFL learners.

The *masu* forms in the corpus were identified and then each token was categorized according to the three major functions that were found in native speakers' data (see Chapter 3). They are the *masu* form in (1) fixed phrases, (2) displays of authority, responsibility or being in charge and (3) speaking in another's voice. These three functions are the major functions of the *masu* form in dinnertime talk in Japanese native speaker families. To see to what extent JFL learners and their host families conformed to the native speaker norms, these three categories were used to tabulate the tokens of the *masu* form used by the learners and their host families.

The transcription conventions used in this study are adapted from conversation analysis (Sacks *et al.*, 1974) with a few modifications. To clearly indicate the *masu* and plain forms in the excerpts, the *masu* form is in bold, and the plain form is underlined.

Transcription conventions:

| | |
|---|---|
| [ | overlapped speech |
| = | latching |
| (0.5) | the number indicates the length of a pause in seconds |
| (.) | unmeasured micropause |
| ( ) | unclear utterance |
| (( )) | commentary |
| :: | sound stretch |
| WORD | loudness |
| ° ° | portions which are delivered in a quieter voice |
| - | cut-off |
| ? | rising intonation |
| . | falling intonation (full stop) |
| @word@ | word said with laughter |
| **kimasu** | the *masu* form |
| <u>kuru</u> | the plain form |

Abbreviations used in word-for-word translations:

| | |
|---|---|
| Cop | various forms of copula verb *be* |
| Lk | linking nominal |
| Neg | negative morpheme |
| Nom | nominalizer |
| O | object marker |
| S | subject marker |

Q        question marker
QT       quotative marker
FP       sentence-final particle
Top      topic marker

In Japanese, there are a large number of English loan words (*gairaigo*), which are assimilated into the Japanese phonological system. In transcribing loan words or English words mixed in a Japanese text, if they are pronounced according to Japanese phonology they are transcribed in *Romaji* reflecting the *katakana* spelling; whereas if they are pronounced according to English phonology, the English spelling is used. For example, if the English word *vitamin* is pronounced [váitəmin], it is spelled /vitamin/ but if it is pronounced [bitamin], it is spelled /bitamin/, reflecting the lack of the /v/ phoneme in Japanese phonology of the English loan word.

## Plan of the Book

This chapter has outlined the theoretical framework in which this book is couched. In the indexical approach, language and context are interdependent, and any linguistic form is potentially indexical. Chapter 2 expands the discussion on indexicality to explore the nature of the context dependency of language. It discusses how social meaning arises and creates a social world. It also introduces Ochs' two-step model of indexical relations, which is central to the analysis of the present study. Before examining style shifts of JFL learners and their host families, Chapter 3 discusses native speakers' norms of the style shift pattern in Japanese family conversation. It first reviews the literature on the *masu* and plain forms and then illustrates from the indexical perspective how Japanese families use the *masu* form in family dinnertime conversation. This chapter argues that the *masu* form is a direct index of the self-presentational stance (i.e. stance of presenting oneself to other(s) when one is literally or figuratively 'on stage' and being watched by others), which further indexes various social identities in social context. Chapters 4, 5 and 6 explore the uses of the *masu* form in the homestay context. Chapters 4 and 5 discuss implicit socialization through use of the *masu* form. Chapter 4 examines how both host family members and learners use the *masu* form to index different social identities. It shows that the host families use the *masu* form in a manner similar to that of the Japanese families discussed in Chapter 3, and that the learners are socialized into the new domain of knowledge about appropriate display of the self-presentational stance. Chapter 5 looks at cases of the *masu* form that are deviant from those of native speakers' usages in the informal context (i.e. 'marked' uses (Myers-Scotton, 1993)) and investigates why the marked uses occur in the homestay context. Chapter 6 examines explicit language socialization through the *masu* form. It illustrates how host family members teach learners polite expressions. Chapter 7 provides implications for L2 pragmatics and pedagogy. This chapter discusses the supportive evidence this study provides for the impact of study abroad experiences on the development of L2 pragmatics. It also compares descriptions found in Japanese language textbooks widely used in the USA and other English-speaking countries and the attested usages of the *masu* form. The chapter also urges researchers and instructors to examine the use of the *masu* and plain forms in diverse social contexts. Chapter 8 concludes the book by summarizing the main points of the book.

## Notes

1.  The analysis of the *masu* form presented in this book reveals that the functions of the *masu* form are not limited to that of 'addressee honorific'.
2.  The terms 'indexical meaning' and 'social meaning' are used interchangeably in this book.
3.  'Modeling' is also known as 'elicited imitation routines' (Ochs, 1990) or as 'prompting' (Demuth, 1986).
4.  In recent years, a growing number of families eat their dinner in silence in front of the TV, or members of a family eat their dinner separately at different times.
5.  As the questionnaire was filled out by the host mother, the responses possibly represent the host mother's view rather than that of all members of the host family.
6.  Yumiko Enyo, who was trained to be an OPI evaluator, assisted me in evaluating the JFL learners' Japanese proficiency level by listening to the recorded dinnertime conversations with their host family members.
7.  Pete's host father is a speaker of the Osaka dialect.
8.  Although the learners and the host families were asked to turn off the TV during the dinner, a few host families did not turn off the TV.
9.  Due to a logistic problem, sometimes the learners and host families were given the questionnaire before they started recording the dinnertime conversations. Filling out the questionnaire before recording the dinnertime conversation may have made the participants behave more carefully while recording than they would otherwise. The questionnaires I provided to the host families and learners, however, did not include questions that directly address the issue of style shift, so any bias caused by filling out the questionnaire first should be minimal.

# Chapter 2
# *Social Meaning and Indexicality*

## Social Meaning

Language is used in time and space. When a sentence is produced in time and space, it evokes a meaning different from that produced in isolation. I will use the term utterance to refer to a sentence in context. The meaning of an utterance may vary depending upon the interactional context in which the utterance occurs, and which it creates at the same time. I refer to such a meaning as social meaning.[1] The use and non-use of honorifics illustrates the nature of social meaning. The Japanese equivalent of the English expression 'Congratulations!' can be uttered with or without the honorific form *goza-imasu* ('to exist') as in *omedetoo gozai-masu* ('congratulation + exist (polite) + masu') or *omedetoo* ('congratulation'). The utterance *omedetoo* ('congratulation') without the honorific form *gozai-masu* can be interpreted as lacking politeness toward the addressee and thus may offend the addressee, if, for example, *omedetoo* ('congratulation') is uttered by a lower status person to a higher status person in a formal setting. Although the propositional content of the utterance expresses congratulations, at another level of meaning, i.e. at the level of social meaning, this utterance may evoke negative affect. Or, consider the utterance, 'She is a great teacher'. This utterance may indicate various social meanings such as the speaker's genuine admiration for the teacher or a sarcastic attitude toward the teacher if it is uttered with a certain tone of voice. If this utterance is produced slowly and loudly, the speaker may be talking to a foreigner (foreigner talk). Intonation patterns may also affect the social meaning of an utterance (Gumperz, 1986).

The social meaning of an utterance may depend on the place an utterance occupies in a conversational sequence (Duranti & Goodwin, 1992; Heritage, 1984; Levinson, 1983; Sacks *et al.*, 1974, 1977). Heritage (1984: 242) writes, 'A speaker's action is context-shaped in that its contribution to an on-going sequence of actions cannot adequately be understood except by reference to the context – including, especially, the immediately preceding configuration of actions – in which it participates.' If the utterance, 'She is a great teacher' occurs following a statement such as 'Next semester I will take a course from Prof. Smith', then the utterance can be interpreted as an encouragement to take the course from Prof. Smith. On the other hand, if this utterance is made following the statement, 'I did not learn anything from Prof. Smith all semester', then the utterance can be interpreted as a complaint from a student. If the addressee knows that the speaker hates Prof. Smith, then this utterance may be interpreted as sarcasm. Social meanings are culturally organized, and speakers from different cultural backgrounds can assign different meanings to the same structure. For example, when a guest is asked by a host(ess), 'How about some coffee?', the guest's answer 'No, thank you' is usually interpreted literally in mainstream American society. In contrast, in Japanese society, 'No, thank you' in such a context is understood as a sign of *enryo* 'rejection of an offer out of politeness'. As a result, the host(ess) gives the guest a cup of coffee anyway. Gumperz (1982) calls misunderstanding between the speaker and the addressee due to different interpretation conventions 'cross talk'. Novices, including both young children and foreign language learners, typically do not frame situations in the same way as adult members, and socialization can be seen as a process of learning conceptual organizations. However, in some instances the adult members may also change their conceptual organization through interactions with a novice. Furthermore, all members of a society do not necessarily share exactly the same conceptual organizations (Ochs & Schieffelin, 1984). These differences bring about ambiguity in interpretation and the participants thus negotiate and clarify social meanings. In this view, culture is an interactive process. Such a process contributes to interpreting a given utterance in a particular context.

Research on social meanings has been carried out within various frameworks. Bateson (1972) and Goffman (1974) introduce the terms frame and key. A frame is a scheme of interpretation. It renders 'what would otherwise be a meaningless aspect of the scene into something that is meaningful' (Goffman, 1974: 21). In other words, without a frame, it is not possible to understand what is going on around us. Without knowing what activity is taking place, it is difficult to make sense of an utterance. Goffman (1974: 43) defines key as 'the set of conventions by which a given activity ... is transformed into something patterned on this activity but seen by the participants to be something quite else.' In other words, a key is a sign that signals how an utterance is to be interpreted in speech context. The speaker's tone of voice and/or intonation can serve as a key which signals whether or not the utterance is sarcastic. For example, the utterance, 'She is a great teacher' can index sarcasm if it is said in a certain tone of voice or intonation. Hymes (1974) also proposes a similar notion of key and Gumperz (1982) uses the term contextualization cue.

The Russian literary critic and philosopher Bakhtin (1981), who also writes under the name of Voloshinov (1973 [1929]), contributes to our understanding of social meanings. He emphasizes that linguistic structures isolated from their context are meaningless and that they merely have the potential of having meaning. Bakhtin (1981) describes the context dependency of an utterance in terms of the notion of voice.[2] According to him, an utterance made in a given situation embodies the speaker/writer's voice, the voice of the addressee, a third party and/or society. These voices contribute to the social meaning of an utterance. The classic example of voice is the case of reported speech. When the speakers/writers report the speech of another, they assume at least three voices in their utterances, namely their own voice, the voice of the addressee and that of the quoted party. Many languages encode a distinction between direct and indirect quotations. In a direct quotation, the voices of the speaker and the quoted party are kept separate from each other ('linear style' (Volosinov, 1978 [1929])). In an indirect quotation, the voices of the speaker and the quoted party are merged ('pictorial style' (Volosinov, 1978 [1929])). The speaker's voice represents his/her own voice as well as that of the quoted party.

The use of voice is not limited to reported speech. We speak in a particular voice from moment to moment in our daily life. Often we hear an expression such as 'as the President of the United States' or 'as a teacher, I cannot say that'. In our daily life, in moment-to-moment interaction, we assume various social identities, i.e. we speak in different voices. Sometimes our opinion is split between different social identities (voices) we assume (e.g. 'As a friend I say that if you like smoking, you might as well enjoy it, but as a doctor I advise you to stop smoking'). In such cases, we speak with the voice of a friend and with the voice of a doctor. The voices of social identities presuppose cultural beliefs, knowledge and expectations in society. In Bakhtin's terms such pre-suppositions constitute the 'social history' of utterances (Bakhtin, 1981). The present book draws upon the notion of 'voice', in particular to account for the meaning of the *masu* form.

## Indexicality

Indexicality is a phenomenon associated with the situatedness of human experience in the creation of meaning. As noted at the beginning of this chapter, we live in time and space and interpret what is going on around us within this frame of time and space. For example, when we see dark clouds over the horizon, we link them to approaching rain, and when we hear a knock on the door, we associate it with someone seeking entry to the room. Indexicality is the function of relating an index to contextual dimensions. We have expectations as to how things are constructed in the physical and temporal world, which helps us associate one sign to an aspect of the context in which we operate. An index is dark clouds in the first case and knocking on the door in the second, which points to the presence of some entity in the context.

Peirce (1955) initially introduced a tricotomy of signs. The three types of signs forming the tricotomy are icons, symbols and indexes. Each of these has a specific semiotic function in language. Icons are signs that are related to the things they stand for by virtue of some direct resemblance. For example, onomatopoeic words are icons. Symbols are signs that are related to the things they stand for by arbitrary relationships agreed upon by those who use them. Symbolic meanings are referred to as referential, descriptive, prepositional or ideational meanings in the linguistic literature. Indexes are signs which are related to the things they stand for because they participate in or are actually part of the event they stand for. Of these signs types, indexes are unique in that they can only be interpreted within an actual context of use while icons and symbols do not need a context of use to be interpreted.

In order to understand linguistic forms as indexes, we need to take the perspective that linguistics forms are tools for interacting with the world (Brown & Levinson, 1978, 1987; Leontyev, 1981a; Vygotsky, 1978). Brown and Levinson (1978: 286) state:

> The social value of the linguistic form of messages can only be ascertained by looking at such forms as tools for doing things, and asking what kinds of things a given form could be doing.

In this view, just as we use an airplane to travel quickly to a faraway destination or use a computer to write an article and send it in a second to the other side of the globe, we use particular linguistic forms to attain a goal. For example, in order to get some help, one uses a polite linguistic form as a tool to make a request (Brown & Levinson, 1978, 1987). Language is a means to create, maintain and change our social world. It is the indexical function of linguistic forms that accomplishes this task.

Classic examples of linguistic indexes are person, space and time deixis (Fillmore, 1971, 1975, 1998; Levinson, 1983; Lyons, 1977). Deictic expressions rely on context for their interpretation. Overwhelmingly, the perspective taken in terms of spatial–temporal location of the speech event is egocentric, i.e. the deictic center is generally the speaker's ego (Hanks, 1992).[3] In other words, these features normally mark the speaker's point of view. Thus, the central person is the speaker; the central place is the location at which the speaker makes an utterance; the central time is the time when an utterance is made by the speaker. Person deixis encodes the role of the participants in the speech event. Pronouns in English are examples of person deixis. For example, the feature *I* indexes the current speaker in the speech event and *you*, the current addressee. *They* indexes the third persons or entities which are neither the current speaker nor the addressee. Place deixis encodes spatial locations relative to the location of the participants in the speech event. This category includes many locative adverbial expressions, demonstratives, definite articles, verbs of motion, etc. Time deixis encodes temporal points and spans of time relative to the time when the utterance is made. Typically, time deixis is found in temporal adverbial phrases (except for calendar-time and clock-time phrases) and in the tense system. Utterances involving time deixis are not clear unless we know when they are uttered. For example, the specific time denoted by the word *yesterday* is only specified by the date of the utterance of this word. Similarly, the past, present or future tense is determined by the time of an utterance. For instance, the past tense of the verb 'to write' in the utterance, 'He wrote a book' denotes that the writing was done prior to the time of this utterance. The meaning of a deictic feature shifts as the contexts shifts. Thus, deictic features are sometimes also called 'shifters' (Silverstein, 1976). For example, the identity of the person referred to by the English pronoun *I* changes as the speaker changes. The linguistic structure, the pronoun *I* in this case, only specifies the meaning 'the current speaker', and the identity of the current speaker changes from moment to moment in the speech context. Thus it is interpretable only if the participants of the speech event know the spatial location of the current speaker or the location pointed to by the current speaker (i.e. 'indexical ground of reference', Hanks, 1990, 1992). The spatial dexis *here*, for example, may not be meaningful if the addressee(s) neither see the location pointed by the speaker nor do they know exactly where the speaker is located. In Hanks' words (1992: 61), '...deixis is a framework for organizing the actor's access to the context of speech at the moment of utterance.'

Indexes are not limited to deictic words. From the point of view of language as action (Austin, 1962), all linguistic structures can function as indexes. As demonstrated by research on pragmatics, sociolinguistics, linguistic anthropology, ethnomethodology and conversational analysis, linguistic forms are constantly interpreted in social context. For example, Garfinkel (1972: 306) notes, '...ways of speaking are essentially indexical (like pronouns), in the sense that part of their meaning and intelligibility always will lie in the situation...'.

Silverstein (1976) expands the notion of index and introduces two categories: referential indexes and non-referential indexes. Referential indexes (e.g. deictic features such as personal pronouns, demonstratives and temporal expressions) do not have any abstract propositional meaning because their references are only in the speech context. Once the reference is picked out, the referential index contributes to the referential meaning of a sentence. On the other hand, non-referential indexes do not contribute to referential meanings but only signal the speech context. Prosody, rhythm and tempo, and shifts in pitch register and selection of a linguistic code, all of which Gumperz refers to as contextualization cues, are typical examples of non-referential indexes.

Furthermore, non-referential indexes include honorifics and pragmatic particles.

## The Creative Aspect of Indexicality

According to Gumperz, contextualization cues provide a framework for interpretation. Some scholars further claim that indexes not only provide an interpretation framework but also have creative power as they are signs which evoke or point to some aspect of context. That aspect becomes the relevant context in the current speech situation. Lyons (1977: 106) defines indexicality as 'some known or assumed connexion between a sign A and its significatum C such that the occurrence of A can be held to imply the presence or existence of C'. In other words, the aspect of the context which is pointed to by an index may have been created itself in the context. Silverstein (1976: 34) further develops this idea and presents a case for the creative power of indexes:

> In some instances, the occurrence of the speech signal is the only overt sign of the contextual parameter, verifiable, perhaps, by other co-occurring behavior in other media, but nevertheless the most salient index of the specific value. Under these circumstances, the indexical token in speech performs its greatest apparent work, seeming to be the very medium through which *the relevant aspect of the context is made to 'exist'* ... (emphasis added by author)

A similar position is expressed by the Soviet sociohistorical school. Lucid (1977: 20) summarizes the sociohistorical position on the creative power of language in his volume on 'Soviet' semiotics:

> Sign systems regulate human behavior, beginning with the instruction given children and continuing through all the programs introduced into the individual by society. A sign system possesses the capacity literally to mold or 'model' the world in its own image, shaping the minds of society's members to fit its structure. *Signs not only passively mirror reality but also actively transform it.* (emphasis added by author)

The tool-like function of language is efficiently achieved by indexes. Fillmore (1975: 76) states that social deixis includes 'the various devices that a language provides for a speaker to be able to establish and maintain a deictic anchoring with a given addressee.' For example, in English, names and titles typically establish social relationships. If a speaker calls an addressee Professor Smith, and the addressee in turn calls the speaker John, the relationship between the two people may be the asymmetrical relationship between a professor and a student. In many languages pronouns establish certain social worlds. For example, a Japanese speaker using the formal first person pronoun *watakushi* ('I') indicates that the speech event is a formal one. When she switches to another first person pronoun *atashi* ('I, female') she indicates that the speech event is informal. Ochs (1988) mentions that the Samoan first person sympathy pronoun *ita* ('poor me') indexes that the speaker is begging. This pronoun helps to establish a different social context from that of the neutral first person pronoun. The tool-like quality is also found in many other linguistic features. For example, as we discussed above, the participants in social events use various voices in their interactions. They may quote a third party's speech, mimic someone else, speak as a teacher, a mother, a friend, etc. These voices again are indexed by linguistic features. Reported speech can be indexed by grammatical markers of indirect speech; for example, mimicking someone can be signaled by a certain voice quality; speaking while assuming a certain social role may be indexed by lexicon and register (e.g. teacher talk). The indexical function of language, thus, establishes social relationships from moment to moment. The way in which these linguistic features establish particular social and psychological realities is similar to the way in which other non-linguistic features in context establish such realities. For example, a particular kind of clothes indicates and helps to define the nature of a social event (e.g. a business meeting, sports event or wedding). Or a particular arrangement of a room helps to define the nature of a social event (e.g. a class, conference, dinner or business meeting). Linguistic indexical signs, in this sense, form part of a larger semiotic system.

Drawing on Bourdieu's (1977) practice theory and Gidden's (1979) theory of structuration, which view social structure as both the medium and outcome of re-productions of practice, this book argues that linguistic structure and social practice mutually affect each other. Speakers' identities influence how they use linguistic forms, and at the same time, their identities are created by the use of these linguistic forms. In discussing indexicality and social meanings, the question arises as to where meanings are created – in the speaker, in the addressee, or in both? In speech act theory (Searle, 1969, 1975, 1979), meaning is primarily associated with the speaker's intentions or the illocutionary force of an utterance. The addressee is seen as a passive recipient who does not have much to contribute to meaning. For example, the sincerity condition for the speech act of an order is that the speaker wants the ordered act performed. The essential condition has to do with the fact that the speaker intends the utterance as an attempt to get the addressee to do the act.

The perspective adopted in this book is that speakers are not passive observers of social custom. Rather they are active agents who choose particular linguistic forms to index who they are, how they feel and what stance they take toward the addressee(s) and the content of talk. Moreover, social meanings of utterances are interactionally constituted. Interpretation is performed socially – jointly among the participants. I am not claiming that speaker's intentions do not play a role in meaning assignment. Rather, intentions are not necessarily the only input to meaning. Although the speaker intends his or her utterance to be a warning, for example, the addressee's response may reframe the warning as something else, such as a joke. In such a case, the meaning of the utterance includes both the speaker's and addressee's understanding (Bakhtin, 1981; Duranti, 1984; Goodwin, 1981; Ochs, 1988; Sacks *et al.*, 1974, 1977).

Any study of indexicality must be rooted in observations of actual language use, particularly language use in social interaction. Much research in linguistics depends on the linguist's native-speaker intuitions and the elicitation of sentences from a native speaker. This research method is designed mainly for the investigation of the referential function of language based on the assumption that language is an invariable phenomenon in a homogeneous speech community (cf. Chomsky, 1965). For studying the indexical function of language, this method is not adequate. As we know from studies of sociolinguistics (e.g. Eckert & Rickford, 2001; Ervin-Tripp, 1972; Hymes, 1972; Labov, 1972), language systematically varies across social contexts. These contexts are indexed by variable linguistic features. When a linguist uses an informant to elicit sentences, the elicitation itself becomes a speech event. Typically such speech events are seen by the informant as formal occasions, and the informant's sentences may index these contexts. While informants are often aware of usage differences in their own language, to conjure up the wide range of contexts and their linguistic indexes is beyond most native speakers' ability. Silverstein (2001) points out that non-referential indexes (e.g. honorifics and particles), non-segmental indexes (e.g. prosodic structures) and creative indexes (e.g. honorifics and particles) are especially difficult for native speakers to bring into consciousness.[4] For this reason, the complex range of meanings of honorifics and pragmatic particles is often beyond a native speaker's consciousness. Studies of these linguistic features based on native speaker's intuition typically identify one salient meaning, but fail to recognize other social meanings that the form might index in context (cf. Agah, 1998). To investigate social meanings of non-referential, creative and/or non-segmental indexes, a more appropriate research method is to record speech in natural settings. Such data reveal the complex relationships between linguistic forms and contexts.

## Indexing Social Contexts: Linguistic Forms and Their Functions

To know how to interpret and understand utterances in context is an important part of our knowledge about language, and part and parcel of what Hymes (1971) has called communicative competence. This knowledge is essential to be a competent speaker in a social group. More recently, Young and He (1998) refer to it as interactional competence, which includes the competence to jointly construct an intersubjective world. How do indexes create contexts? Ochs (1988, 1990, 1996) observes that only a few linguistic indexes universally have a one-to-one mapping between form and context, and that most can occur in a wide range of contexts and with different meanings. Co-occurring linguistic and non-linguistic features narrow down the range of their possible social meanings to a more specific one. For example, rising intonation can mark uncertainty, question, doubt and request for confirmation. The place the utterance with rising intonation occupies in the sequential organization of the talk and/or the propositional content of the utterance can specify the social meaning of rising intonation. Another example comes from recent research on gender and language. There are few linguistic forms that are directly linked to the female or male speaker. In English, for example, the expression, 'What a lovely house!' is typically considered as an example of female speech (cf. Lakoff, 1975). The lexical item *lovely*, however, does not always index the female gender, for it is not exclusively used by women. Even in Japanese, which is often regarded as an example of a gendered language, only few linguistic forms are directly tied to female or male speech. Sentence-final forms, including sentence-final particles, are typically classified into female or male speech forms (cf. Ide, 1982). However, recent research indicates that most sentence-final forms are not exclusively used by one gender (Matsumoto, 2002; Okamoto, 1995). Male and female social identities are thus not directly indexed by linguistic forms but rather evoked in context in a complex manner. In other words, most social information is not grammaticized but implicated in context.

What model captures the complex relations held between linguistic features and their social meanings? Ochs (1990, 1996, 2002) proposes a model of indexical relations in which restricted sets of linguistic resources function as building blocks and index a broad range of social contexts. This model is grounded in the understanding that in addition to the temporal and spatial frame, social context is constituted by four fundamental dimensions. They are ACTS (goal-oriented behavior, e.g. responding to a question), STANCES, IDENTITIES and ACTIVITIES (sequences of acts). In other words, social context is constituted by what we do (ACTS and ACTIVITIES), what and how we feel and know (affective and epistemic STANCES), and who we are (IDENTITY).

Ochs (1993, 2002) argues that acts and stances are the basic building blocks of more the complex dimensions of activity and identity. A sequence of giving a personal account may index the activity of narrating. The act of asking a quiz question may index the identity of a teacher. A stance can index an act or an identity. Indexing of the epistemic stance of uncertainty can help constitute the social act of question and the social relationship of lower social status. Ochs (1988) proposes a two-step model of indexical relations that accounts for complex indexical relations (Figure 2.1).

In this model, contextual dimension 1 is indexed by a linguistic feature in an unmediated fashion whereas contextual dimension 2 is a more complex dimension evoked by dimension 1 and mediated by a given situational context. This process is generative. In some cases, contextual dimension 2 further helps to index another contextual dimension. The indexing of the speaker's affect helps to define the speaker's social identity; the indexing of the speaker's epistemic stance helps to constitute a particular social relationship, and so on.

Particular acts and stances are expected in certain social identities and activities. For example, in an academic counseling session of an American university, the counselor is expected to give advice and information as well as solicit information, and the student is expected to request information, permission and advice (Bardovi-Harlig & Hartford, 1990). Thus, the counselor's expert status is in part created by the acts of giving advice, information and soliciting information. The counselor's identity as an expert can also be constituted by his acts of initiating the topic of the student's identity and defining it (He, 1995). In contrast, the student's novice status is in part constituted by the social acts of accommodating the counselor's definition and requesting information, permission and advice. An epistemic stance of uncertainty can constitute different identities for the counselor and the student. He (1995) demonstrates that the counselor's epistemic stance of uncertainty is interpreted as a

| Linguistic → resource | Contextual ----> dimension 1 | Contextual dimension 2 |
|---|---|---|
| | Direct index | Indirect index |
| | Affective stance | Act |
| | Epistemic stance | Identity |
| | Act | Activity |
| → Direct indexical relation | | |
| --- > Indirect indexical relation | | |

**Figure 2.1** Indexical relations

professional guess that he makes from his experience as a counselor whereas the student's expression of uncertainty indexes her as an inexperienced novice. This is because different responsibilities and roles are expected of each in the academic counseling session in an American university.

As He (1995) discusses, the construction of identities and activities is mediated by the cultural ideologies of a social group. A link between a particular act/stance and a particular identity may differ from culture to culture or from group to group. For example, in Japanese society, the act of apologizing at the beginning of a speech constitutes the social identity of a good speaker, but in other societies, such an act may not index a good speaker, but an insecure speaker. In sum, social meanings (e.g. social identities and activities) are emergent products of social interaction through interlocutors' joint orientation to culturally appropriate interpretation of the situation at hand.

## Linguistic Indexes of Affective and Epistemic Stances

Central to Ochs' two-step model of indexicality are linguistic indexes of affective and epistemic stances, which have 'an especially privileged role in the construction of social life' (Ochs, 1996: 420). In other words, linguistic structures that mark affective or epistemic stances are major ingredients of social contexts. In this view, non-referential indexes, which do not contribute to the referential meaning, play an important role in the construction of social meaning. They are one of the most powerful resources available for indexing social context. Ochs (1996: 410) defines the two stances as follows. She states:

> *affective stance* refers to a mood, attitude, feeling, and disposition, as well as degrees of emotional intensity vis-à-vis some focus of concern; (Ochs & Schieffelin, 1984, Labov, 1984, Levy, 1984)

> *epistemic stance* refers to knowledge or belief vis-a vis some focus of concern, including degrees of certainty of knowledge, degrees of commitment to truth of propositions, and sources of knowledge, among other epistemic qualities. (Chafe & Nichols, 1986)

Linguistic indexes that mark affective and epistemic stances are numerous. Affective markers include diminutives, quantifiers, sentential adverbs, intonation and particles, among others. Epistemic markers are evidentials that include sentential moods, inflections, hedges and particles. Non-referential indexes are mostly affective or epistemic stance markers. A number of studies on linguistic indexes of the affective and epistemic stances (i.e. affect and evidential markers) show that these indexes have a broad range of indexical functions which constitute social identity, social relationship, speech acts and speech activities, among others

(Besnier, 1990; Chafe & Nichols, 1986; Cook, 1990b, 1992; Fox, 2001; He, 1995; Hill & Irvine, 1993; Mushin, 2001; Ochs, 1988, 1996).

Ochs' model allows us to describe the social meanings of non-referential indexes such as sentence-final particles and honorifics. For example, Japanese has a number of sentence-final particles which do not carry direct referential meaning. Typically they occur in face-to-face interaction and they can index various speech acts. Thus, they are essential in sense making in face-to-face interaction. Ochs (1988) proposes that the Japanese sentence-final particles typically associated with gender (e.g. *ze, zo* and *wa*) be analyzed as a direct index of the affective stance and as an indirect index of the speaker's gender identity. For example, she explains that the particle *wa* directly indexes the affective stance of softness and hesitancy. The speaker's gender is evoked by direct indexing of this affective stance mediated by the gender ideology in Japanese society, which is partly defined in terms of the affective disposition. In other words, the soft and gentle disposition, which is an expected affective disposition for females, has a constitutive relation with the affective softness of *wa* to evoke the female gender.

The sentence-final particles index not only the identity of the speaker but also speech acts. I will illustrate how the affective stance of the Japanese sentence-final particles can constitute speech acts as well as identity by drawing on an example of the particle *zo* from naturally occurring conversations between a mother and child. The sentence-final particle *zo* has been described as a male particle and is perceived as sounding 'forceful' (e.g. Ide, 1982; McGloin, 1990).[5] Its social meaning is, however, not limited to gender identity, and it indexes speech acts such as encouragement and threats. Ochs' model of indexical relations can account for complexities associated with particles such as *zo* by positing an affective stance as a direct index (contextual dimension 1), and the gender identity and speech acts as indirect indexes (contextual dimension 2). In Example (1), the mother's use of *zo* indirectly indexes the speech act of encouragement. In this instance, the assertive attitude, which has traditionally been associated with male identity, is backgrounded. In this example, the one-year-old child, is eating dinner without the mother's assistance. The mother is encouraging him to continue to do so. Without the particle *zo*, the mother's utterance would not clearly index the act of encouragement, but simply constitute a statement of a fact.[6]

[The mother and Yuu are eating dinner.] (Cook, 1997)
**Mother:** yuu-chan hitori de taberareru **zo**.
        Yuu      oneself   eat-able    FP
        'Yuu, you can eat by yourself *zo*'

The particle *zo* emphasizes the mother's encouraging attitude toward the boy (perhaps in English it can be expressed with 'come on, you can eat by yourself!'). Example (2) shows that the particle *zo* can index the speech act of threat. Here *zo* occurs in the utterance of a hero in a children's story book.

(2) [The mother is reading to the child a storybook about a robot called Flash King. Below is a line said by Flash King, the hero of the story.] (Cook, 1997)

**Flash King:** kore kara mo minna de waru mono o taosu zo.
this from also all　　　bad　guy　O beat　FP
'(We = Flash King and others) will beat the evil robots from now on *zo*.'

If *zo* did not occur in (2), the utterance would sound less threatening. Flash King's assertive attitude directly indexed by *zo* helps constitute the speech act of threat.

Figure 2.2 shows that the particle *zo* directly indexes the affective stance of assertive attitude (contextual dimension 1), which helps constitute other social dimensions (contextual dimension 2) such as the social identity of the speaker and speech acts.

In this model, the male gender often associated with *zo* is indexed through the indexing of the affective stance of assertive attitude. This is so because the male gender in Japanese society is in part defined in terms

| Linguistic → resource | Contextual ----> dimension 1 | Contextual dimension 2 |
|---|---|---|
| *Zo* | **Affective stance** | **Identity** |
| | Assertive attitude | Male gender |
| | | **Acts** |
| | | Threat |
| | | Encouragement |
| | | (The list is not exhaustive.) |
| → Direct indexical relation | | |
| --- > Indirect indexical relation | | |

**Figure 2.2** Indexical relations of *Zo*

of this characteristic. It also accounts for instances in which the particle *zo* indexes speech acts such as encouragement and threats.

In Cook (1990b, 1992), I discuss in detail how the Japanese sentence-final particles *no* and *ne* help constitute various dimensions of social context. For example, the particle *ne* directly indexes the affective stance of the affective common ground between the speaker and the addressee, and this social meaning (contextual dimension 1) helps constitute the speech acts of opening of talk, introducing a new topic, displaying and seeking agreement and confirmation, among others (contextual dimension 2). The particle *no*, on the other hand, directly indexes group authority in the realm of knowledge (i.e. fact) (contextual dimension 1), and this social meaning helps constitute the speech acts of explanation, persuasion and make-believe, among others (contextual dimension 2). The strength of this model is that it can account for the complexity of social worlds because the contextual dimension 2 includes a range of contextual dimensions. This means that a given index has the potential to evoke a number of acts, activities, stances and identities – theoretically as many as the number of social contexts in which it occurs. Ochs' model thus makes it possible to explain multiple social meanings associated with a given linguistic form without setting up separate categories for the same linguistic form, or ignoring the potential of various other social connotations associated with linguistic forms.

## Markedness in Social Meaning

The ways in which linguistic structures evoke social meanings in context are often conventionalized, and members of a social group share interpretation conventions. For example, indirect speech acts (Searle, 1975), in particular, exist because of the conventionalized sense-making processes shared by a social group. The cooperative principle of conversation and the flouting of the maxims of conversation (Grice, 1975) also suggest a group norm of interpretation. Similarly, the notion of 'preference organization' (Pomerantz, 1984) in conversation analysis rests on the shared interpretation convention. Conversely, cross talk (Gumperz, 1982) occurs when speakers from different social groups misunderstand the social meaning of an utterance due to their different interpretation norms. Hanks (1996: 237) asserts that acting in habitual ways is the nature of social actors and that this disposition 'tends to stabilize their practices, making them repeatable and therefore expectable'. Thus, members of a social group at some level share knowledge of preferred or expected associations between a particular linguistic structure and a particular social meaning in a given social situation. Myers-Scotton (1993), for example, argues that this knowledge is part of communicative competence, and accounts for this knowledge by the theory of markedness. Speakers know which linguistic choices are unmarked or marked and how each choice is interpreted. They choose the unmarked form more frequently as it is expected and conventionalized. Language socialization is a process of learning the unmarked and marked associations between linguistic structures and social meanings in a given social situation (Ochs, 1996). This is how the norms of a social group are produced and reproduced.

As speakers are not passive observers of the linguistic and social norms of society, sometimes they do not follow the conventional linguistic choice in a given social situation. Myers-Scotton's (1993) markedness model can account for non-conventional interpretation of social meaning. Studying the phenomenon of code switching, she states:

> ... markedness has a normative basis within the community, and speakers also know the consequences of making marked or un-expected choices. Because the unmarked choice is 'safer' (i.e. it conveys no surprises because it indexes an expected interpersonal relationship), speakers generally make this choice. But not always. Speakers assess the potential costs and rewards of all alternative choices, and make their decisions, typically unconsciously. (Myers-Scotton, 1993: 75)

Myers-Scotton's proposal accounts for the socially shared nature of interpretation norms, and yet it also allows for individual choices. Members of a social group use language to create identities and activities in interaction. In this process their tacit knowledge of which linguistic choices are unmarked or marked in a given social situation allows them to choose how to construct their social identities and activities. In this book, I will use the notion of markedness to discuss speech style choices, for the notion of markedness is useful for accounting for the phenomena of codeswitching (cf. Myers-Scotton) and style shifts. Chapter 5 shows that there are marked patterns of *masu* uses associated with conversation in contact situation, which differ from the normative uses of the *masu* form associated with Japanese family conversation.

## Conclusion

Linguistic indexes are resources that create, maintain and negotiate social acts, activities and identities. Affect indexes can create or attempt to elicit and express fear, devotion and solidarity. Indexes of epistemology can create the idea that a certain statement is true or valid or doubtful. Social meanings directly indexed by linguistic forms further constitute various social categories.

Through indexes, members of society shape the social worlds in which they live (Bakhtin, 1981; Leontyev, 1981a, 1981b; Vygotsky, 1978). Indexes as a linguistic resource aid in the formation of the self as well. Our identity is formed by social relations with others and by the reflexive nature of language (i.e. the function of language that presupposes, represents and characterizes its own nature) with respect to situations (Bakhtin, 1981; Vygotsky, 1978). The response of others to our own utterances may redefine a situation and give new meaning to our own utterances (Cook, 2006a; Ochs *et al.*, 1989, 1992). In this process, we may redefine social situations.

## Notes

1. The term 'social meaning' is used synonymously with the terms, 'pragmatic meaning' and 'indexical meaning' in this book.
2. The notion of 'voice' is closely related to the sociological notion of 'role', but the conceptualization of the two terms differs. While the notion of 'voice' underscores the linguistic construction of social personae, that of 'role' implies parts played in interactional settings (cf. Keane, 2001).
3. Wetzel (1985) argues that in Japanese the deictic center is not the speaker's individual ego but the speaker's collective ego, which includes the speaker and his or her group.
4. Creative indexes are typically non-referential.
5. Both sentence-final particles *zo* and *ze* are referred to as male particle, but to discuss how the two particles differ in social meaning is beyond the scope of this book.
6. Although a statement in English 'You can eat by yourself' may index an encouragement, a statement in Japanese 'hitori de taberareru' ('You can eat by yourself') normally constitutes a statement of fact. By adding the particle *zo*, the utterance can clearly be interpreted as an encouragement in this context.

## Chapter 3
# *Functions of the* Masu *Form*

Japanese style shifts involve shifts between so-called 'addressee honorifics', the *masu* form and its non-honorific counterpart, the plain form. Typically, addressee honorifics are defined as honorifics that indicate politeness toward the addressee even when the addressee is not mentioned in the sentence. The *masu* form has been viewed as the addressee honorific in Japanese (Comrie, 1976; Martin, 1964, 2004) and has been discussed extensively in the literature. This chapter first discusses previously proposed accounts and then introduces the indexical account of the *masu* form so that readers will better understand the nature of the Japanese style shift. It addresses the role of the social context in indexical processes and shows that the social meaning of politeness associated with the *masu* form is its interpretation in the *soto* ('out-group/outside') context. In the *uchi* ('in-group/inside') context, the *masu* form primarily indexes participants' social identities. This chapter also illustrates how Japanese family members shift between the two forms during dinnertime conversation, and proposes a normative style shift pattern in Japanese family conversation.

## Previous Accounts of the *Masu* Form

Japanese has an addressee honorific, *masu* form, and its non-honorific counterpart, the plain form. Table 3.1 lists the *masu* and plain forms.[1]

In this book, the term *masu* form includes the present (*-masu*) and past tense, (*-mashita*), the gerund (*-mashite*), and the copular present (*desu*) and the past tense of *desu* (*deshita*).[2] The plain form includes the present (*-u* or *-ru*) and past tense (*-ta*), the gerund (*-te*), the copular present (*da*) and past tense (*datta*) forms as well as bare nominals, which are considered as a form of copula deletion (*hon da/desu* ('is a book') → *hon Ø* ('a book')). In all the Japanese examples given in the rest of the book, the *masu* form is in bold, and the plain form is underlined.

Examples (1a) and (1b) are identical in referential meaning but differ in social meaning.

(1a)  Taro ga Hanako to  **dekake-masu**. [*masu* form]
        S        with  go out
      'Taro goes out with Hanako.'

(1b)  Taro ga Hanako to  dekake-ru. [plain form]
        S        with  go out
      'Taro goes out with Hanko.'

**Table 3.1** Three clause types and gerund in the *masu* and plain forms

| Clause type | Masu form | Plain form |
|---|---|---|
| Verbal | Verb stem -mas-u (present)<br>Verb stem -mas-en (negative)<br>Verb stem -mashi-ta (past)<br>Verb stem -mashi-te (gerund) | Verb stem -(r)u (present)<br>Verb stem -nai (negative)<br>Verb stem -ta (past)<br>Verb stem -(t)te (gerund) |
| Adjectival | Adj + copula<br>  des-u (present)<br>  deshi-ta (past)<br>  deshi-te (gerund) | Adj<br>-i (present)<br>-kat-ta (past)<br>-kute (gerund) |
| Nominal | Nom + copula<br>  des-u (present)<br>  deshi-ta (past)<br>  deshi-te (gerund) | Nom + copula<br>  da (present)<br>  dat-ta (past)<br>  de (gerund) |

In (1a) the verb 'to go out' is in the *masu* form (*dekakemasu*) while in (1b) it is in the plain form (*dekakeru*). In the case of subordination the verb of the main clause can occur in either the *masu* form or the plain form; the verb in the subordinate clause usually remains in the plain form.[3]

(2a)  [[Taro ga   Hanako to    dekakeru toki] itsumo ame ga **furi-masu**]
                                                                    [*masu* form]
        Taro S     Hanako with go out    when   always rain S fall
          'When  Taro goes out with Hanako, it always rains.'

(2a)  [[Taro ga   Hanako to    dekakeru toki] itsumo ame ga fur-u]
                                                                    [plain form]
        Taro S     Hanako with go out    when always rain S  fall
          'When Taro goes out with Hanako, it always rains.'

Besides the above usages, in spoken discourse the speaker sometimes inserts the *masu* form of the copula *desu* after a phrase or a clause. In such cases, the sentence-final particle *ne* often follows. The insertion of *desu* does not alter the referential meaning of the sentence, but does change its social meaning.

(3a) Taro ga Hanako to dekakeru   toki
          S         with go out      when
       'When Taro goes out with Hanako'

(3b) Taro ga **desu** ne Hanako to dekakeru  toki   **desu**  ne
          S Cop FP              with go out    when    Cop    FP
       'When Taro goes out with Hanako'

As these examples illustrate, when the plain form is the verb of the main clause, it contrasts with the *masu* form with respect to social meaning. The plain forms discussed in this book are instances in which they occur in the main clause.

What is the function of the *masu* form? In other words, what does the *masu* form index? As the *masu* form has a clear morphological marking contrasted with the plain form, a number of scholars studying Japanese have investigated the functions of the *masu* form. Most of the previous studies have focused on only one dimension of its social meaning, namely politeness/formality, and investigated what triggers the shift between polite and non-polite speech levels. First, I will discuss previous proposals regarding the *masu* form below.

## Rule-based usage of the *masu* form

In Japanese, the *masu* form is called *teineitai* ('polite form') and the plain form, *futsuutai* ('ordinary form'). In this view, Examples (1a) and (2a) are *teinei* ('polite'), but (1b) and (2b) are not polite (i.e. they are neutral). Some scholars call the *teineitai* ('polite') form a formal form (e.g. Makino, 1996; Wetzel, 1995). The informal form is for intimates, and the formal form is for non-intimates. The *masu* form is also referred to as an 'addressee honorific' (Comrie, 1976; Martin, 1964). Honorifics are defined as 'direct grammatical encodings of relative social status between participants, or between participants and persons or things referred to in the communicative events' (Brown & Levinson, 1987: 179). In this view, addressee honorifics directly encode the speaker's politeness toward the addressee, marking the relative status of the speaker and the addressee. Martin (1964) proposes that factors influencing the speaker's choice include outgroupness, position, age and sex differences. He proposes that the speaker chooses the *masu* form when he or she speaks to someone outside his or her group, or to a higher-status person in terms of social position, age or sex. Contrary to these claims, however, we find numerous counter-examples in which the *masu* form marks neither the relative status of the participants nor out-groupness (cf. Cook, 1997, 1998; Okamoto, 1999).

Many scholars take the view that the *masu* form marks polite speech and have proposed a rule-based analysis of the *masu* form (e.g. Harada, 1976; Ide, 1982; Ide & Yoshida, 1999; Martin, 1964; Neustupny, 1978; Niyekawa, 1991). The basic assumption of previous studies on speech style is that there is a one-to-one relationship between the speech style and the context of its use. Niyekawa's proposal of speech levels (1991) exemplifies the rule-based view of Japanese speech styles. According to her proposal, there are four speech levels in Japanese: the neutral speech-style level and three polite-speech styles. The neutral speech-style level

(N-level) corresponds to an informal relationship. At this level, there are male and female speech styles as indicated in (4a). The *masu* form is associated with the three polite speech-style levels (P-levels). The P-0 level (4b) incorporates only the *masu* form, while the P-1 (4c) and P-2 (4d) levels combine the *masu* form and the referent honorifics both exalting (subject honorific) and humbling (object honorific) forms.

(4)    'When you went yesterday, was it crowded?'
(4a)   N: M:   Tanaka-kun ga kinoo      itta toki,   <u>kondeta</u> ka(i)?
                Tanaka         S yesterday went when  crowded Q
            F:  Tanaka-san ga kinoo      itta toki,   <u>kondeta</u> (no)?
                Tanaka         S yesterday went when  crowded FP

(4b)   P-0:  Tanaka-san ga kinoo      itta toki, konde (**i**)**mashita** ka?
               Tanaka         S yesterday went when crowded exist Q

(4c)   P-1:  Tanaka-san ga kinoo irasshatta      toki, konde **imashita** ka?
               Tanaka         S yesterday went SH when crowded exist Q

(4d)   P-2:  Kachoo ga kinoo oide ni natta toki, konde **imashita** deshoo ka?
              Tanaka  S yesterday went SH when crowded exist Cop Q

(Niyekawa, 1991: 83)
[Gloss, underlining and bold facing were added to the original]

While the neutral level is equated with informal contexts such as in conversations between family members or close friends, the P-levels are associated with formal relationships. However, examining naturally occurring speech, we find that most speakers are not single speech-level speakers in a given social situation. It is not uncommon for speakers to change speech styles throughout the course of talk with the same addressee in the same setting. For example, teachers shift between the two forms in teaching a class (cf. Cook, 1996b; Wade, 2003). Japanese mothers as well sometimes shift from the plain form to the *masu* form, for example, when serving food and scolding her child at home (see discussion in section on 'Serving food').

From the perspective that the *masu* form is a linguistic marker of polite speech, Ide (1982) proposes the following social rules of politeness in Japanese society.

Ground rules:
Rule 1 – Be polite to a person of a higher social status
Rule 2 – Be polite to a person with power
Rule 3 – Be polite to an older person

Overriding rule:
Be polite in a formal setting.                    (Ide, 1982: 366–371)

Ide gives the following examples to illustrate how the rules work.

(5a) (A policeman: talking to the neighborhood doctor)
    Ii      o-tenki **desu** ne.                       [masu]
    Good  weather     SENTENCE FINAL PARTICLE
    'Fine day, isn't it?'

(5b) (A policeman: talking to the neighborhood carpenter)
    Ii      o-tenki <u>da</u>  ne.                     [plain]
    Good  weather     SENTENCE FINAL PARTICLE
    'Fine day, isn't it?'

                             (Ide, 1982: 367 (examples (24a) and (24b))

(6a) (Customer) Miruku <u>aru</u> (  ) [plain]
             milk    exist
             'Is there milk?'

(6b) (Merchant) Hai **arimasu**. [masu]
              Yes exist
              'Yes, there is.'

                          (Ide, 1982: 367 (examples (25a) and (25b))
[Underlining and bold facing were added to the original]

Ide explains that Rule 1 is operating in Examples (5a) and (5b). The speaker uses the polite speech-level marker, the *masu* form, in talking to an addressee of a higher social status (5a), whereas he or she does not use it in talking to an addressee of a lower social status (5b). Rule 2 is operating in examples (6a) and (6b). While the customer speaks to the merchant in the plain form, the merchant speaks in the *masu* form to the customer, who has more power because he or she is paying the merchant. Ide (1989) calls this type of behavior – based upon socially-agreed-upon rules of etiquette – *wakimae* ('discernment'). She claims that the notion of politeness in Japanese society is best described by *wakimae*, which is obligatory. She describes how professors and students interact with each other in a university seminar class:

> ... it is an obligatory *wakimae* for a student to choose honorific forms in a seminar. His/Her choice of honorifics indexes his/her sense of place in the situational context through expression of a formal attitude to the setting and a deferential attitude toward the professor, either as the addressee or as the bystander. The professor will speak with honorifics indexing his/her sense of place in the formal setting, the seminar. He/she may speak without honorifics outside of class, but the students will not reciprocate in non-honorific forms even in an informal setting. (Ide, 1992: 300)

In this perspective, use of the *masu* and plain forms is regulated by social rules (*wakimae*), and any usage that deviates from the rules is perceived as a violation or incorrect usage. This view is prescriptive and often adopted in *keigo* ('honorifics') usage books written for native Japanese speakers as well as Japanese language textbooks for JFL learners. However, this static rule-based analysis does not capture the dynamic nature of human interaction.

Based on naturally occurring data, Okamoto (1999) reports that in conversation between a professor and a student, even the student can use the plain form in exclamatory expressions and soliloquy-like remarks. In my study of academic consultation in Japanese universities (Cook, 2006b) as well, the student freely shifts to the plain form in exclamatory expressions and soliloquy-like remarks. Example (7) is from a consultation between a male professor of linguistics and a male student in the professor's office at a university in Tokyo.[4] The professor asks the student a question in line 1 using the *masu* form. According to the notion of *wakimae*, this use of the *masu* form is interpreted as the professor's indexing his sense of place in the formal setting, an academic consultation. However, we note two 'violations' of *wakimae* in this segment. The first 'violation' is the student's use of the plain form in lines 6 and 7, where he makes soliloquy-like remarks. The second is the professor's comment on the characteristics of the thesis in line 8. He shifts to the plain form here.

(7) P (professor), and S (student)

1 P: ano ichiban:: kore ga sono: mondai  da    tte iu,
     well most     this S    that  problem Cop QT say
     soo iu   na- nante iu   ka soo iu  no **arimasu** ka?
     So  say wh- what  say Q  so  say Nom exist   Q
     'uh this one is the number one problem, is there any sort of- that
     sort of thing?'

2 S: e:tto ((coughs))
     well
     'Well'

3 P: nan- ste- e: pinkaa to    sono binsu no koko kore ga tadashii toka ne,
     what- st- uh Pinker and that Vince Lk here this  S  correct  etc.  FP
     soo iu   no
     so   say Nom
     'wel- Ste- uh this one by Pinker and Vince is correct, it's that sort
     of thing'

4 S: ee:to
     'Well'

5 P: mata koko wa <u>okashii</u> toka     ((sniffling)) (3.0)
    also this   Top strange etc
    'or this part is strange, etc.'

6 →S: doko <u>datta</u> kke na (12.0) ((sniffling and turning pages of
                                         the book))
    where Cop FP FP
    'Where was it, I wonder.'

7 →S: ano:: nan- nan <u>datta</u> kke   na
    well wha- what Cop FP     FP
    'uh, I wonder what- what that was.'

8 →P: kore ronbun to shite wa  sugoi nagai ronbun <u>da</u>   yo  ne (  )
    this thesis   as     Top very  long  thesis  Cop FP FP
    'This is very long as a thesis, right? (   )'

9 S: soo **desu** ne
    so  Cop  FP
    'That is right'

            [
10 P:        ne
            FP
            'right.'

Do the professor and the student in this example act in an impolite manner, violating the social etiquette of Japanese society? In this example, neither the professor nor the student reacts negatively to the utterances that end in the plain form. This fact suggests that these uses of the plain form do not index impoliteness. Examples such as (7) provide evidence that rigid social rules cannot fully explain the intricacies of social life.

The rule-based analysis does not adequately account for all usages of the *masu* and plain forms.[5] In fact, as documented in the literature on Japanese style shifts, usages of *masu* that violate the politeness rules such as those found in Example (7) are not uncommon (Cook, 1996a, 1996b, 1997, 1998, 2006b; Dunn, 1999; Matsumoto, 2002; Maynard, 1993; Megumi, 2002; Okamoto, 1998, 1999). The rule-based analysis views the participants of a speech event as passive observers of social rules. Participants in most social events, however, are active agents who create events with both verbal and non-verbal actions. As demonstrated by Cook (1998, 2006b), Okamoto (1999), Matsumoto (2002) and others, whether or not to use the *masu* form at any moment of interaction is ultimately a choice the speaker makes in order to achieve his/her communicative goal.

## The *masu* form as a marker of distance, speech to others and *soto*

In the literature, politeness associated with the *masu* form is also linked to concepts such as distance, speech to others and *soto* ('outside/out-group' relationship).

Some scholars claim that the *masu* form is a marker of interpersonal or psychological distance (Hinds, 1978; Ikuta, 1983; Jorden & Noda, 1987; Shibatani, 1990). Based on his findings from natural interview data, Hinds (1978) claims that the *masu* form is chosen when there is a perceived social distance between the interlocutors. Ikuta (1983), who studied a TV interview program, proposes that the *masu* form indicates [+ distance], and the plain form [ − distance] in interpersonal relationships. She claims that speakers obligatorily choose one of the forms according to the social situation, but they can shift to a level appropriate to their momentary feelings. The explanation that the *masu* form indexes interpersonal or psychological distance is in line with the notion of 'negative politeness' (Brown & Levinson, 1978, 1987) and accounts for many uses of the *masu* form. This analysis, however, does not account for uses of the *masu* form if interpersonal or psychological distance is not a manifestation of cold affect. For instance, a mother can often speak in the *masu* form when she serves food to children (see Example (13) below). Why does she do so in this instance? It would seem strange if the mother were withdrawing herself from being warm and distancing herself when serving food to the children, for the mealtime is a time of sharing among family members. How 'interpersonal distance' is employed in interaction is highly complex. As we can see from this example, the notion of interpersonal or psychological distance does not fully capture the complexity of *masu* usages.

Other scholars associate the *masu* form with speech to others, while the plain form marks speech to oneself (Kindaichi, 1982; Makino, 1996, 2002; Maynard, 1991, 1993). Maynard (1991, 1993), whose study includes both intimate conversation and written prose, has contributed to our knowledge about style mixing. She distinguishes the naked plain form (the plain form without any sentence-final particle) and the non-naked plain form (the plain form with a sentence-final particle), and maintains that the non-naked plain form is morphologically less committed.[6] Working with conversational data, she has proposed that this is the form that is more likely to occur when the speaker's awareness of the addressee is low. She explains that the speaker's low awareness of the addressee is achieved when he or she psychologically perceives no barrier between him- or herself and the addressee. She offers a framework that links the human relationship to the morphological choice:

> The more the speaking self is aware of 'thou' as a separate
> and potentially opposing entity, the more elaborate the markers for
> discourse modality become, one of which is the *desu/masu* ending.
>
> (Maynard, 1993: 179)

Thus, according to Maynard, contexts in which the naked plain form is likely to occur are those in which the speaker's awareness of the addressee is low. These are instances in which the speaker does not deliberately address the addressee such as (i) an abrupt remembrance or a sudden emotional surge; (ii) a narrative-internal point of view; and (iii) echoing questions and jointly creating an utterance.[7] In other words, the naked plain form typically occurs when the speaker does not design his or her utterance in order to interactionally accommodate the addressee. In contrast, the *masu* form is more likely to occur in contexts in which the speaker's awareness of the addressee is high. These are instances in which the speaker deliberately addresses the addressee such as in (1) formal relationships and (2) presenting main information directly addressed to the addressee. Although Maynard's observation is insightful, it does not explain why immediate family members sometimes use the *masu* form in informal settings.

Some proposals (e.g. Makino, 2002; Sukle, 1994) link the *masu* and plain forms to *soto* ('outside/out-group') and *uchi* ('inside/in-group'), an important cultural distinction in Japanese society (Bachnik, 1994; Bachnik & Quinn, 1994; Lebra, 1976). The *uchi/soto* ('inside/outside') orientations organize Japanese self, society and language. While *uchi* evokes the notions of familiarity, proximity, inclusion, certainty and control, *soto* evokes unfamiliarity, distance, exclusion, uncertainty and lack of control (Quinn, 1994a). Although this distinction exists in every society, because it organizes the self, society and language, it is particularly meaningful within Japanese society. *Uchi/soto* defines different sets of behavioral patterns (Bachnik & Quinn, 1994; Lebra, 1976). The Japanese language has a number of expressions that contain the word *uchi* or *soto* (Quinn, 1994b; Wetzel, 1994). For example, the word *uchi* is used as the first person reference (my group). There are two different sets of kinship terms in Japanese, one referring to the *uchi* members when talking to a *soto* member (e.g. *haha* 'my or our mother') and the other referring to the *soto* members (e.g. *okaasan* 'your or someone else's mother').[8] Japanese also has pairs of lexical items, one of which refers to a referent that originates in Japan, and another that originates overseas (Moeran, 1988). For example, *tennoo* refers to the Japanese emperor (*uchi*) while *kootei* refers to emperors outside of Japan (*soto*). As *uchi* ('in-group/inside') and *soto* ('out-group/outside') are indexical, what group is *uchi* or *soto* is defined situationally. One's relatives are *uchi* in some social situations but are positioned as *soto* in others. However, the prototypical *uchi* is one's immediate family.

Makino (2002: 123) considers the plain form as the form 'primarily used when speaking with a person or persons in *uchi* space, a space in which casual communication takes place' and the *masu* form as the form 'primarily used when speaking with a person or persons in *soto* space, a space in which formal interactions take place'. That is, mutual *masu* exchanges indicate a polite, formal or 'outside' (*soto*) relationship between the interlocutors, whereas mutual plain form exchanges indicate an informal or 'inside' (*uchi*) relationship. Sukle (1994) investigates directives in four different locations (a railway ticket window, a post office window, a neighborhood vegetable market and a middle-class family).[9] He found that the frequency of the *masu* form used in directives is proportionate to the degree of distance between interlocutors appropriate to the location. In other words, at a railway ticket window and a post office window, which are both considered to be *soto* ('out-group/ outside') contexts, only the *masu* form occurred, whereas in family conversation, which is a typical *uchi* ('ingroup/inside') context, the plain form was mainly used. The *masu* form is also associated with *omote* ('front'), a Japanese cultural notion related to *soto* ('out-group/outside') (Dunn, 1999).[10] Relating the *masu* and plain form to the notions of *soto* ('out-group/outside') and *uchi* ('in-group/inside') respectively, however, cannot explain the non-reciprocal use of these forms (also see Matsumoto & Okamoto, 2003 for criticism of Sukle, 1994). For example, in a situation in which a professor speaks to a student in the plain form while the student speaks to the professor in the *masu* form, it is at least confusing to say that two interlocutors create the *uchi* and *soto* space simultaneously in the same interaction. This problem arises from directly linking the linguistic forms (the *masu* and plain forms) with contextual features (*soto* and *uchi*). As noted in Chapter 2, most linguistic forms do not directly index contextual dimensions. Thus, the *masu* and plain forms do not directly index *soto* ('out-group/outside') and *uchi* ('ingroup/inside') respectively. In sum, most previous studies have assumed that the *masu* and plain forms are directly linked to only one social meaning and they have not taken into account that these forms are indexical in nature.

As I discuss below, politeness or formality typically associated with the *masu* form is an interpretation based on other related concepts. In other words, there is no one-to-one direct relationship between the *masu* form and politeness or formality. Rather, the *masu* form has a broad range of social meaning that arises out of communicative practice situated in social context.

## An Indexical Account of the *Masu* Form

### The *masu* form as a marker of a self-presentational stance[11]

A full description of the *masu* form can only be made with reference to a theory of indexicality. In this section, drawing on Ochs' model of indexicality, I present an indexical account of the social meanings of the *masu* form. Drawing on examples from dinnertime conversations in Japanese families (Cook, 1996a, 1997), I discuss how the direct index of the *masu* form evokes indirect indexical meaning. The data base used below comes from nine hours of audio-recorded dinnertime conversations from three different Japanese families (Families O, M, and T), who all are educated middle-class residents of the Tokyo area. Each family consists of the parents and two or three children (3–7 years old).[12] Other family conversation excerpts cited are from the research of Nakamura (2002) and Takagi (2002).

Figure 3.1 illustrates the indexical relations of the *masu* form. In this model, the linguistic form (the *masu* form) directly indexes the

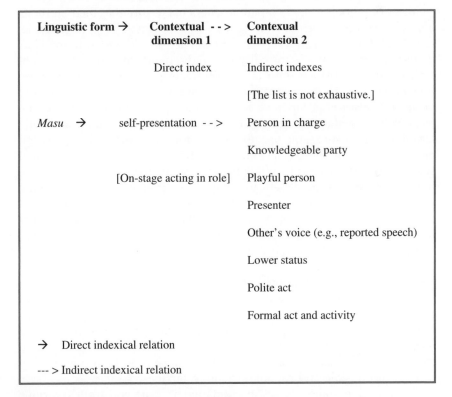

| Linguistic form → | Contextual --> dimension 1 | Contexual dimension 2 |
|---|---|---|
| | Direct index | Indirect indexes |
| | | [The list is not exhaustive.] |
| *Masu* → | self-presentation --> | Person in charge |
| | | Knowledgeable party |
| | [On-stage acting in role] | Playful person |
| | | Presenter |
| | | Other's voice (e.g., reported speech) |
| | | Lower status |
| | | Polite act |
| | | Formal act and activity |
| → Direct indexical relation | | |
| --- > Indirect indexical relation | | |

**Figure 3.1** Indexical relations of the *masu* form

self-presentational stance, which evokes various social identities and acts/activities in different contexts.[13]

The *masu* form directly indexes the self-presentational stance. This stance is characterized by the speaker's heightened awareness of the addressee (c.f. Maynard, 1993). The notion, 'self-presentational stance' is defined as the self which presents an on-stage display of a positive social role to the addressee.[14] It is a particular affective stance of presenting oneself to other(s) when one is literally or figuratively 'on stage' and being watched by others. In Japanese, the terms *shisei o tadasu* ('to hold oneself up') or *kichin to suru* ('to do something neatly') describe this affective stance. In Japanese society, to assume the posture of *shisei o tadasu* ('to hold oneself up') shows one's proper and responsible attitude when engaging in activities. For example, Japanese children are trained to assume the posture of *shisei o tadasu* before they start every class in the elementary school. At the beginning of a class, the teacher or student representative calls out 'shisei o tadashite kudasai ('Please hold yourself up')' as the students stand up by their desk. Once they straighten themselves up, they bow to the teacher and then the class begins. Even in elementary schools outside Japan, teachers make sure that their students hold themselves up before starting the class. Kanagy (1999), for example, reports that a teacher in a Japanese immersion kindergarten in the USA corrects the children's posture (back straight, hands in lap) and does not start taking attendance until all the students have the correct posture (*shisei o tadasu*). These observations indicate how important the posture of *shisei o tadasu* is in Japanese society to show one's good side. By the term 'self-presentational stance' I mean the Japanese notion of *shisei o tadasu*. In other words, the use of the *masu* form is a linguistic expression of the posture of *shisei o tadasu*. The notion of the self-presentational stance (or *shisei o tadasu*) I am talking about is related to Goffman's (1959) notion of 'presentation of self' to others. The difference is that while the Goffmanian 'self-presentation' takes place whenever an individual encounters others, the self-presentational stance (or *shisei o tadasu*) occurs in a more restricted context, namely when an individual becomes more self-conscious of their own behavior (i.e. literally or figuratively on stage being watched by others). In other words, an individual is not likely to assume the self-presentational stance when he or she is relaxed, feels intimate with others and/or does not care about how others evaluate him or her (cf. Lebra, 1976). This stance can be expressed either verbally or non-verbally. While the verbal display of this stance is the use of the *masu* form, the non-verbal display includes a straight posture and formal clothes among other things. This affective stance is an important part of being a responsible and capable person in Japanese society.

The affective stance of self-presentation in part constitutes various social identities in Japanese society. Thus, the *masu* form can indirectly index various social identities and activities such as those of a person in charge (e.g. parent, teacher), a knowledgeable party (e.g. teacher, other authority figures) and a presenter (e.g. newscaster, interviewer). It also indirectly indexes another's voice (e.g. reported speech), and a lower-status person in some non-reciprocal exchanges between the *masu* and plain form, among others. These social identities are in part created by the self-presentational stance, for the display of this stance is indicative of a responsible or good social persona in Japanese society. For example, a mutual *masu* exchange between the professor and student in Example (7) above can index that they are speaking in their professional capacity (i.e. professor and student). To recapitulate, the *masu* form indexes that the speaker is speaking in some social capacity of self-presentation, which further infers various social identities of a responsible or of a good persona acting in character.

## Mediation of the *uchi* and *soto* contexts: Politeness and formality

In this section, I discuss how the social meaning of politeness and formality typically associated with the *masu* form arises in interactional context. These social meanings of the *masu* form are mediated by the *uchi* ('in-group/inside') or *soto* ('out-group/outside') context.

The meaning of politeness associated with the *masu* form is fore-grounded by the *soto* context. In the *soto* context, in which less intimacy exists between the speaker and addressee, the speaker's display of the self-presentational stance is socially expected (cf. Lebra, 1976), and an absence of this stance may index improper and impolite behavior. As polite behavior is expected in this context, the self-presentational stance evokes the social meaning of politeness. This does not mean that social identities are not indexed by the *masu* form in the *soto* ('outside/out-group') context. Both social identities and politeness are simultaneously indexed through the self-presentational stance. For example, when the professor and student both speak in the *masu* form, they are enacting the social identities of 'professor' and 'student'; at the same time their *masu* use is interpreted as polite behavior. However, because displaying politeness through the good side of a persona (i.e. *shisei o tadasu*) is expected in the *soto* ('out-group/outside') context, the social meaning of politeness is foregrounded. This is why native speakers of Japanese perceive the *masu* form as a marker of politeness. As the social identities indexed by the *masu* form in the *soto* context are not so salient as the indexing of politeness, these social meanings are beyond native speakers' consciousness (cf. Silverstein, 2001). In contrast, in the *uchi* ('in-group/ inside') context, in which intimacy and spontaneity are the norm (cf. Lebra, 1976), a display of the self-presentational stance is not socially expected. Therefore, an absence of this stance is not an impolite act. Thus, a display of this stance in this context foregrounds the speaker's identity rather than a polite behavior.

The *masu* form can also index formality. Formality is a complex notion. Irvine (1979) proposes that formality has four different aspects: (1) increased code structuring; (2) code consistency; (3) invocation of positional identities; and (4) emergence of a central situational focus. Each aspect can index formality but often more than one aspect co-occurs to create formality in the same social occasion. The *masu* form is perceived as a marker of formality when at least two aspects co-occur in the speech situation – when the *masu* form highlights the speaker's social identity (i.e. invocation of propositional identities) and its use is sustained (i.e. code consistency). As the sustained use of the *masu* form occurs in, and indexes, the *soto* context, the social meaning of formality is also mediated by the *soto* context.

The identity of a lower-status person is created by the display of self-presentation to someone of a higher status. Although in general in the *soto* ('out-group/outside') context, a display of the self-presentational stance is expected, it is more likely that a higher-status person does not sustain this stance when talking to a lower-status person. This is perhaps because a person with higher status cares less about how he or she is evaluated by a person of lower status, and is more inclined to act intimately toward a person of lower status. The resulting non-reciprocal exchange of the *masu* and plain forms in the *soto* ('out-group/outside') context may index a status difference between interlocutors. In other words, exchanging two different verbal forms can indicate different social statuses. In such an instance, the lower-status person's *masu* form can be interpreted as a way of showing politeness to a higher-status person because a display of politeness is socially expected.

An example of non-reciprocal exchange of the *masu* and plain forms between a mother and a child provides further evidence that the social meaning of politeness is not a direct index of the *masu* form and that a non-reciprocal exchange of these forms does not automatically mean that the user of the *masu* form is a lower-status or younger person. Rather, such social meaning is mediated by the social context in which the form occurs. Example (8) illustrates this point. In this example, using *masu*, the mother is asking her son H whether he wants jam or chocolate to put on his toast. Note that the son responds to the mother's question in the plain form, which is the form in which he mostly speaks to the mother.

(8) [Family O] (Cook, 1997:702)

1 → M: sa      jamu **desu** ka?
        well   jam   Cop  Q
        'Well, do you want jam?'

2 → M: apurikotto jamu **desu** ka  choko      **desu**  ka?
     apricot   jam  Cop  Q chocolate  Cop   Q
     'Do you want apricot jam or chocholate?'

  H: boku wa jamu da̲    na
      'I     Top jam Cop   FP
      'I want jam.'

  M: hai hai
     yes yes
     'Yes, yes'

In family conversation (a typical *uchi* 'in-group/inside' context), the mother speaks to the child in the plain form most of the time. Then why does she speak in the *masu* form here? Apparently, the mother's use of the *masu* form does not index a display of politeness to the child. Note that in this example the mother uses the *masu* form when she offers food to the child. As I discuss below, the *masu* form in Example (8) highlights the social identity of the 'mother' who is responsible for providing food to the family. The important point is that the social meaning of politeness or formality is not directly linked to the linguistic form of *masu* but rather is an outcome of interaction mediated by the *uchi* or *soto* context. In sum, the foregoing discussion indicates that the social meanings of the *masu* form are context dependent and vary from context to context or even from moment to moment.

This analysis has at least four advantages over the previous analyses. First, it incorporates and advances Maynard's (1991, 1993) insight that the *masu* form is more likely to occur when the speaker's awareness of the addressee is high. It is reasonable to say that the speaker is most likely to display the self-presentational stance when he or she is aware of being watched by the addressee(s). Second, this analysis can explain what most previous proposals (in particular, those claiming that the *masu* form is a marker of politeness) cannot adequately account for. For instance, it can account for the use of *masu* by a parent to the child. Third, it can account for various shades of social meaning arising in different communicative contexts. Fourth, it captures the dynamic nature of social interaction, in which the meaning of a linguistic form is part of interactional processes. In sum, the model given in Figure 3.1 does not directly assign a linguistic form to the social categories that are constructed in interaction. Thus it captures more fully the dynamic nature of social interaction.

## The Pattern of the *Masu* Form Usages in Japanese Family Conversation

In many cultures, family conversation at home is one of the most intimate contexts (cf. Blum-Kulka, 1997) and is the context in which children first acquire language and are socialized. In this sense, in the Japanese setting it is a typical *uchi* ('in-group/inside') context, where young Japanese children first learn appropriate use of the *masu* and plain forms.

Family dinnertime conversation is a speech event in which the interactants are typically relaxed and 'off stage'. To index intimacy, informality and spontaneity, Japanese immediate family members today mostly use the plain form (often with co-occurring affect markers such as sentence particles) regardless of differences in age and rank (e.g. parents versus children). This practice contrasts with the use of address and reference terms among family members. Among Japanese family members, typically, the younger members call the older members by kinship terms, and the older members call the younger members by their first name (see Suzuki, 1984). This practice is observed in Western societies as well but in a more limited fashion. While in most Western societies, the child typically calls only the parents and grandparents by kinship terms, in Japanese society, younger siblings call older siblings by kinship terms (i.e. *oneesan* 'older sister' and *oniisan* 'older brother') while they are called by their first name. Thus, with regards to address and reference terms, Japanese families are more clearly rank-ordered than American families. In this context, reciprocal use of the plain form, which is the norm in the family, allows family members to index informal, equal and spontaneous relationships.

It is generally believed that, as the plain form is the norm in the family context, the *masu* form does not occur. Therefore, only a few studies have examined use of the *masu* form in family conversation. However, the family members sometimes shift to the *masu* form. Sukle (1994) studied a family dinnertime conversation among parents and two college-age daughters in a middle-class household in Tokyo. He found that the *masu* form is used in a small percentage of family conversation. Out of a total of 453 utterances in the corpus of his data, he found that 3.8% of all utterances were in the *masu* form, 30.7% in the plain form and 65.6% in fragment (i.e. incomplete sentences).[15] When do the members of a Japanese family habitually shift to the *masu* form in family conversation? This section discusses normative uses of the *masu* form in Japanese family conversation.

The existing research on use of the *masu* form within families reveals a pattern of *masu* form use among family members. For example, Clancy (1985), who studied interactions between young children (ages 1–3 years old) and their parents at home, reports that mothers use *masu* in the following social contexts: (1) playing a teacher's role, (2) correcting a child's behavior, (3) reading a storybook, (4) quoting the speech of a socially high-status person such as a doctor and (5) performing a host/ guest role-play. Clancy (1985: 444) notes that the mothers in her data sometimes shift to *masu* when they playfully take on the role of a teacher:[16]

> For example, mothers sometimes used the −*mas* level in requesting that the child perform, as in *Nani o utatte kureru n desu ka?* ('What will you sing for us?') or *Midori wa dore desu ka?* ('Which is the green one?') addressed to a girl of 2;1 years. In such contexts, the mother seems to step momentarily out of her ordinary role to become a kind of teacher, and these situations have the feel of assumed formality which characterizes the longer routines. Mothers seem to enjoy these playful code-switching sequences, in which they briefly adopt a different attitude or role towards their child...

Cook (1997) also found that the *masu* form is used when the participants speak in another's voice, utter a set formula and are in charge of matters related to their responsibility. In family conversation, then, shifts to the *masu* form habitually occur within a range of well defined social functions: (1) uttering a set formula, (2) using 'voices' (Bakhtin, 1981) to display a variety of social identities, which include a person in charge, a knowledgeable party, a presenter and (3) quoting the voice outside the home.

As discussed above, the politeness interpretation of the *masu* form is foregrounded when the self-presentational stance is expected (e.g. *soto* or 'out-group/outside' context). In the *uchi* ('in-group/inside') context (e.g. family conversation), in which such a stance is not expected (except for set formulas), the *masu* form is mainly used as a resource for displaying various social identities. Japanese children learn to use the *masu* form in the *uchi* ('in-group/inside') context before learning to use it in the *soto* ('out-group/outside'). This means that they first learn to use the form when parents enact different social identities through the affective stance of self-presentation. Later, children use the *masu* form as a marker of politeness to people in *soto* relationships. It seems that most children start to prefer to speak to outsiders in the *masu* form around the time when they reach puberty, when they become more conscious of their behavior.[17] Apparently, the affective stance of self-presentation associated with the *masu* form is more fundamental than politeness in the sense that it is the social meaning young children first come to understand in the *uchi* ('in-group/inside') context.

In what follows, based on data from previous studies, I illustrate habitual usages of the *masu* form in Japanese family conversation. The family members may shift to the *masu* form when they (1) express set formulas such as *itadakimasu* (a polite phrase before eating), (2) index a variety of social identities and (3) use reported speech.

## Set formulas

Some set formulas that are used daily in family conversation are only used in the *masu* form. Expressions such as *itte kimasu* or a more polite variant *itte mairimasu* and *itadakimasu* are good examples. *Itte kimasu* (or *itte mairimasu*) is said as one leaves one's own house or a place to which he or she belongs. For example, all family members say *itte kimasu* or *itte mairimasu* as they leave the house. *Itadakimasu*, which is the humble form of the verb *to receive*, is a set formula said by everyone just before eating or drinking, meaning 'thank you for what I am about to receive'. It is similar to the French expression, *bon appétit*, but it differs from *bon appétit* in the sense that *itadakimasu* is said by everyone before every meal and snack. Example (9), in which the father, mother and their child Aya start to eat dinner, shows that everyone in the family, including three-year-old Aya, says *itadakimasu* as they begin dinner. The parents even say the phrase two times.

(9) [Family M] (family conversation data, Cook)

1 F: **itadakima:su**
   receive
   'I am going to receive.'

2 M: **itadakima:su**
   receive
   'I am going to receive.'

3    aya-chan mo kore itadaite mo  ii  wa yo.
    Aya     also this  eat    also good FP FP
    'Aya, you may eat this.'

4 A: **itadakimasu**
   receive
   'I am going to receive.'

5 M: **itadakimasu**
   receive
   'I am going to receive.'

6    hai. aya-chan, osushi tsukutte miyoo ka
    yes Aya     sushi make  try    Q
    'OK, Aya, shall we try to make sushi?'

7 F: **itadakima:su**
   receive
   'I am going to receive.'

*Itte kimasu* (or *itte mairimasu*) and *itadakimasu* are set formulas that children hear family members say and which they are told to say all the time. In particular, children eat at least three meals and also eat snacks a couple of times a day, so they frequently hear their caregivers say *itadakimasu* at a very young age. As these set formulas are only available in the *masu* form, even when the family members are infrequent users of the *masu* form, they use the *masu* form when expressing these set formulas. Thus, Japanese children grow up at home using both plain and *masu* forms.

## Being in charge: Constructing the social identity of a parent

In family conversation between parents and children, perhaps the most prominent use of the *masu* form is to construct parental identity. Teaching children, correcting children's behavior and serving food are primary responsibilities of parents, in particular those of the mother. When parents are in charge of these activities, they may shift to the *masu* form. This use of the *masu* form contrasts with that used by lower-status speakers to indicate politeness toward a higher-status person.

### Correcting children's behavior

The *masu* form in the parents' speech can occur when correcting children's behavior, or when teaching them something they do not know. In these instances, a parents' use of the *masu* form indexes his or her identity as the 'parent' responsible for correcting the child's inappropriate behavior, but does not index politeness to the child. In (10), a three-year-old child A is climbing on the dinner table. The father tells her that climbing on the table shows bad manners. In these examples, the father employs the *masu* form to correct the child's behavior.

(10) [Family M] (Cook, 1997: 703)

F: otsukue no ue, ogyoogi warui **desu** yo, sore wa.
   desk     LK top manner bad  Cop FP that Top
   'On top of the table, that's bad manners, that is.'

Example (11) comes from Takagi's data (2002). The family is eating noodles for dinner. In line 2 the father simply tells the child that he does not want to eat the noodles. Here he uses the plain form. Then the child puts the noodles in the mother's mouth. When she takes them out of her mother's mouth, she immediately holds them out to the father. This time the father rejects her offer because he does not want to eat food that was already in someone else's mouth. In line 6, he does so by shifting to the *masu* form. Both in lines 2 and 6, the father is rejecting the child's offer but he uses different stances. In line 2 he rejects her offer by stating his personal desire. In contrast, in line 6, he is talking to the child as a 'father/parent'. In this utterance, the reason why he does not want to eat the food the child offers to him is objectively stated as a social norm. Teaching the child social norms is one of the important responsibilities of the parents. Thus, the *masu* form used by the father in line 6 indexes that the father is acting in his role of father/parent.

(11) (Takagi's data) F (father), M (mother), and A (child, girl about two years old)

1  A: ((Picks up a noodle from her bowl with her left hand and holds it up toward F.))

2   F: toosan ira(h)nai. ((Turns away his head.))
     father need Neg
     'I don't want it.'

3  A: ((Brings her left hand toward M.))

4  M: ((Pretends to take a bite of the noodle.))

5  A: ((Quickly puts the noodle in M's mouth, then takes it out and holds it out to F again.))

6-> F: (1.0) na(hhh) (.) ippen kuchi ni iretamono **irimasen**.
                   once mouth in put in thing need Neg
     'I don't want things that have been already in someone else's mouth.'

7  A: ((Holds the noodle up toward M.))

Clancy (1985) reports similar examples. For instance, when a child broke off the nose of his Snoopy toy, his mother shifted to the *masu* form, saying, *Ikenai* **desu** *ne* 'That's not nice, is it?' Nakamura's (2002) data also illustrate that mothers often use the *masu* form when they scold their children.

*Teaching children – a knowledgeable person – a parent/teacher*
Another important responsibility of parents is to teach their child. Parents often shift to the *masu* form when they teach their child something that he or she does not know. In Example (12), the mother is talking to her sons, K and H. She shifts to the *masu* form when she realizes that Child K is not able to do some simple math. Here the primary recipient of the mother's questions is the older child K, who is seven years old.

(12) [Family O] (family conversation data, Cook)
M (Mother), K (child, age seven), and H (child, age five)

1 M: sanji    ni deta to shite hachiji    ni kaeru  to shitara    nanjikan?
     3 o'clock at leave suppose 8 o'clock at return suppose how many hours
     'If I leave at three and come back at eight, how many hours (will I be gone)?'

2 H: Da dan ((utters a nonsense word))

3 K: rokujikan da. rokujikan sanjuppun.
    6 hours   Cop 6 hours  30 minutes
    'Six hours. Six hours and thirty minutes.'

4 M: sanji     ni dete hachiji    ni kaeru to shitara? keesan shite.
    3 o'clock at leave 8 o'clock at return suppose  calculate
    'If I leave at three and come back at eight? Calculate.'

5 H: cha uto: ((utters a nonsense word.))

6 K: ((long pause))

7 M: (  ) nigate ne, kazu ne, kazoete ikeba ii ja nai
       not good FP Kazu FP count  go if good not
    '(  ) You're not good at it Kazu. All you need to do is count.'

8 H: ashita     sa:-
    tomorrow FP
    'Tomorrow-'

9 K: demo boku kanji dake ga tokui  de sansuu wa anmari tokui ja nai =
    but  I     kanji only S good at and maths Top very good at   Neg
    'But I'm only good at Chinese characters and not very good at math.'

10 H: = ja hachi-
     well eight
     'uh, eight-'

11 → M: sanji     kara hachiji    made wa nan jikan **desu** ka?
       3 o'clock from 8 o'clock till   Top what hours Cop  Q
       'How many hours are there between three o'clock and eight
       o'clock?'

12 H: hachi-
    eight
    'Eight-'

13 M: yatte, hiro. san kara hachi made ikutsu    aru no?
    do   Hiro  three from eight till how many exist FP
    'Count Hiro. How many hours are there between three and eight?'

14 K: gojikan.
    5 hours
    'Five hours.'

15 M: gojikan.
    5 hours
    'Five hours.'

The mother asks her son how many hours she would be gone if she leaves home at three o'clock and returns at eight. K gives a wrong answer in line 3. The mother repeats the question in line 4, but K does not respond to her question. The mother takes K's long pause as an indication that he does not know the answer, so she comments that K is not good at math in line 7. K explains in line 9 that he is good at Chinese characters but not math. Up to this point, both the mother and K are speaking in the plain form. But in line 11, instead of acknowledging K's excuse, the mother repeats the same question but this time in the *masu* form. The fact that she does not acknowledge K's excuse indicates that it is not acceptable to her. It is at this point that the mother shifts to the *masu* form to index the voice of a teacher.

*Serving food – the mother*

In Japanese society, cooking and serving food to family members is an important responsibility associated with the identity of the mother. Mothers often shift to the *masu* form when they serve or talk about food they cook. This is another expression of the self-presentational stance when engaging in activity in which the speaker is in charge. Example (13) illustrates this use of the *masu* form. Here the mother speaks in the *masu* form to her young children when she offers them an omelet. The *masu* form foregrounds her identity as a mother.

(13) [In Family T the mother is offering food to the children, D (age five), C (age three) and Y (age one).] (Cook, 1997:702)

1 – > tamagoyaki mo **arimasu** yo.
     omelet       also exist     FP
     'There is also an omelet.'

2   chii-chan, ohashi no tsukaikata        ga   ii   ja <u>nai</u> no.
     Chii        chopstick LK way of using S good   not   FP
     'Chii, (you) use chopsticks well, don't you?'
     ((Y wants more food))

3   ((gives food to Y)) hai manma yuu-tan.
                         yes food    Yuu
                         'Yes, food, Yuu-chan.'

4   ((to C)) chihiro-chan moo sukoshi koo massugu suwaranai
             Chihiro       more little this way straight sit not
             to okoboshi- okoboshi <u>suru</u> kara ne
             if spill       spill      do    so    FP

     'Chihiro, if you do not sit straight, you will spill.'

5 – > ((to Y)) tamatama mo **arimasu** yo, yuu-chan
      egg      also exist   FP Yuu
      'Yuu, there are also eggs'

In line 1, the mother marks her utterance in the *masu* form when she offers the omelet to the children. In line 5 she uses it again when she offers some eggs to the one-year-old child, Y. Here we note that the mother uses the nursery word *tamatama* ('eggs') when she talks to Y. The nursery word suggests that the utterance containing the *masu* form is exclusively addressed to the toddler, Y. Use of the *masu* form in Example (13) indexes the mother's identity as the person who is in charge of cooking and serving food.

*Household chores – a parent/mother*

There are other household chores that parents preside over. These include regulating children's behavior at home, such as putting children to bed, asking children to help with household chores, regulating TV time for children, as well as playing with children. Example (14) illustrates a case in which the mother shifts to the *masu* form to announce it is time for her children to watch TV.

(14) [Family O] (Cook, 1997:703)

1    K: terebi tsukete
        TV   turn on
        'Turn on the TV.'

2    M: moo sukoshi mada. Mada <u>hachiji</u> yo
        more little   not yet still 8 o'clock FP
        'A little while, not yet. It's still not eight o'clock yet.'

3  K: moo     hachiji   <u>da</u> yo
      already 8 o'clock Cop FP
      'It's already eight o'clock.'

4 M: <u>mada</u> yo.
    not yet FP
    'Not yet.'
    ((several minutes later))

5 – > M: ja:   terebi **tsukemasu** ka?
        well TV   turn on   Q
        'Well shall we turn on the TV?'

In line 1, Child K asks to turn on the TV, but the mother rejects his request. Her utterance that it is still eight o'clock is in the plain form followed by the emphatic particle *yo*. K argues back saying that it's already eight o'clock, using the plain form as well as the particle *yo*. The mother rejects his request once more using the emphatic particle *yo*. But several minutes later, in line 5, she decides that it is time to turn on the TV and states *terebi tsukemasu ka* ('shall we turn on the TV?'). The shifts to the *masu* form occurs in this utterance, which foregrounds her identity as the authority who regulates the TV time for the children.

One of Nakamura's examples (2002: 26) also falls into this category. In (15), the mother, who was speaking in the plain form, shifts to the *masu* form when she asks the child, who is two and half years old, if he has finished his meal. The mother is the person who regulates the beginning and ending of the child's meal, and the *masu* form here is indexing this parental responsibility. The child also responds to her in the *masu* form. As I discuss below, this use of *masu* is a display of the child acting as a good child.[18]

(15) (Nakamura, 2002:26)

Mother: moo       gohan tabe-**owarimashita** ka?
          Already meal     eat-finish           Q
          'Have (you) finished eating (your) meal already?'

Child: mada **desu**.
        not yet Cop
        'Not yet.'

I have shown that parents in Japanese family conversation shift to the *masu* form to index their responsibility and duties in the household. By so doing, they foreground the parental identity that comes with these responsibilities. Family members' shift to the *masu* form does not occur in random fashion. When it occurs, it may fall within a range of certain social acts related to parental responsibilities and duties.

It is important to note, however, that not all instances of parents' responsibility and duties are marked with the *masu* form. For example, in Example (14), the mother does not speak in the *masu* form in lines 2 and 4. When the mother speaks to her child in the plain form, it does not mean that she is not a mother. In such an instance, she is a mother, but she is not placing her social identity as a mother in the foreground of the interaction. Again, it is a choice the speaker makes to mark the utterance with the *masu* form to foreground his or her social identity in the immediate speech context.

In sum, parents may shift to the *masu* form when they are in charge of actions that are related to their responsibility at home.

## Quoting others: Social identities outside the home

From time to time, participants in family conversation use the *masu* form when they enact social identities other than their own, or when they quote their own voice in talking to outsiders. They often do so by employing reported speech.

For example, parents may quote an authority figure such as the child's doctor as in Example (16). Here the father talks to a 3-year-old child and quotes the doctor's words using the *masu* form in reported speech. Quoting different categories of people using the *masu* form teaches children appropriate social contexts outside of the home in which the *masu* form is used.

(16) [Family M] (family conversation data, Cook)

F: ashita    wa Tanaka-sensei aya-chan puuru itte mo ii **desu** yo.
   tomorrow Top Tanaka Dr.  Aya       pool go also good Cop FP
   tte itta  n datte ne
   QT said Nom Cop FP
   'Dr. Tanaka (said), 'Aya, it is OK to go swimming in the swimming pool
   Tomorrow (*masu* form).'

Another instance of the *masu* form used in reported speech can be seen in Example (17). Here, the mother is talking to the father about swimming classes for their children. She talked to a teacher at the nearby Yamato elementary school. She quotes the teacher's voice using the *masu* form.

(17) [Family O] (family conversation data, Cook)

M: demo, ano yamatoshoo         no hito       to kyoo atte ne,
   but   uh  Yamato elementary LK person with today met FP
   chotto oshaberi shita n dakedo kekkyoku
   a little chat    did Nom but  after all
   'ichikawa-shi no suiee kyooshitsu to shite **yarimasu**' tte.
   Ichikawa city LK swimming class as    do        QT
   'But I saw the teacher of Yamato elementary school today and we talked a little. It turned out that she said, "We'll be holding swimming classes as a part of classes offered by Ichikawa-city (*masu* form)."

By shifting to the *masu* form, the family members also quote their own voice addressed to member(s) of an outgroup. In Example (18), the mother shifts to the *masu* form when she quotes herself when discussing the need to report her son's absence to his teacher.

(18) [Family O] (family conversation data, Cook)

M: 'kega shita kara oyasumi **shimasu**' tte renraku shinakutcha.
   injury did so    absent  do       QT contact have to
   'I have to contact (the teacher), to say, "(my son) got injured so he will be absent (from school) (*masu* form)."'

These examples show that by shifting to the *masu* form to quote the voices of outsiders and of their own, parents convey to children how certain categories of people outside the home speak as well as how to talk to people outside the home.

The *masu* form can also index a shift in the speaker's footing to a playful mood. In the following conversation, the mother and two children, K and H, are eating dinner. K marks his playful comments by constructing the voice of an advertisement in the *masu* form.

(19) [Family O] (family conversation data, Cook)

1 K: kondo    koora sukunakute ii kara, kono kurai de ii kara.
   this time coke  little amount good so this much    good so
   'Now (I want) some coke just a little. Just about this much.'

2 H: umai na    oishii na
   delicious FP delicious FP
   'Delicious. Delicious.'

3 M: ja    yusuide irasshai yo.
   Well rinse    go       FP
   'Well, rinse (the glass).'

4 H: boku yusuganakute mo heeki da yo. boku nareteru mon.
   I    no rinse        also OK Cop FP I    used to   FP
   'I don't mind if I don't rise it. I am used to it (not being rinsed).'

5 M: ii   no?[19]
   good FP
   'Is it OK?'

6 H: ii    yo (.) doose   aji   wa kawaranai   shi.
   good FP anyway    taste Top change not and
   'It's OK. The taste doesn't change.'

7 →K: gyuunyuu to koora mazeru to oishisoo da  shi  ne. gyuunyuu
    milk        and coke mix    if delicious Cop and FP  milk
    ando  koora **desu**.
    and   coke  Cop
    'Mixing milk and coke seems delicious too. It's milk and coke.'

Children K and H were drinking milk but then they wanted some coke. The mother told them to rinse the glasses they were using to drink milk. However, in line 4, H asserts that he does not mind drinking coke from the same glass without rinsing it, and in line 7, K supports H, using the *masu* form and the English borrowing *ando* ('and'), reflecting a style typically used in advertisements. In this example, in which the children are not complying with their mother, K's use of an advertisement-like slogan indexes playfulness.

## Children's social knowledge

Through daily interactions with their parents, by age three, Japanese children know appropriate uses of the *masu* form both inside and outside the home (Clancy, 1985; Cook, 1997; Fukuda, 2005; Nakamura, 2002). Children may shift to the *masu* form when they display their responsibilities at home. In this sense, acquisition of the *masu* form goes hand in hand with acquiring sociocultural knowledge. Children's responsibilities are not the same as those of their parents. They are expected to be good children who listen to their parents and learn about the world. When they are conforming to such parental expectations, children tend to use the *masu* form. Children at the age of three can act out the role of a 'good child' or an 'expert' using the *masu* form (Cook, 1997). This also suggests that children as young as three years old have already been socialized into displaying their good side when parents expect them to behave well. For example, in family O, five-year-old Child H uses the *masu* form when claiming that he is a good child at kindergarten. This follows a complaint by his mother that he is not listening to her.

(20) (family conversation data, Cook)

H: Yoochien     de wa yoku **kiitemasu** yo
    Kindergarten in Top well listen     FP
    'I listen (to my teacher) certainly well at kindergarten'

Being a good child also entails being able to apologize when the child makes a mistake or does not behave. Nakamura (2002) reports that the children in her data often shift to the *masu* form when apologizing as shown in (21). Here the boy, aged two-and-a-half, spilt his milk and was scolded by his mother. He apologizes using the *masu* form.

(21) Apologizing for spilling his milk. (Nakamura, 2002: 28)

Child: Gomennasai. Moo     **shimasen**.
    Sorry     any more do Neg
    '(I'm) sorry.    (I) won't do (it) again'.

In these examples we have seen that young Japanese children can shift to the *masu* form to convey to their parents that they are good children.

## Socialization through the use of the *masu* form

From the discussion above, it is clear that participants use the plain form for the most part in Japanese family conversation, but there is a habitual shifting pattern to the *masu* form. Shifts to the *masu* form indirectly index various social identities related to responsibilities in the family and the reporting of interaction with people outside the family. For example, parents make this shift when they are teaching children, in control of household chores, and cooking and serving food among others. In these instances, the parent's use of the *masu* form is equivalent to saying 'as a parent I am telling you'. The parents' daily practice of how and when to use the voice of 'mother', 'father', 'parent' or other social identities through use of the *masu* form socializes children in culturally important ways: first, it teaches children when to be on stage in ways appropriate to their role at home. For example, the mother's use of the *masu* form when serving food to the family teaches children that doing so is the mother's responsibility. Secondly, it teaches children that when one is in charge or takes responsibility, displaying a self-presentational stance (i.e. *shisei o tadasu* or *kichin to suru*) is part of taking responsibility. Shift to the *masu* form implicitly instructs children when to show their good side and when and how to be responsible at home. Furthermore, the *masu* form is a linguistic tool to express various voices in society or what Bakhtin (1981) calls 'heteroglossia'. It is used to index other people's voices, for example, the voices of people outside the family or one's own voice when talking to outsiders. Through use of the *masu* form, both parents and children utilize other voices to teach social norms and to be playful. From daily interaction with parents at home, Japanese children learn to differentiate and display different voices, both personal and social. In this manner, within the bounds of intimate family interaction at home, occasional display of self-presentational stance through the use of the *masu* form is an important tool in socializing children.

Use of the *masu* form at home prepares children to display their social identities in contexts outside the home (e.g. classroom). The way in which the *masu* form is used in many social situations outside the home is consistent with the way in which it is used at home (e.g. Cook, 1996a). For example, elementary school students use the *masu* form when they participate in the *happyoo* ('presentation') activity (Anderson, 1995; Cook, 1996b). When giving a *happyoo*, students are literally on stage, for they stand up in front of the class or by their own seat and present their opinion to the whole class. They mark their self-presentational stance with use of the *masu* form during the *happyoo* activity. When they finish their *happyoo*, they shift to the plain form. The *masu* form indexes the students' identity as players in the *happyoo* activity.

## Normative Uses of the *Masu* Form in Family Conversation

A particular style shifting pattern is conventionally associated with a particular social context. In family conversation, which is a typical *uchi* ('in-group/inside') context, besides appearing in set formulas, the *masu* form indexes various social identities that foreground the responsibilities and authority of family members, and marks the voices of other people. In other words, the preferred stance in family conversation is intimacy indexed by the plain form with other stances (e.g. display of certain social identities, voices of other people) and set formulas indexed by the *masu* form. These are the normative uses of the *masu* form in family conversation. On the other hand, in the family, the *masu* form occurs neither in reactive tokens nor in questions/answers/statements in which the speaker is not expressing his or her responsibility and/or authority. These uses of the *masu* form are typically associated with the *soto* ('out-group/outside') context (see Chapter 5 for further discussion). Here, it is important to emphasize that participants, as active agents in social interactions, choose the *masu* forms to accomplish their interactional goals (e.g. Cook, 1996a, 1996b; Okamoto, 1999). They are not passively observing prescribed social norms. Although the pattern described above is the norm and most expected, there is a range of variation across speakers with respect to the use of linguistic forms.[20] Figure 3.2 schematizes the normative patterns of the use of the *masu* form in family conversation (*uchi* context).

Although members of a Japanese family have choices as to when to shift to the *masu* form, their choices are constrained by the structure of expectations and preferences of local practice. The members of middle-class Japanese families in the Tokyo area from which this data is taken tacitly know a range of social meanings of the *masu* form in family conversation. As I mentioned above, it is also important to note that not all instances of being in charge of household tasks, for example, are marked by the *masu* form. What Figure 3.2 indicates is that shifts to the *masu* form in family talk may occur in the specific acts that constitute the indirect indexes listed in this figure. Family members also tacitly know that to use the *masu* form in ways deviant from the norm of family conversation (e.g. to give a reactive token in the *masu* form) may index a *soto* ('out-group/outside') context. Such knowledge is communicative competence of middle-class Japanese native speakers.

| Linguistic form | Stance | Indirect indexes |
|---|---|---|
| *Masu* form → | On-stage → self-presentational stance | A person in charge Knowledgeable party Playing Quoting others Set formula |

**Figure 3.2** Normative uses of the *masu* form in family conversation

## Conclusion

The fluidity of social meanings of the *masu* form is accounted for by the indexical model. In this model, the *masu* form is directly linked to the affective stance of self-presentation (*shisei o tadasu* 'to hold oneself up'), which is an important social disposition for a responsible member of Japanese society. This stance (direct index) helps constitute other social meanings such as social identity and politeness (indirect indexes). In this process, social contexts influence the interpretation of the *masu* form. Thus, in the *uchi* ('in-group/inside') context, the *masu* form foregrounds social identities. In contrast, in the *soto* ('out-group/outside') context, the *masu* form indexes politeness because politeness is socially expected in this context.

In Japanese family dinnertime conversation, there is a normative style shift pattern. While the participants mainly use the plain form to index spontaneity and intimacy, they may shift to the *masu* form when they (1) utter a set formula, (2) display various social identities and (3) speak as outsiders or in their own voice when talking to an outsider. The *masu* form is a resource for parents to show their responsibilities and rights as 'parents', and for children to show their responsibilities as 'children'.

## Notes

1. The *masu* form is also referred to as the 'polite or formal style' and 'distal style', and the plain form as the 'non-polite style', 'informal style', 'direct style' and '*da*-style'.
2. In this book, the tentative form of *desu* (*deshoo*) and the request form (*kudasai*) are not included in the analysis. The plain counterpart of *deshoo*, which is *daroo*, sounds rough even in informal conversation and for that reason is typically used only by men in informal contexts. Therefore, although *deshoo* is a *masu* form, it is used even in informal conversation by both women and men. As a contrast between *deshoo* (the *masu* form) and *daroo* (the plain form) is not salient in most talk, I did not include *deshoo* as the *masu* form in the present analysis. The request form of *masu*, *kudasai*, is not included either, in order to be consistent with the Japanese native speaker family conversation data (Cook, 1996a, 1997).
3. The verb in the subordinate clause can be in the *masu* form, but this sounds hyperpolite (cf. Makino, 2002). In conversation, the *masu* form may occur in a *kara* ('because') or *kedo* ('but') clause without the main clause. In such instances, the *kara* or *kedo* clause is more like a main clause, i.e. *kara* or *kedo* functions as a pragmatic sentence-final particle rather than a conjunction. In this book, the *masu* and plain forms that occur in *kara* and *kedo* clauses are counted as instances of the *masu* and plain forms, respectively.
4. Example (7) comes from the data corpus I collected for a larger project on academic consultation sessions between university professors and students.
5. Brown and Levinson (1978, 1987) note that rule-based analysis can work for well bounded ritualized speech events like greetings.

6. Maynard refers to what I call 'the plain form' as 'the abrupt form'. I did not discuss the concept of the naked plain form earlier in this chapter where I explained the linguistic structure of the *masu* form because most scholars who study Japanese style shifts work within the dichotomous framework of the *masu* and plain forms and do not recognize the naked plain form as a category that has significant social meaning.

7. It is not clear to me why joint constructions are cases in which the speaker's awareness of the addressee is low.

8. In conversation between *uchi* ('outside/outgroup') members, the term *okaasan*, for example, is used as an address or reference term. In this case, *okaasan* means 'Mom', 'my mother' or 'our mother'.

9. In his study, Sukle included the request form, *-te kudasai*, in the *masu* form.

10. For further discussion on the notions of *uchi/soto* and *omote/ura*, see Lebra (1976) and Bachnik and Quinn (1994).

11. In describing the *masu* form, I used the terms 'the disciplined mode' in Cook (1996a, 1996b) and 'the mode of self for public presentation' in Cook (1997). In this chapter, I use the term 'self-presentational stance' because it is simpler and makes more sense in relation to the indexical model proposed by Ochs. I am not changing the analysis by using a different term. The terms used in my previous publications express the identical concept as the term 'the self-presentational stance'.

12. Excerpts from my previous publications are cited by date and page number(s), and those which did not appear previously have no date and page number(s).

13. As shown in Figure 3.1, the *masu* form foregrounds different aspects of context. However, not all social meanings of the *masu* form are within the reach of the native speakers' consciousness (Silverstein, 2001), and yet the *masu* form is a powerful tool for language socialization of the novice.

14. The role cannot have a negative social value such as the role of a rebel.

15. Sukle counted the request form, *kudasi*, as a *masu* form. He defines fragments as utterances without the *masu* or plain form.

16. Clancy (1985) does not present the frequency of the mothers' use of the *masu* form in conversation with her children.

17. As I discuss below, by the age of three, children learn that one of the functions of the *masu* form is to talk to outsiders. However, when the child is young, it seems that they are allowed to speak to outsiders in the plain form. This is perhaps because the ability to speak to outsiders in the *masu* form is considered as a sign of maturity and young children are not expected to show the presentational stance to outsiders. Most children begin to speak to outsiders using the *masu* form around the time when they go to junior high school (12 years old).

18. This analysis is mine. Nakamura (2002) uses this example to demonstrate that the child follows the speech style used by his mother.

19. *No* is classified as a nominalizer, but when it occurs at the end of an utterance, its primary pragmatic function is that of a sentence-final particle (see Cook, 1990b).

20. In my own data of family conversations, there was no use of the *masu* form deviant from the norm.

## Chapter 4
# Identity Construction Through Use of the Masu Form: JFL Learners and Host Families

One of the important tenets of Ochs and Schieffelin's language socialization model is that novices are implicitly socialized through the use of language. As discussed in Chapter 3, although most interactions among immediate Japanese family members are carried out in the plain form, shifting to the *masu* form allows speakers to express a variety of social identities related to their position in the family, and to enact the voices of outsiders as well as their own voices when talking to outsiders. Culturally and linguistically, JFL learners are similar to Japanese children in that they are novice members of the (host) family.[1] In this sense, dinnertime conversations (as well as other interactions) provide learners with opportunities for language socialization. This chapter examines uses of the *masu* form by host families and learners. The findings are in line with those discussed in Chapter 3; i.e. besides set formulas, the *masu* form is used when speakers display the social identity of (1) someone in charge of matters at hand or someone who is displaying authority, or (2) someone enacting the voice of someone else or their own voice when talking to others (ventriloquism).[2]

## Previous Studies on JFL Learners' Acquisition of the *Masu* Form

Before discussing the present data, I will review the literature on JFL learners' acquisition of the *masu* form. To date, only a few studies have examined JFL learners' acquisition of the *masu* form. Most of these studies, which investigated style shifts in the classroom setting, assume that the *masu* form is a marker of politeness and/or formality.

Yamashita (1996), Rounds *et al.* (1997) and Kanagy (1999) came to similar conclusions regarding Japanese teachers' uses of the *masu* form in the classroom. Yamashita (1996) investigated the style shifts of a Japanese instructor in a college JFL classroom, and Rounds *et al.* (1997) and Kanagy (1999) studied style shifts of teachers in a Japanese language immersion classroom in an American elementary school and a kindergarten. These studies found that while the teachers investigated mostly used the *masu* form in the classroom, they occasionally shifted to the plain form when they spoke to students in a more intimate manner. In particular, shifts to the plain form were observed when the teachers paraphrased complex sentences, scaffolded the content matter, and gave feedback to the students' answers. The findings of these studies are consistent with those of Cook (1996b), who examined the teachers' style shifts in first-language Japanese elementary school classrooms. These studies suggest that JFL learners are exposed to style shifts similar to those that occur in Japanese elementary school classrooms.

One of the important factors in acquiring a foreign language is noticing (Schmidt, 1993, 1995, 2001); that is, in order for learning to take place, learners have to pay conscious attention to a linguistic form and its associated contexts. Research indicates, however, that not only JFL learners but also Japanese language instructors are not conscious of style shifts. Wade (2003) analyzed style shifts of students and teachers in six Japanese language classrooms in both the USA and Japan. She provides evidence for the non-conscious nature of style shifts and further suggests that the teachers' shifting patterns do not match the prescriptive description of appropriate speech style usage. She found that the teachers' style shifts were intricately related to the different identities they play (e.g. teacher, interviewer and conversationalist)[3] in their interaction with the students as well as different stances (e.g. formal or casual) they took toward the students and the content of talk.[4]

JFL learners do not readily notice style shifts, and it is rather difficult for JFL learners to acquire an appropriate speech style through direct instruction in the classroom. To find out to what extent JFL learners' conscious attention to style shifts helps the acquisition of appropriate uses of the *masu* and plain forms, Ishida (2001) examined beginning-level JFL learners' awareness of the *masu* and plain forms over a period of three consecutive semesters. He asked three learners to observe Japanese native speakers' style shifts outside of the classroom and to keep journals on their observations. Although he found that the learners did not start to notice style shifts till the third semester, he also reported, based on the role-play data, that the learners were gradually able to appropriately shift speech styles.

Another question is whether or not JFL learners are able to notice style shifts and recognize social meaning indexed by the shift after the initial introduction of style shifts in the classroom. In Cook (2001), I examined the pragmatic judgments of 120 second-year American JFL learners after two and half semesters of typical foreign language instruction at the university level. This study found that 81% of second-year JFL learners did not notice examples of inappropriate speech style (i.e. the use of the plain form where the *masu* form is expected as well as use of sentence-final particles where absence of such particles is the norm) in an on-line listening comprehension task. However, it did not determine whether the students' failure to notice inappropriateness was due to cognitive or sociocultural factors. In other words, it is not clear from the study whether the students' failure in noticing inappropriateness was due to their inability to recognize the presence of the sentence-final particles and the plain form in the on-line task, or their ignorance of Japanese sociocultural norms. In order to see if fourth-year JFL learners can recognize inappropriate speech style, I also examined the pragmatic judgment of 53 fourth-year JFL learners in an on-line comprehension task employing the same material used in the 2001 study (Cook, 2002a). Compared with the 2001 study, this study found a marked improvement at the fourth-year level. Forty-seven percent of the fourth-year level JFL students successfully judged the use of inappropriate speech styles in an on-line listening comprehension task. However, 53% still failed at the fourth-year level. Reasons for their failure were found to be cognitive as well as sociocultural. These studies indicate that JFL learners find it difficult to notice and use appropriate speech styles at the beginning level, and that even after studying Japanese for more than three years, some JFL learners are still not capable of detecting pragmatic inappropriateness. These studies also suggest that paying close attention to class instruction and/or having frequent contact with native speakers in both formal and informal social contexts may help students succeed in pragmatic judgments of speech styles.

In order to investigate learners' uses of the *masu* form, other researchers have interviewed JFL learners after they returned from Japan to their home institution. In Marriott's study (1993), 11 Australian high school students who spent a year in Japan were interviewed by native speakers of Japanese. Marriott hypothesized that the students who studied Japanese longest prior to their departure to Japan would use the *masu* form more frequently than those who studied Japanese for a shorter period, for JFL learners typically learn the *masu* form first in the JFL classroom (see discussion in Chapter 7). However, the study did not confirm this hypothesis. Regardless of the length of Japanese study prior to leaving for Japan, most of the students used the plain form in the interview context – a context in which the *masu* form would normally be expected.

Taking a similar approach, Iwasaki (2005) interviewed JFL learners after their return from Japan, but came to a different conclusion than Marriott (1995). In Iwasaki's study, five male college students were given an Oral Proficiency Interview (OPI) soon after they came back to Japan. Only two students overused the plain form in the OPI interview. Then two years after they returned, in order to obtain their retrospective evaluation of their study-in-Japan experiences, Iwasaki interviewed the four students.[5] On the topic of speech styles, the three students who did not overuse the plain form in the OPI interview mentioned that due to some social engagements such as participation in extracurricular activities, they noticed the importance of the appropriate use of the *masu* form during their stay in Japan. In contrast, the student who overused the plain form in the OPI interview reported that he used the plain form as the default form mainly due to a lack of negative feedback. Iwasaki's study suggests that there are individual variations, depending on the type of experiences learners have, with respect to the acquisition of the appropriate use of the *masu* form during study abroad. However, the sample size of Iwasaki's study is too small to draw any definitive conclusion on individual experiences during study abroad. I will return to the topic of the length of stay and the acquisition of pragmatics in Chapter 7.

McMeekin's study (2007) is the only study that qualitatively examined style shifts in the homestay context. Her data came from conversations between five pairs of JFL learners and their host families who participated in an eight-week summer study abroad program in Japan. The learners' Japanese proficiency levels range from intermediate to low advanced on the OPI scale. Three 50-minute recordings were made for each learner and host family pair (one from the beginning, middle and the end of the study abroad period). Her findings are that while the host family members use the plain form over 80% of the time, the learners overwhelmingly use the *masu* form. The first recordings show that the intermediate-level learners use the *masu* form over 92% of the time while the advanced-level learner uses it over 56% of the time. Her data show that the learners, at least four out of five, exhibit some indications of shift to plain form use. Comparing the ratio of the plain and *masu* form uses over eight weeks (three recordings – one from the beginning, middle and the end of the program), it was found that all the learners except for one gradually increased the plain form uses and decreased the *masu* form uses. Although the rate of the learners' increase of the plain form is small, McMeekin's study demonstrates that the learners were socialized to use more plain forms by participating in daily interactions with the host family members who mostly spoke to them in the plain form. I will return to the issue of the learners' shift from *masu*-form dominance to plain-form dominance in Chapter 7.

In sum, the common assumption in most previous studies on JFL learners' style shift is that there is a one-to-one relationship between speech style and the social context. In other words, the plain form is used in informal situations such as when talking to peers while the *masu* form is used in formal situations such as an interview or when talking to a teacher. As discussed in Chapters 1 and 2, this assumption does not reflect the multiple social meanings of the *masu* form in everyday conversation. As a result, we still do not know whether or how JFL learners learn appropriate uses of the *masu* form in a host family setting and whether host family members shift to the *masu* form the way Japanese family members do.

## Uses of the *Masu* Form in Dinnertime Talk: The Learners and the Host Families

The present data reveal that although there are individual variations, host family members and JFL learners mostly use the plain form in dinnertime conversation and only sometimes shift to the *masu* form.[6] In other words, the plain form is the dominant speech style regardless of the learner's Japanese proficiency level, their length of Japanese study prior to coming to Japan and/or the host family members' age and gender. Plain form exchanges between learners and host family members indicate that interactionally they are co-constructing the *uchi* ('in-group/inside') context. What is remarkable is that no participant is a single speech style speaker. For the most part, the way in which the *masu* form is used in this context is similar to how Japanese native speaker families use the *masu* form to create different social identities in interaction, rather than as a marker of politeness. Furthermore, there is no instance in the data in which host family members correct the learner with respect to *masu* or plain form usage during dinnertime talk.

Because the plain form is the dominant speech style that both learners and host family members employ in dinnertime talk, I will first illustrate use of the plain form with two different examples. Example (1) involves a novice-level learner and his host sister and Example (2), an advanced-level learner and her host parents. Example (1) is a conversation between Tom and the host sister, who is also a college student. They are talking about what time they went to bed the night before. The entire conversation is carried out in the plain form, which indexes the informal and spontaneous nature of their talk.

(1) Tom 012802

1  HS: kinoo    wa  nanji    ni  neta  no?
       yesterday Top what time at slept  FP
       'What time did you go to bed yesterday?'

2  T: (.) kinoo (.) sanji
       yesterday 3 o'clock
       'yesterday, three o'clock.'

3  HS: SANJI?          nande? (.) benkyoo? =
        3 o'clock        why      study
        'Three o'clock?  Why?   Were you studying?'

4  T: = nn chigau [((laughs))
       no not right
       'No, that's not it.'

5  HS:          [(<u>denwa</u>?)
                 telephone
                 'telephone?'

6  T: aa:: e-mail (   ) =
      'uh e-mail.'

7  HS: = a- demo watashi motto <u>osoi</u> (2.0) motto <u>osoi</u>
            uh but I          more late          more late
            'uh but I (went to bed) much later, much later.'

8  T: a- (   )
      'uh- (   )'

9  HS: yoji   ni betto ni haitte (0.3) dakedo (.) <u>nemurenakatta</u>
            4 o'clock at bed in enter          but          sleep can not
            'I went to bed at four, but I couldn't sleep.'

       (1.0)

10  T: dooshite
       why
       'Why?'

       (1.0)

11  HS: ano sono mae    no   hi ni ippai <u>neta</u> kara =
             well that before LK day at a lot slept so
             'Well, because I slept a lot the day before.'

12  T: = ((laughs))

13  HF: = ((laughs))

14  T: wakatta
        understood
        'I understand.'

Plain form exchanges are not limited to talk between peers (i.e. learners and their host brother/sister). Reciprocal plain form usage is also observed between learners and their host parents. Example (2) is a conversation between Ellen and her host parents. The topic of the conversation in (2) is 'sleep' as well. The entire conversation is carried out in the plain form regardless of the age/or gender differences between Ellen and her host parents.

(2) Ellen 020302

1   E: a: yooku <u>neta</u> kyoo ((laughs))
        uh well slept today
        'uh I slept well today.'

2   HM: [((laughs))

3   HF: [<u>neta</u>?
        slept
        'Did you sleep?'

4   E: [(      )

5   HM: [demo (ame ga futte) nerareru   n   <u>da</u>   yo =
        but     rain  S falling sleep can Mom Cop FP
        'But (it rained so) we could sleep.'

6   HF: = soo kyoo wa otoosan mo [tsukare <u>toreta</u>
        so today Top father also fatigue removed
        'So I also don't feel tired today.'

7   E:                        [hayaku <u>neru</u>? u:n          ((to HF))
                              early   slep  um
                              'Will you go to bed early? um'

8   HM: hayaku <u>neru</u>? =      ((to HF))
        early     sleep
        'Will you go to bed early?'

9   HF: = <u>nenai</u>       yo
        sleep Neg FP
        'I won't.'

10  E: [((laughs))

11  HM: [((laughs))

12  HF: kyoo  shime        da mon seekyuusho <u>kakanakya</u>
        today settling day Cop Nom  bill       write must
        'Today is the settling day, so I've got to prepare bills.'

The above examples demonstrate that dinnertime conversations between JFL learners and host family members are conducted mainly in the plain form regardless of the participants' age and/or gender and the learner's Japanese proficiency level. This practice indexes that they feel close and uninhibited. Thus, like Japanese family members, the host families and the JFL learners staying with them construct a close relationship by using the plain form most of the time.

Sometimes, however, they shift to the *masu* form. Table 4.1 shows the frequencies of the *masu* form per 2000 words in the speech between JFL learners and their host families. In Table 4.1, only data from conversations between the learner and the immediate host family members were included in the tabulation. Two dinnertime conversations (one of Rick's host family and one of Mary's host family) were excluded from the tabulation because guests were present. The presence of a guest may affect the speech style of the participants, in particular that of the host family members. In order to compare the frequencies of the *masu* form between the host family and the JFL learner, the utterances of the families and the learners were separated, and the frequencies of the *masu* form were calculated for each group.[7] The total number of instances of the *masu* form was divided by the total number of words spoken in each corpus, which was then multiplied by 2000.[8] This yielded a frequency index per 2000 words for both the host family and the JFL learner in each family.

Table 4.1 shows that the host families used the *masu* form on an average of 8.6 times per 2000 words, whereas JFL learners used the form

**Table 4.1** Frequencies of *masu* form in the speech of host families and JFL learners

|  | *Host family's frequency per 2000 words* | *JFL student's frequency per 2000 words* |
|---|---|---|
| Host family/Alice (novice) | 4.9 | 11.9 |
| Host family/Tom (novice) | 1.3 | 21.5 |
| Host family/Kate (novice) | 29.2 | 46.1 |
| Host family/Rick (intermediate/low) | 2.1 | 9.5 |
| Host family/Greg (intermediate) | 23.4 | 30.6 |
| Host family/Skip (advanced/low) | 3.0 | 3.0 |
| Host family/Pete (advanced) | 2.6 | 11.1 |
| Host family/Mary (advanced) | 9.2 | 4.3 |
| Host family/Ellen (advanced) | 1.8 | 3.7 |
| Average | 8.6 | 15.7 |

15.7 times. Overall, the frequency measures of all host families, except for those of Kate and Greg, are less than 10 cases per 2000 words. The frequency with which some host families used the form is substantially lower than the average. For example, Tom's host family used the *masu* form only 1.3 times per 2000 words. The host families of Rick, Skip, Pete and Ellen used it less than 4 times per 2000 words. In contrast, the host families of Alice, Kate, Greg and Mary had a higher ratio.

As I will describe in more detail in Chapter 5, the difference between families is partly due to their dinnertime activities. For example, Mary's host father was in charge of video-recording the family dinnertime conversation. He set up the camera, and made sure that everyone was in the picture. He often used *masu* when attending to his immediate task. In Alice's family, there were small children. For this reason, the host mother seems to index her identity as a 'mother' more often by shifting to the *masu* form. Greg and Kate's respective host mothers showed much higher frequency ratios. They liked to teach about Japanese customs and language, and they often shifted to the *masu* form while doing so. Besides playing a teacher's role, Kate's host mother also used the *masu* form in quoting others. It is important to point out, however, that use of the self-presentational stance indexed by the *masu* form is, at least to some extent, a personal choice. For example, not all cases of the host mother's act of serving food co-occur with the *masu* form. Thus, the frequency of the *masu* form partly depends upon the type of activity the host families engage in, as well as the stance they choose to take toward both the content of talk and the addressees.

As for the JFL learners, the frequencies also vary from learner to learner. Due to the small sample size, it is not possible to determine whether the learners' proficiency level influenced the frequency with which they used the *masu* form. However, in the present sample, as implied in Table 4.1, there is a correlation between frequency of use and Japanese proficiency. Advanced-level learners tended to use the *masu* form less frequently than intermediate- and novice-level learners. In addition, it should be noted that, in general, use of the *masu* form by the host family does not necessarily influence the learner's use. But at the same time, we note that the two learners with the highest *masu* frequencies (Kate and Greg) had a host family who employed the *masu* form with a comparatively high frequency. Moreover, aside from Mary, the learners' frequency in using the *masu* form is higher than that of their host families.

How do participants in dinnertime conversation use the *masu* form? Are there differences between host families and JFL learners? To address these questions, I tabulated instances of the *masu* form used by the learners and the host families according to the three major functional categories found in the speech of Japanese families. These include (1) a display of various social identities (e.g. someone with authority or someone in charge of the matter at hand) and (2) the quoting of someone else's or one's own voice, (3) set formulas and (4) others (i.e. uses of the *masu* not consistent with those normally found in Japanese family conversations). With respect to the host families' responsibility and authority, only clear cases are included. The host families' display of knowledge about Japanese culture, social customs and language, and the learners' display of knowledge about their own culture and language are counted. Responsibilities included tasks at hand, and cooking and serving food (i.e. the host mother's responsibility). Other topics may also be related to the responsibility of the host family. For example, the host mother's questions about the learner's daily life such as 'Is your Japanese exam tomorrow?' could be interpreted as the host mother's responsibility. However, as asking about the learner's schedule may or may not reflect the speaker's sense of responsibility as 'host mother', in this study, they are not counted as part of the first category in Figure 4.1. Figure 4.1 shows the percentages of the different functional categories of the *masu* form in the speech of the host families and the JFL learners.[9]

We find in Figure 4.1 that both the host families and the learners used the *masu* form in the three major functional categories found in Japanese family talk. Of all the instances of the *masu* form that occur in the speech of the host families, 27.4% fall into the category of a display of particular social identities; 22.6% come into the category of quoting someone else's or one's own voice; 8.8% are set formulas; and 2.4% are unknown uses.[10] The first three categories are normative uses of the *masu* form in Japanese family conversation. In contrast, the remaining 38.8% are uses that did not occur in dinnertime talk in Japanese families. Among the instances of

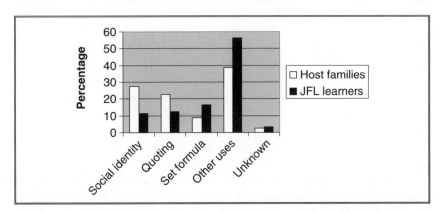

**Figure 4.1** Functions of *masu* in the speech of host families and learners

the *masu* form that occur in the speech of the JFL learners, 11.3% fall into the category of displaying social identities; 12.5% into the category of reported speech; 16.5% into set formulas; and 3.4% are unknown uses. The percentage of the learners' *masu* form uses that do not conform to those of native speakers in the *uchi* context is 56.3%, which is much higher than that of the host families. This means that 61.2% of the host families' and 43.7% of the JFL learners' uses of the *masu* form conform to the shifting pattern observed in family conversations of native speakers of Japanese. Furthermore, with respect to the frequencies of the first three functional categories, there is an inverse relation between the host families and the JFL learners. The set formula that occurred most in the data is *itadakimasu*, a phrase said before eating.

In sum, Figure 4.1 shows that many uses of the *masu* form in the data fall within the same three social activities in which the shift to the *masu* form is found in Japanese family conversation. Below, I focus on shifts to the *masu* form in the first two categories in Figure 4.1, namely a display of social identities and reported speech. Through these shifts, JFL learners are socialized into appropriate ways of displaying the self-presentational stance.

## Indexing Social Identities Through the Self-presentational Stance

Both host family members and learners shift to the *masu* form when they engage in activities in which they are in charge, display knowledge and quote others. When the *masu* form co-occurs with such social acts, its direct index, the self-presentational stance evokes certain social identities. By shifting to the *masu* form, host parents construct their social identity as 'host parents' who not only serve food but also teach the learner something about Japanese culture and language. For example, the host mother's shift to the *masu* form when she teaches Japanese social customs to the learner constitutes her social identity as a 'host mother', the person responsible for teaching Japanese culture to the learner. The JFL learners also sometimes shift to the *masu* form when they teach host family members about their home country and English. In these instances, they display their social identity of 'English teacher' to their host family.

In sum, usage of the *masu* form in family conversation is often linked to the speaker's expected social identities in the homestay context. In what follows, I discuss in detail how different social identities are displayed through use of the *masu* form in dinnertime conversation between the JFL learners and their host families.

## A person in charge

The participants often shift to the *masu* form when they are in charge of, or responsible for, an immediate situational goal at hand. For example, the host mother tends to shift to the *masu* form when she serves food to the family, and the learner may do so when he or she sets up the video camera and recorder.[11] In these instances, the *masu* form indexes that the speaker is someone who is in charge.

*Serving food*

Cooking and serving food are important responsibilities of the host mother. In all host families in the data, the host mother takes the sole responsibility for preparing meals. The host mothers of Alice, Kate, Rick, Greg, Pete and Mary sometimes shift to the *masu* form when they are serving food or talking about the food which they just prepared.[12] The *masu* form in these instances highlights the host mother's identity as the provider of food in the household. Tom and Ellen's host mothers speak in the plain form when serving food. As I discussed above, speakers can choose not to speak in the *masu* form even when they are in charge of an activity. Tom and Ellen's host mothers chose not to enact the identity of 'mother' when serving food.

Some host mothers often shift to the *masu* form when they offer food or talk about what they cook, but shift back to the plain form when the topic changes. This supports the interpretation that a shift to the *masu* form indexes their social identity as 'host mother'. Examples (3) and (4) are cases in point. Example (3) comes from Mary's host family. In this example, Mary's host mother speaks in the *masu* form when offering food to Mary, but shifts back to the plain form when she acknowledges Mary's food preference.

(3) Mary 012802

1 → HM: hai tabete mite kudasai. kimuchi mo **arimasu** yo
      yes eating try  please   kimchee too exist      FP
      'Yes, please eat.        There is also kimchee.'

2   M:   [((laughs))

3   HF:  [((laughs))

4   HM:  [((laughs))

5   M:   hai
        yes
        'yes'

6    HF: hai
        yes
        'yes'

7    HM: Mary-san suki da  kara ne:   [kimuchi
         Mary     like Cop so   FP    kimchee
         'Mary, you like kimchee.'

8    M:                              [un
                                     yeah
                                     'yeah.'

In line 1 Mary's host mother speaks in the *masu* form as she offers
kimchee to Mary.[13] Note that this utterance contrasts with that in line 7,
in which she shifts to the plain form as she states Mary's food preference.
The plain form here indexes that she is not highlighting her role as a 'host
mother' because she is no longer offering the food to Mary.

In Example (4), Greg and his host mother are sitting at the table and
are just about to eat dinner.

(4) Greg 011302

1    HM: doozo =
         please
         'Please'

2    G: = hai (2.0) nn soba?
         yes      um soba noodles
         'yes'    'uh soba noodles?'

3    HM: kyoo    wa   ne yakisoba =
         today   Top FP fried noodles
         'It's fried noodles today'

4    G: = un
         yeah
         'Yeah'

5 → HM: hisashiburi ni      yakisoba      o **tsukurimashita**.
         after a long time fried noodles O made
         'I cooked fried noodles for the first time in a long time.'

6    G: un un (0.4) nn?
         yeah yeah um
         'Yeah yeah'

7  HM: itsumo raisu <u>da</u> kara[14]
       always rice Cop because
       'Because we usually have rice.'

8  G: un itsumo gohan <u>da</u> kara =
      yeah always rice Cop because
      'uh huh because we usually have rice.'

9  HM: = un gohan <u>da</u> kara     ne un.
         yeah rice Cop because FP yeah
         'yeah, because we usually have rice.'

10 G: un
      uh huh
      'uh huh'

11 HM: toki ni wa? yakisoba     toka ((laughs))
         time at Top fried noodles etc.
         'Sometimes food like fried noodles.'

12 G: un
      yeah
      'yeah'

The utterances in the plain form in lines 2 and 3 are a question/answer adjacency pair. In line 4 Greg provides an acknowledgement token, *un* ('yeah'). Then in line 5, shifting to the *masu* form, the host mother paraphrases what she said in line 3, foregrounding her role as cook. Note that when she states the reason for a change (i.e. they usually have rice) in lines 7 and 9, she switches back to the plain form. The contrast between line 5 and lines 7 and 9 highlights the host mother's role as provider. She is presenting herself as someone who is in charge of cooking a variety of food for the household.

Shifting to the *masu* form when offering food is optional. Ellen's host mother does not shift forms when she offers steamed clams that she cooked, as shown in Example (5).

(5) Ellen 020402

1  HM: kore wa ne: asari no sakamushi tte ne =
         this Top FP clams LK sake steam QT FP
         'This is called steamed clams with *sake*.'

2  E: = un
      uh huh
      'uh huh'

3   HM: osake de ne: =
        sake with FP
        'with *sake*'


4   E: un =
       uh huh
       'uh huh'


5 → HM: = <u>musu</u> no
           steam   FP
           'we steam them.'


6   E: aa      [soo <u>na</u> no                        [hu:n
       oh       so Cop FP
       'Oh, is that so?'  'uhm'


7 → HM:      [osake irete <u>musu</u> no      kore [asari
             sake put in steam FP          this clam
             'We steam the clams with sake.'


8   E: un
       'uh huh'


9 → HM: osake na   n   <u>da</u>  yo
        sake Cop Nom Cop FP
        'It's *sake*, you know.'


In Example (5), the host mother is offering steamed clams to Ellen.
Rather than focusing on her role (using the *masu* form), she explains how
to steam them in the plain form with the sentence-final particle *no*, which
implies that this cooking style is a general practice in society (cf. Aoki,
1986; Cook, 1990b).[15] She is not interactionally highlighting her social
identity as a 'host mother' who is responsible for cooking, but rather
reporting the general practice as a member of Japanese society (a stance
indexed by the particle *no*). While doing so, she is simultaneously
displaying an intimate and casual relationship with Ellen through her
use of the plain form.

### The person in charge of recording

A situational goal common to all the JFL learners in the present study
is the task of ensuring the successful recording of the dinnertime
conversation. For data collection, I asked the learners to take charge of
recording dinnertime conversations by setting up the video camera and
the cassette tape-recorder just before dinnertime. In this sense, the JFL

learners are in charge of recording the conversation, including turning on and off the recording devices. In some host families, family members also took responsibility for successfully recording the conversation. Sometimes one of the devices was turned on before the other. Therefore, in nine segments of data, the participants happened to record the procedures of setting up or turning off one of the recording devices.[16] The JFL learner and/or the host family talked about starting and/or finishing the recording. Table 4.2 lists the participants who talked about beginning and ending the recording and the linguistic form they used. It indicates that when they are in charge of recording the conversation, only the advanced-level learners and their host families shift to the *masu* form.

In particular, Mary's host father took complete charge of the task of recording. In Example (6), the host mother and Mary are at the table starting to eat dinner. The host father has set up the video camera and is about to sit at the table with the host mother and Mary to be video-recorded.

**Table 4.2** Responsibility for the immediate goal: The recording of dinnertime conversation

| Participants: JFL learner and host family | Linguistic marking of the social acts (starting and/or ending the recording of dinnertime talk) |
|---|---|
| Tom (novice) & HF (dinner 1) | Tom-plain form<br>Host mother-plain form |
| Rick (Inter-low) & HF (dinner 1) | Rick-plain form<br>Host sister-plain form |
| Rick (Inter-low) & HF (dinner 2) | Rick-plain form<br>Host brother-plain form |
| Pete (advanced) & HF (dinner 1) | Pete-*masu* form<br>Host father-*masu* form |
| Pete (advanced) & HF (dinner 2) | Pete-*masu* form |
| Pete (advanced) & HF (dinner 3) | Pete-*masu* form<br>Host father-*masu* form |
| Ellen (advanced) & HF (dinner1) | Ellen-*masu* form |
| Mary (advanced) & HF (dinner 1) | Host father-*masu* form |
| Mary (advanced) & HF (dinner 2) | Host father-*masu* form<br>Host mother-*masu* form<br>Mary-*masu* form |

(6) Mary 012802

1    HM: [oishii?
          delicious
          'Is it delicious?'

2    M: [oishii [oishii            un
         delicious delicious yeah
         'It's delicious delicious yeah.'

3    HM:        [honto?
                really
                'Really?'

4  → HF: ja: boku kore kara **hairimasu** kara ne ((standing by the tripod))
         Well I this from enter          because FP
         'Well, I am going to get in the picture now.'

5    M: ((giggles))

6    HM: [(    )

7  → HF: [chotto **ugokashimasu**.
         A little move
         'I am going to move (the camera) a bit.'

8  →      boku ga **hairimasu**
          I    S enter
          'I am going to get in the picture.'

As he announces his move in relation to the video-recording, the host father uses the *masu* form. The instances of *masu* in the host father's speech in this example index that he is in charge of and responsible for the immediate goal of the situation, which is videotaping the dinner. His uses of the *masu* form are contrasted with the plain form used by Mary and the host mother in lines 1 to 3, where they are talking about the taste of the food. His use of the *masu* form also contrasts his usual use of the plain form when talking to Mary and the host mother.

In Pete's host family, the host father and Pete are jointly taking charge of the recording. Both of them shift to the *masu* form when they take care of the recording, but shift back to the plain form to clarify Pete's ambiguous statement.

(7) Pete 010603[17]

1  HF: ano hito    no seikaku    na   n     daroo na? [are
        that person LK character Cop Nom Cop Cop that
        'That's his (Bush's) personality maybe? that'

2   P:                                                    [un
                                                          yeah
                                                          'yeah'

3  HM: shooganai         ne?
        can't be helped FP
        'Can't be helped.'

4  HG: un
        uh huh
        'uh huh'

5  HF: shooganai        tashika ni soo ya  to omou yo
        can't be helped surely     so Cop QT think FP
        'Can't be helped. I think it sure is.'

6  P: soo   na    n     da  un
       so   Cop   Nom   Cop yeah
       'yeah, that's true.'

7  HF: soo ya      to omo[u
        so  Cop     QT think
        'I think so.'

8  HG:                   [ne?
                          FP
                          'right?'

9 → HF: moo sorosoro **owarimashita** ne (  ) [daijoobu **desu** ka?
        already soon  finished         FP        all right  Cop  FP
        'It (the tape)'s almost finished, right? (  ) Is it all right?'

10  P:                                        [soo **desu** ne
                                               so  Cop FP
                                               'That's right'

        [a    tomatteru wa @(kore wa)@
        oh stop          Top this    Top
        'Oh, it has stopped, this'

11 HF: [((laughs))

12  HM: <u>owachatta?</u> [moo     <u>owatta</u> no?
           finished     already  finished FP
           'Has it finished? Has it already finished?'

13  P:                   [ore wa    <u>owatta</u> kara   ne
                          I   Top  finished because FP
                          'I have finished so'

14  HF: <u>chigau</u> [<u>chigau</u>     moo     sono a- are ga
           disagree disagree already that uh that S
           'No, no already well th- that'

15  HM:         [iya  iya iya
                 no   no no
                 'No no no'

16  HF: rokuon   ga moo     owatteru n   ja <u>nai</u>
           recording S already finished Nom Neg
           'It's that the recording has already finished, isn't it?

17  →   mada [**haittemasu**?
           still   recording
           'Is it still recording?'

18 → P:       [su      iya iya iya **owarimasu**
               su      no no no finished
               'No no no, it's finishing.'

19 → HF: owaru n desho?
           finish Nom Cop
           'It's finishing?'

20  HM: owa-
           finish-
           'finish-'

21 → P: ja    **owarimasu**
           well finish
           'OK, let's finish (recording).'

In Example (7), Pete, his host mother, host father and host grandmother are talking about President Bush in lines 1 through 8 using the
plain form. In line 9, looking at the cassette tape-recorder placed on
the dining table, the host father, shifting to the *masu* form, says that the

tape is about to finish. In line 10, Pete gives an acknowledgement token (*soo desu ne*) in the *masu* form as he looks at the cassette tape-recorder. Then he says in the plain form, *a tomatteru wa kore wa* ('oh it has stopped, this'). His plain form here is reflecting a soliloquy-like remark.[18] Then using the plain form, the host mother asks if the recording has finished (line 12). Although she does not encode the subject NP,[19] as the topic is still on the recording, it is understood here that it is the recording that has finished.[20] Apparently, Pete mistakes the host mother's utterance in line 12 for a question if he has finished his dinner. Here he says in the plain form *ore wa owatta kara ne* ('I have finished so'), which encodes the subject NP (*ore* 'I'). The encoding of the subject NP makes his agency emphatic here. His utterance in line 13 implies that it is Pete's dinner that is finished rather than the recording. Both the host father and host mother attempt to repair Pete's remark. In line 14, the host father starts to repair Pete's utterance by saying *chigau chigau* ('no no') in the plain form. He tries to say that the recording is finished but cannot come up with the right word, so he says *are ga* ('that + subject marker') while searching for the right word (cf. Kitano, 1999). In line 15, the host mother overlaps with the host father and says *iya iya iya* ('no no no'). In line 16 the host father continues to clarify the miscommunication created by Pete by stating that it is the recording that has finished. Note that while he is trying to resolve the miscommunication, the host father speaks in the plain form. Once the trouble is repaired, then both host father and Pete start to talk about finishing the tape-recording by shifting back to the *masu* form. From line 17 to the end of this example, speaking in the *masu* form, both the host father and Pete take the stance of being in charge of recording the dinnertime conversation, which is contrasted with the plain form used while Pete and his host family are talking about President Bush and while the host parents are trying to repair Pete's utterance. Here again, the *masu* form is a tool used to create the social identity of someone who is in charge of the activity at hand.

## Authority: A teacher of language and culture

The self-presentational stance indexed by the *masu* form can also position the speaker as a knowledgeable person. In the context of dinnertime talk between the JFL learner and the host family, the type of knowledge participants display tends to focus on their respective social customs and language.

Just as Japanese parents do with their children, some host mothers sometimes shift to the *masu* form when they explain to the JFL learner something that they assume is new to the learner, in particular regarding Japanese social customs and language. This use of *masu* indexes the identity of a knowledgeable person who is disseminating new information. In the present data, two host mothers (those of Kate and Greg) show frequent shifts to the *masu* form, especially when prefacing their utterance with the phrase, *nihon de wa* ('in Japan'). The JFL learners as well sometimes tell the host family members about their home country and teach them English. Some learners, including Tom, who is a novice-level learner, shift to the *masu* form in these cases, thus indexing their identity as a teacher.

In Example (8), Greg and his host mother are talking about Japanese words borrowed from English. The host mother shifts to the *masu* form when she tells him what a gas station is called in Japanese.

(8) Greg 012702

1  G: tatoeba       gasu    sutando? a @ [sonna koto iwanai@ eego-
      for example gasolin stand       uh  that sort thing say Neg English
      amerika de
      America in
      'For example *gasu sutando*. We don't say that in English- in
      America.'

2  HM:                                          [aa
                                                 oh
                                                 'oh'

3  HM: aa gasorin    sutando?
         oh gasolin   stand
         'uh (you mean) *gasorin sutando*?'

4  G: soo
      so
      'Yes.'

5 → HM: u::n gasorin sutando **iimasu** yo nihon ja
        uh    gasolin stand   say      FP Japan in
        'uh, we say *gasorin sutando* in Japan.'

6  G: soo
      so
      'Is that so?'

7  HM: moo minna      gasorin sutando       ja amerika    ja iwanai?
        now everyone gasoline stand       well America in say Neg
        'Everyone (says) *gasourin sutando*. So you don't say that in
        America?'

8   G: un (0.8)   <u>iwanai</u>
         uh          say Neg
         'uh'        'We don't (say that).'

9   HM: hu:n     amerika wa    nan te   <u>yuu</u> no?
          uh huh  America Top  what QT say Nom
          'uh huh, what do you call it in America?'

10  G: gas- gas station?
        'Gas, gas station.'

In line 1 Greg provides what he thinks is an example of a loan word from English, *gasu sutando* ('gas stand') meaning 'gas station'. However, the correct loan word in Japanese is *gasorin sutando* ('gasoline stand'). In line 3, by rephrasing the word, the host mother asks whether he meant *gasorin sutando* ('gasoline stand'), and in line 4 she asserts that in Japan people use the word, *gasorin sutando* (instead of *gasu sutando*). In this utterance, she shifts to the *masu* form, which is followed by the emphatic sentence-final particle *yo*. Then in line 7 she asks him if people use the word *gasoline stand* in the USA, and when he responds negatively to her question after a short pause, in line 9 she asks what people call it. She asks these questions shifting back to the plain form, because she is no longer playing the role of a teacher of the Japanese language.

When the JFL learners explain to the host family members something about their home country and English, they sometimes shift to the *masu* form. Such use of *masu* indexes the learner as the knowledgeable party or an English teacher.

In Example (9), the host mother is talking about the loan from English *maneejimento* ('management'). Note that Greg shifts to the *masu* form when he responds to his host mother's question about the English equivalent of *maneejimento*.

(9) Greg 011302

1   HM: nihongo demo ne: maneejimento tte nihogo    <u>da</u> kedo
         Japanese in also FP management QT Japanese Cop but
         'In Japanese, the word, 'maneejimento' is Japanese.'

2   G: aa <u>soo</u>
        oh so
        'Is that right?'

3   HM: ma- nihongo wa <u>MANE:JIMENTO</u>
          well Japanese Top management
          'Well, the Japanese word is MANEEJIMENTO.'

4   G: aa <u>soo</u> ((laughs))
     oh so
     'Is that right?'

5   HM: eego    wa chigau desho?
        English Top different Cop
        'It's different in English, right?'

6  → G: chotto **chigaimasu**
        little   different
        'It's a little different.'

In line 1, the host mother expresses that in Japanese the loan word from English *maneejimento* (meaning *management* in English) is used and that it is considered as a Japanese word. She pronounces the word with the Japanese phonology [maneejimento]. In line 3, she states again in a louder voice that the word *maneejimento* is a Japanese word. Up to this point, the conversation is carried out in the plain form.[21] Then she asks Greg if the word is pronounced differently in English. In line 6 Greg provides an answer shifting to the *masu* form. As he is an authority on the English language in this context, the *masu* form in line 6 indexes his identity as an English teacher.

## A presenter

Sometimes, there are opportunities for the participants to present themselves in front of a captive audience at the dinner table. In particular, when they are conscious of the video camera, they sometimes give a formal presentation to the people at the dinner table as well as to potential viewers of the video. On such occasions, use of the *masu* form indexes the social identity of a presenter.[22] In Example (10), Mary and her host parents are sitting around the dinner table. Mary is eating an apple for dessert. The host father is reading a newspaper.

(10) Mary 012802

1   M: @ watashi no ringo o tabeteru sugata dake@
           I      LK apple O eat      figure only
        'Only a picture of me eating an apple'

2   HF: <u>utsutteru</u>?    ((leans over and looks at the video camera))
        showing
        'Is it recording (on the screen).'

3   HM: <u>utsutteru</u> no yo papa
        showing  FP FP daddy
        'Dad, you are showing (on the screen), you know.'

4  HF: <u>utsutteru?</u>
       showing
       'Am I being filmed (on the screen)?'

5  → ja    boku ringo **tabemasu**
       well I    apple eat
       'Well then, I'm going to eat an apple.'

6  HM: un
       uh huh
       'uh huh'

Mary looks at the video camera screen and comments about her image on the screen, and the host father co-constructs her utterance in line 2, which prompts all participants to orient to the video camera. As the host father leaned over and looked toward the video camera, now his face is on the video screen. In line 5 he prefaces his forthcoming utterance with *ja* ('well then'), which indicates that his following action is contingent on being video-recorded. He is conscious of being video-taped when he announces in the *masu* form that he is going to eat an apple. In lines 1 through 4, the participants are commenting on what is appearing on the screen but not intentionally acting in front of the camera. While these utterances are made in the plain form, the host father shifts to the *masu* form when he performs in front of the video camera. This use of *masu* indexes being on stage and presenting oneself to an audience.

A few minutes later, Mary's host brother comes home and joins the dinner. Mary formally introduces her host brother in front of the video camera.

(11) Mary 012802

1  →M: oniichan no    takashi    de **gozaimasu** ((laughs))
       older brother Takashi    Cop
       'This is my older brother Takashi.'

2  HF: [((laughs))

3  HM: [((laughs))

4  HB: <u>totteru</u>    no =
       recording FP
       'Is it recording?'

5  M:  = [((laughs))

6  HF:  = [((laughs))

Here in line 1, as she presents her host brother in front of the video camera, Mary not only speaks in the *masu* form but also uses the 'super-polite' form of the copula, *gozaimasu*. This contrasts with the host brother's question in line 4, which is in the plain form. Here, while Mary is conscious of being video-taped, the host brother, who has just come home, guesses that the video-taping is being conducted in the living room but that he is not yet part of it. His plain form in line 4 indexes that he is not acting on stage.

## Self-presentational Stance as an Individual Choice

I would like to remind readers that not all instances of social acts such as serving food, taking charge of tasks at hand and disseminating information are marked by the *masu* form. Whether or not each instance of such social acts co-occurs with the *masu* form is in part the individual speaker's choice. Example (12) illustrates this. In this example, the host mother shifts between the plain and *masu* forms when she tells Kate the meaning of Japanese phrases.

(12) Kate 060904

1   HM: hora   'me de kagu'      'me de taberu' to <u>onnaji</u> (0.5)
          see    eye with smell   eye with eat    with same
          'See, "to smell with one's eyes" is the same as "to eat with one's eyes"'

2   K: <u>kagu</u>?
        smell
        '*Kagu* (to smell)?'

3   HM: 'me de kagu'      noozu de ne
          eye with smell   nose with FP
          ' "to smell with one's eyes", with one's nose'

4   K: u:n un
        un mhmm'
        'un mhmm'

5 → HM: de nioi         o kagu   no     o kagu to iu    n     **desu**
          And fragrance O smell   Nom   O smell QT say   Nom   Cop
          'And we say "kagu" to mean smell fragrance.'

6   K: aa <u>kagu</u> (0.5)
       oh smell
       'Oh *kagu* (smell)'

7 → HM: futsuu wa noozu de: (.) ii     nioi       tte kagu to
         usually Top nose with good fragrance QT smell QT
         iu   n     **desu** kedo:
         say Nom   Cop   but
         'Usually, saying "Oh this has a good fragrance," we smell with
         our nose.'

8        sore o ima chotto 'me de     kagu' tte iu   no    wa
         that O now little   eye with smell QT say Nom Top
         yappari me de     mita toki ni:
         after all eye with saw  time at
         'Saying "smell that with one's eyes" is when we see something
         with our eyes'

9 → ano konaida   'me de taberu' tte **imashita** yo ne (.) de me de <u>kagu</u>
       uh  the other day eye with eat QT said   FP FP and eye with smell
       'uh, I said the phrase "to eat with one's eyes" the other day. And
       we also say, "to smell with one's eyes".'

10 → nihonjin  wa  kono 'me de     miru' to iu    no    o
        Japanese Top this  eye with see    QT say Nom O
        totemo daiji ni suru no kamo <u>shirenai</u>
        very important do Nom maybe
        'Japanese may place a lot of importance on "seeing with
        one's eyes".'

        (3.0)

11  K: a:
       oh
       'Oh'

In line 1 the host mother is explaining the phrase 'to smell with one's
eyes', but Kate does not know the meaning of the verb *kagu* ('to smell').
The host mother starts to explain the meaning of the word, *kagu* ('to
smell') in line 7 and continues to remind Kate that she taught her the
other day the Japanese phrase 'to eat with one's eyes'. She uses the *masu*
form in these utterances, which positions her in the identity of a teacher.
But in line 10 she shifts back to the plain form to tell Kate that Japanese
may place a lot of importance on the phrase, 'to see with one's eyes'.

When the host mother describes to Kate some aspects of the Japanese language or culture using the *masu* form, she foregrounds her identity as a teacher or host mother. In referential terms, the *masu* form in these instances is equivalent to saying, 'as a host mother or as a teacher, I am speaking to you'. In contrast, when she uses the plain form, due to the absence of the self-presentational stance, her social identity as a teacher is backgrounded. Therefore, her utterance takes on a more personal nature.

## Direct Quotation: Voices of Society

From the Bakhtinian perspective, whenever we speak, our utterances are populated with the voices of other people. Bakhtin (1981) refers to this phenomenon as 'heteroglossia'. Language has a number of grammatical devices that encode different voices, and among them is reported speech. Bakhtin (1981) states that reported speech is the most self-conscious in that it is reflexive. Reported speech can be either direct or indirect speech. Direct speech (or direct quotation), however, is not necessarily a verbatim report of what was actually said. In naturally occurring talk, reported speech is generally not reported, but in Tannen's words (1989: 105), it 'is creatively constructed by a current speaker in a current situation'. It is the act of taking on another person's identity temporarily (Tannen, 2005) and is a discourse strategy that effectively communicates different 'voices' in one's utterance.

A shift to the *masu* form often denotes a direct quotation in Japanese. The *masu* form in a direct quotation plays an important role in communicating different voices in society. In English, indirect speech is differentiated from direct speech by a personal and/or temporal deictic switch adapted to the viewpoint of the reporter as shown in Examples (13a) and (13b).

(13a) John said, '*I will* see *you tomorrow*.' * [direct speech]

(13b) John said that '*he would* see *me the next day*.' * [indirect speech]

*The deictics are indicated in italics in (13a and b).

In contrast, in Japanese it is not always easy to distinguish direct from indirect speech because Japanese normally does not encode the pronouns for person or object references, and complementary clauses do not change tense or word order (Coulmas, 1986). The structure of reported speech in Japanese is given in (14).

(14) _____X_____ *to* V

Where X can be a sentence, a clause, a word or an onomatopoetic expression.

(Coulmas, 1986: 164)

In (14), X is the quoted speech, *to* is a quotative particle and V is the predicate verb of saying or thinking that expresses the act of reporting. In informal interactions such as family conversations, however, the quotative particle *to* is replaced by its informal counterpart *tte*, and the verb for saying or thinking that encodes the act of reporting may be omitted. Examples (13a) and (13b) are given in Japanese in (15a) and (15b) to illustrate these features of Japanese reported speech.

(15a) John wa 'ashita      (watashi wa) (anata ni) <u>au</u>/**aimasu'** to <u>itta/</u>
      **iimashita**.
      John Top tomorrow (I      Top)      (you with) see          QT said
      'John said, "I will see you tomorrow."'      [direct speech]

(15b) John wa   ashita      (kare ga) (watashi ni) <u>au</u>   to   <u>itta</u>/**iimashita**.
      John Top   tomorrow   (he   S) (I   with) see QT said
      'John said that he would see me the next day.' [indirect speech]

In direct speech (Example (15a)), the verb in the quoted speech is in the plain or *masu* form, whereas in indirect speech (Example (15b)) it is only in the plain form because an indirect quotation (i.e. speech reported rather than being quoted directly) grammatically requires the plain form in the embedded clause. In addition, in Japanese when the referent of the subject, object or oblique is understood in context, normally it is not encoded. On the one hand, due to the absence of a pronominal deictic switch, when the quoted voice is in the plain form, it is not possible to grammatically distinguish direct from indirect speech. On the other, the occurrence of the *masu* form in the quoted voice indicates direct speech. As the quoted voice is not necessarily a verbatim report of what was actually said, direct quotation requires the speaker's sociocultural knowledge regarding in what social contexts speakers typically employ the *masu* form. For example, in directly quoting a student who is talking to the professor, the reporter is likely to choose the *masu* form, which is more appropriate and normally expected in this given social situation. Using the *masu* form, the host families as well as the learners speak in the voices of various categories of people in Japanese society, ranging from that of a mailman to those of themselves in social contexts removed from the family setting. Thus, direct quotations involving the *masu* form index the voices of people outside of the intimate family setting and thus implicitly socialize the learners to use appropriate voices in various social contexts outside the family (i.e. *soto* 'out-group/outside').

## The voice of a third party

To index conversational involvement, the host family members creatively construct voices of various categories of people. Sometimes they quote what others have said, and other times they quote what they think others might say. When they directly quote people outside the family setting, they often speak in the *masu* form. Ellen's host mother, who is an infrequent user of the *masu* form, does shift to *masu* when she takes on the voices of others. In Example (16), when she narrates how her daughter, Emi, met her husband, Ellen's host mother animates the voice of Emi's future husband when he came to see Emi in the hospital. Just before this excerpt, the host mother told Ellen about the skiing trip that her daughter Emi took with her friends sometime before she got married. When Emi ate lunch on the way to the destination, she got really sick and was taken to the hospital. When the host mother was staying with Emi in the hospital, Emi's boyfriend came to visit the hospital.

(16) Ellen 20402

```
1   HM: soide  sa  emi  ga =
         and   FP  Emi  S
         'And Emi'

2   E:  = un =
         uh huh
         'uh huh'

3   HM: = sono toki ni sono issho ni ita   kono unten shita otoko no ko? ga
         that time at that together existed this drive did male LK child S
         'at that time uh the guy who was with her, who was the driver'

4        ano: iya: ano: nan da (gogo)    gurai yuugata kana: kite kurete
         well no well what Cop afternoon about evening FP came give
         'well, no well uh he came to see her in the afternoon, evening'

5        soide ne: keeki motte kite   kureta no =
         and  FP  cake  bring came give   FP
         'and  he  brought some cake.'

6   E:  = unn
         uh huh
         'uh huh'
```

7 → HM: 'ikaga:- doo **desu** ka' tte =
　　　　how　　how Cop FP QT
　　　　'(He said,) how- how is she?'


8　E: = nn =
　　　uhm
　　　'uhm'


(( four lines omitted))


9　HM: = kite kureta no　　ga ima no <u>kare</u>
　　　　came give Nom　S　now LK he
　　　　'the one who came to see her is her present husband.'


10　E: nnn
　　　uh huh
　　　'uh huh'


In line 7, the host mother said that Emi's boyfriend asked her, 'how is she (Emi)?' As the host mother animates his voice, she shifts to the *masu* form. Furthermore, she first uses *ikaga*, the formal form of *doo* ('how'), but self-repairs to *doo* the informal form of 'how'. This repair suggests that the host mother is consciously choosing the most appropriate level of politeness for his voice in the given context.

In the next example, Greg's host mother uses a direct quotation to represent the voice of a particular segment of society. Just prior to this excerpt, she was telling Greg that as the USA is a multiracial country, Americans tolerate other races more than Japanese do. She describes American society using the word, *hooyooryoku ga aru* ('has the capacity for tolerance'). In lines 5–10 she is explaining to Greg the meaning of this expression.

(17) Greg 012702

1　HM: 'hooyooryoku　　　　　ga <u>aru</u>' tte yuu　n　<u>da</u>　kedo
　　　　capacity for tolerance S　exist QT say　Nom Cop but
　　　　'We call it "to have the capacity for tolerance".'


2　G: un
　　　yeah
　　　'Yeah'


3　HM: hooyooryoku?　　　　un
　　　capacity for tolerance yeah
　　　'The capacity for tolerance? yes'

4   G: hai
      yes
      'Yes'

5   HM: hooyooryoku           tte yuu no    wa ironna- ironna    imi
       capacity for tolerance QT say  Nom Top various various meaning
       <u>aru</u> kedo (.)
       exist but
       'The capacity for tolerance can have many meanings.'

6      koo        chotto <u>ookii</u> un
       this way little   big    uh
       'this, sort of big uh'

7  →  'aa anta chigau kuni  <u>da</u> kara (.) aa  chotto **komarimasu'** toka tte
       uh you different country Cop so  uh little   trouble          etc.  QT
       'Saying something like, "uh, because you are from a different
       country, it gives us a trouble"'

8      soo n    ja <u>nai</u>  wake ne?
       so Nom Neg       FP     FP
       'is not so (the capacity for tolerance).'

9      un ironna kuni      no hito      to nakayoku      shite
       uhm various countries Lk people  with good terms  do
       'uhm to be on good terms with people from different countries'

10  G: hai
      yes
      'Yes'

11  HM: un <u>ikeru</u>? iku mitai na <u>kimochi</u>?
       uhm can go go like Cop feeling
       'uhm to be able to do so. The intention to do so (is the capacity
       for tolerance).'

12  G: un =
      yeah
      'Yeah'

Note that Greg's host mother speaks in the plain form except for her
utterance in line 7. Here shifting to the *masu* form, she quotes the
hypothetical voice of a narrow-minded segment of Japanese society as an
example of people who are not tolerant. The direct quotation describes
vividly the opinion of those who are narrow-minded.

## A playful person

The *masu* form that marks the voice of a third party is sometimes employed as a tool to index playfulness. When co-occurring with laughter or other linguistic or non-linguistic features, it can foreground a shift in 'footing' (Goffman, 1981), from a serious character to a playful one. Or to use Bateson's term (1972), the self-presentational stance indexed by the *masu* form 'keys' playfulness. Example (18) illustrates how the use of the *masu* form can index playfulness. In this example, Tom, the host mother and the host sister are sitting around the table having just finished dinner. Tom has just eaten some Italian chocolate for dessert. By using the *masu* form, the host sister teases Tom with an obvious lie that the chocolate contains poison.

(18) Tom 01280

```
1   T: oishii      oishii ((laughs)) sono kyandii wa oishii
        delicious delicious          that candy    Top delicious
        'It's delicious, delicious. That candy is delicious.'
```

((Host sister looks at the chocolate wrapping)) (2.0)

```
2 → HS: kono chokoreeto ni wa (0.5) doku  ga  haitte imasu
        this chocolate    in Top       poison S   containing exist
        'This chocolate contains poison.'
```

    (2.0)

```
3   T: where? doko
              where
        'Where? Where?'
```

```
4   HS: [ano chokoreeto ni wa
         that chocolate   in Top
         'In that chocolate'
```

```
5   HM: [(     ) sukoshi tabeta kara
               a little  ate    because
        '(     ) ate a little so'
```

```
6 → HS: doku  ga   haitte imasu
        poison S    containing exist
        'It contains poison.'
```

    (3.0)

7   T: [((laughs))

8   HS: [hitotsu dake
        one      only
        'only one'

9   T: ((laughs))

        (2.0)

10  HS: anata  ga tabeta (1.0) [choko        ni[23]
        you    S   ate          chocolate   in
        'the one that you ate'

11  T:                              [nn
                                     uhm
                                     'uhm'

Just prior to this excerpt, the host sister asked Tom to translate the Italian written on the chocolate wrapping paper into Japanese, but Tom said that he does not understand Italian. In line 1, Tom makes up a false translation. Here his laugh indexes that he is joking. Immediately after Tom's repetition of the word *oishii* ('delicious') in line 1, the host sister also makes up a false translation by saying that there is some poison (*doku*) in the chocolate. Her statement is obviously false, and thus violates the Grician maxim of quality (Grice, 1975). Instead of laughing, she pronounces this utterance in the *masu* form with a serious tone of voice. Her *masu* form represents the voice of the chocolate maker addressed to the customer. A two-second pause after line 2 indicates that Tom is having trouble understanding his host sister's statement. His repetition of the word *where* both in English and Japanese in line 3 suggests that his pause is triggered by his confusion of the word *doku* ('poison') with *doko* ('where'). As a novice-level learner, perhaps he never encountered the word *doku* ('*poison*').[24] Because of the confusion of the word *doku* ('poison') with *doko* ('where'), the host sister's statement did not make sense to him. The host sister interprets his utterance in line 3 as a request for clarification, so she attempts to clarify her previous utterance by repeating it while maintaining the *masu* form. After a three-second pause, Tom starts laughing, which signals that he has figured out that the host sister is teasing him. The *masu* form is sometimes utilized in a playful manner.

## Learners' use of direct quotations

A direct quotation is a form of ventriloquy, and a speaker who animates the voice of others needs to have sociolinguistic knowledge as to how a certain category of people typically speak in a given social context. As already argued in Chapter 3, Japanese children acquire sociolinguistic competence as to how others typically speak in various social contexts outside the family. They demonstrate such knowledge by role-playing with caregivers or peers. Adult JFL learners do not engage in role-plays with their host family. However, the host family members' use of direct quotations may help them acquire such sociolinguistic knowledge. In fact, the learners' use of direct quotation is a good indication that they are acquiring sociolinguistic competence in Japanese.

In the current study, only three advanced learners (Skip, Pete and Mary) shift to the *masu* form when they engage in ventriloquy. They have acquired the communicative competence to link a particular social identity to a particular speech style and express the voices of others using direct quotations. The other learners in this study do not use the *masu* form in direct quotations.

Sometimes the host mother and the learner jointly construct a dialogue. In Example (19), both the host mother and the learner Mary co-construct a dialogue between the mailman and Mary, by shifting to the *masu* form.

(19) Mary 020402

1  HM:    a::::: (0.5) are   wa? okaasan okutte <u>kureta</u> no? =
            oh         that Top mother send    give   FP
            'Oh:: is that something that your mother sent to you?'

2  M:  = ee chigau       watashi ano intaanetto de chuumon <u>shita</u> no =
          uhm different  I       uh  internet    by order       did   FP
          'uhm, no. I ordered it through the internet.'

3  HM: = a: soo <u>na</u> no: =
          oh so Cop FP
          'Oh, is that so.'

4  M: = hajimete [intaanetto de chuumon <u>shita</u> no
          first time internet    by order      did   FP
          'It's the first time that I ordered something through the Internet.'

5  HM:              [hu:n
                     oh
                     'Oh::'

6  HM: hu:n <u>soo</u> (2.0)
          oh   so
          'Oh, is that so?'

7  HM: are  wa    Igirisu kara  kita  no? =
           that Top England from  came  FP
           'Did that come from England?'

8  M: n amerika kara =
       no America from
       'No, from the United States.'

9  HM: = amerika kara a::: ((sniff)) (2.0)
            America from oh
            'From the States oh::'

10 → yuubinya-san Eego na n de yubi sashite 'koo yuu hito **imasu** [ka' tte
     ((laughs))
     mailman English Cop cause finger point this say person exist Q QT
     'Because it was written in English, the mailman pointed at the
     package and said, "Does this person live here?"'

11 HF:                                                           [((laughs))

12 → M: 'a: watashi **desu**' tte
         oh I        Cop    QT
         '(I said,) "Oh, it's me" '

13 HM: [((laughs))

14 HF: [((laughs))

   Up to line 9, both Mary and her host mother speak in the plain form.
Then in line 10, when the host mother mimics the voice of the mailman,
she shifts to the *masu* form. In line 12 Mary also quotes herself in the *masu*
form, responding to the mailman. As Mary was not at home at the time
the mailman delivered the package, her utterance is not what she
actually said but rather what she thinks she would say in this particular
context. The host mother and Mary co-construct the conversation
between the mailman and Mary, which vividly recreates the scene of
the mailman delivering a package to Mary. This example indicates that
Mary has acquired the sociolinguistic competence for reporting a
conversation with an outsider such as a mailman.
   Example (20) provides another demonstration of sociolinguistic
competence by an advanced-level learner. In this example, Pete is
narrating his experience as a vendor in a Sunday flea market in a park
in Tokyo. He is talking about a strange customer who insisted on
paying only 100 yen even when Pete told him the item cost 1000 yen.

Narrating the event, Pete constructs the dialogue he had with the customer.

(20) Pete 010603

1 → P: de    'a sore wa    sen          en **desu** kedo'  tte ittara
         and   uh that Top thousand yen Cop but      QT said when
         'And when I said to him, "that's 1000 yen"'

2 → P: 'ja <u>hyaku</u>        en' ((laughs))
         well hundred    yen
         '(he said,) "Well, here's 100 yen".'

3 →      'wa kitsui <u>kana</u>' to  omotte
         oh   harsh FP     QT think
         '"Oh, that's harsh" I thought and'

4 →      'cho- chotto  matte **kudasai'**
         lit   little   wait  please
         '(I said,) "Please wait a mi- minute".'

5 →      'iya <u>matanai</u>' tte yutte pu tte [koo yatte moo sugu kaette kite
         no wait Neg QT said pyu QT this do more soon return come
     '(he said,) "No, I won't wait" and he swiftly left but came back soon'

6 HM:                                    [((laughs))                 un
                                                                     yeah
                                                                     'yeah'

7 → P: 'ja <u>hyaku</u>  en?'
         well hundred yen
         '(he said,) "Here's 100 yen".'

8 →   'iya: mada **desu'**
      no   still Cop
      '(I said,) "No, it's not enough".'

9 HM: un
      uh huh
      'uh huh'

Note that in this excerpt, Pete uses the *masu* form when he speaks in his own voice as a vendor (lines 1, 4 and 5) but shifts to the plain form to construct the customer's voice (lines 2, 5 and 7) as well as his inner thoughts (line 3). Typically, Japanese store clerks speak politely using honorific language including the *masu* form, while the customer may not due to the higher status granted to customers in Japanese society (cf. Okamoto, 1998).[25] Pete's shifting pattern in the constructed dialogue reflects this tendency in Japanese sales talk, which suggests that Pete has acquired tacit sociolinguistic knowledge about the appropriate behavior for a store clerk and a customer. Furthermore, in line 3, he quotes his inner thoughts. He distinguishes between his voice as a vendor and the voice of his own inner thoughts by shifting from the *masu* form to the plain form. Example (20) demonstrates Pete's skillful manipulation of the *masu* and plain forms to index different voices.

The interaction with the host family is a locus of socialization for JFL learners. Participation in this social scene helps them acquire the ability to appropriately display social identities in various social contexts. By shifting to the *masu* form, the Japanese host family members speak with various 'voices' (Bakhtin, 1981) in Japanese society. They take on the voices of various social identities such as mailman, customer and the voice of a group in society holding a particular opinion. The present data suggest that the learners are socialized to quote people from different social categories as they become more competent in Japanese, and that the JFL learners with an advanced proficiency-level can construct a dialogue by assessing the speech styles appropriate for the social identity of the quoted party.

## Conclusion

This chapter has focused on ways in which the host families construct different social identities and represent a variety of voices in society through the use of the *masu* form in interaction with JFL learners. By using the *masu* form, the participants in family conversation construct social identities in two ways: one is to foreground a particular aspect of their social identity (e.g. the host mother), and the other is to quote themselves or other people in a different context. Both strategies are tools to create a range of social identities both in and outside the family context. The foregrounding of an aspect of the participants' social identity is often linked to their duties, responsibilities and/or authority in the immediate social context. Through this use of the *masu* form, the learners are socialized into a new domain of knowledge concerning the self-presentational stance. The *masu* form in constructed dialogue represents a voice removed from the here and now of dinnertime talk, representing the *soto* social context. The learners learn how people outside of the family talk through direct quotations. Thus, the *masu* form is a building block for a variety of social identities and a tool to implicitly socialize learners to become competent in displaying a range of social identities.

Figure 4.2 summarizes the indexical relations of the *masu* form in the *uchi* context, which schematizes how the *masu* form constructs different social identities in interaction.

Indirect indexes listed in Figure 4.2 are by no means intended to be exhaustive, but in the homestay context, social identities that are indirectly indexed are related to the expected identities that host family members and JFL learners assume. The *masu* form, which directly indexes the affective stance of self-presentation, foregrounds expected responsibilities associated with particular social identities in the home-stay context. The host mother's authority in this context, for example, is linked to her knowledge of Japanese culture and language. On the other hand, the JFL learner's authority resides in his or her knowledge of English and the cultural practice of his or her home country. In reported speech (direct speech), the *masu* form can construct a wide variety of

| Linguistic → resource | Contextual    ---- > dimension 1 | Contextual dimension 2 |
|---|---|---|
| *Masu* | Direct index | Indirect index |
| → | | (the list is not exhaustive) |
| | (Affective stance)  - -> | (Identity) |
| | Self-presentational stance | Authority- -> Host mother or father                                   Teacher |
| | | Responsibility- -> Host mother or father                                          Someone in charge of                                          a task at hand |
| | | Presenter |
| | | Quoting other social identities |
| | | (typically of the *soto* 'out-group' context) |
| → Direct indexical relation | | |
| --- > Indirect indexical relation | | |

**Figure 4.2** Unmarked indexical relations of the *masu* form in homestay context

voices outside the home in Japanese society. It can be utilized in a playful way as well.

Previous research on the learner's acquisition of the *masu* form investigated use in formal contexts because of the general assumption that the *masu* form does not occur in informal talk. In the homestay context, it is true that both host family members and JFL learners speak mostly in the plain form, and that the *masu* form occurs rather infrequently. However, this chapter demonstrates the importance of examining the *masu* form in the homestay context. When talking to the learner, for the most part, host family members use the *masu* form to construct certain social identities and to quote others just as Japanese parents do with their children. Even novice-level learners at times can index a particular social identity by using the *masu* form. In this way, talk with the host family provides invaluable learning experiences. In the Japanese language classroom, typical instruction provides only one of the social meanings of the *masu* form, politeness or formality (more discussion on this issue in Chapter 7). This chapter has demonstrated that by participating in dinnertime talk with the host family, JFL learners are socialized into the multiple social meanings of the *masu* form evoked through its direct index, the affective stance of self-presentation.

## Notes

1. According to the questionnaires, most of the host families felt that the learner was a part of the family, and most of the learners felt that they were treated as a daughter or a son of the host family. The subjective evaluations of the participants' social identities will be discussed in Chapter 5.
2. Some shifts do not conform to the unmarked patterns observed in Japanese families. These marked shifts are discussed in Chapter 5.
3. In the foreign language classes Wade (2003) observed, sometimes as a class activity the teachers took on the role of an interviewer interviewing students.
4. Wade (2003) finds two functions of teacher talk in her data, namely 'formal stance' and 'casual stance'. What she calls 'formal stance' is equivalent to the notion of 'self-presentational stance' that I propose. In her data the formal stance teachers take occurred to highlight the positional identities of the teacher (e.g. teacher as controller of the classroom discourse; teacher as lecturer, modeler and evaluator).
5. The fifth student was not interviewed two years after his return from Japan. Furthermore, it is not clear in which language (Japanese or English) these interviews were conducted in Iwasaki's study.
6. The finding of McMeekin's study (2007), which shows that the learners use the *masu* form most of the time, seems to contradict that of the present study, but the difference between the two studies is the learners' length of stay with the host family. I will return to this issue in Chapter 7. I will also discuss in more detail differences in shift patterns between the JFL learners and the host families in Chapter 5.
7. I am not listing separate frequencies for the individual family members because of the following reasons: (1) as shown in Examples (1) and (2), there is little or no difference in speech style among family members with different

age groups; (2) in every host family, the host mother dominates the conversation with the JFL learner, and the contribution of the rest of the family members in the conversation is not substantial. As the focus of this study is not to compare each host family member's frequencies using the *masu* form vis-à-vis that of the learner, listing separate frequencies for the individual family members does not contribute much to the study.

8.  As Japanese is an agglutinative language, it is not always clear what constitutes a word. For the consistency of word counts, the data were transcribed according to the CHAT *wakachigaki* system (MacWhinney & Oshima-Takane, 1998).

9.  It is important to note here that not all the instances of the social acts of displaying a particular social identity and quoting voices are expressed in the *masu* form.

10.  The unknown uses are those for which it is hard to define their function due to unclear utterances.

11.  One of the reviewers mentioned that shifting to the *masu* form when a host family member takes care of recording the conversation is an observer's effect because he or she would not normally use the form. I disagree with the reviewer in that as a native speaker of Japanese, I have observed that speakers' shift to the *masu* form often occurs when they take charge of some task at hand such as cleaning a room.

12.  In Skip's family, the activity of serving food does not occur in the data.

13.  *Kimchee* are Korean pickled vegetables, which taste hot and spicy and have a strong garlic smell. Japanese think that foreigners, in particular Westerners, do not like *kimchee*. The laughter of the host parents and Mary that immediately follows the mother's offering of *kimchee* to Mary seems to have to do with this Japanese assumption about *kimchee*.

14.  In lines 7, 8, and 9, the host mother's utterance ends with *kara* 'because,' which syntactically constructs a subordinate clause. Although the verbs in most subordinate clauses are normally in the plain form in Japanese, in the *kara* clause, the *masu* form occurs as well. Therefore, in the *kara* clause, the form of the predicate verbal contrasts with its social meaning.

15.  *No* is grammatically a nominalizer and pragmatically functions as a sentence-final particle if it occurs sentence-finally. It indexes shared or common knowledge among the interlocutors or in community (Cook, 1990b). Japanese conversation generally does not encode subject pronouns. The utterance in line 7 does not have a subject pronoun. To reflect the meaning of the particle *no*, the sentence is translated with the pronoun 'we' rather than 'I'.

16.  In other segments of conversations, the participants turned off the recording devices after they finished dinner or stopped talking. Therefore, the topic of turning off the recorder was not recorded.

17.  HG is the host grandmother.

18.  The plain form is utilized for speech to oneself (cf. Maynard, 1993; Okamoto, 1999).

19.  In Japanese, it is the norm not to encode the subject as it is generally understood that the subject is the topic discussed immediately prior to the current utterance.

20.  Non-native speakers of Japanese may think that the host mother's utterance in line 12 is ambiguous because she does not state what is finished. However, it is normal not to encode the subject pronoun in Japanese, and

the fact that the host father does not ask for clarification indicates that her utterance is not a source of misunderstanding here.

21. *Deshoo* is the tentative form of the *masu* form (cf. Jorden & Noda, 1987), but as I mentioned earlier, since in conversation this form is typically not contrasted with the plain form *daroo*, I do not count it as an instance of the *masu* form in this study.

22. It is also possible to interpret the *masu* form in these occasions as a marker of politeness, for showing the good side of a person in front of an audience is a polite act.

23. The verb *tabeta* 'ate' in this utterance is in the plain form, but since it occurs in a subordinate clause, it does not index any social meaning. Therefore, it is not the case that the host sister shifted to the plain form while she is still joking.

24. The word *doku* ('poison') does not appear in most beginning Japanese textbooks whereas the word *doko* ('where') is one of the words that is introduced early in beginning Japanese textbooks.

25. While in Japanese society store clerks in general speak politely using the *masu* form and referent honorifics, street vendors may speak in the plain form as demonstrated in Okamoto (1998). Pete may not yet be aware of this sociolinguisitc information.

## Chapter 5
# Marked and Unmarked Uses of the Masu Form in the Homestay Context

As discussed in earlier chapters, the *masu* form in Japanese family conversation is intricately interwoven with social identities. It can index the social identities of the participants who are displaying playfulness, the voices of others, responsibility or authority related to expected social roles. As these uses of the *masu* form and its use in set formulas are the majority in the *uchi* ('in-group/inside') circle of family conversation, they are considered as unmarked (i.e. habitual) uses in this context. In contrast, some *masu* usages rarely occur in this context. They are occurrences of the *masu* form (1) in reactive tokens and fillers and (2) in the speech acts of questions, answers and statements that do not evoke the authority or responsibility of the speaker's social identity relevant to the social context.[1] These uses of the *masu* form occur mostly in *soto* ('out-group/outside') context, such as an interview or academic consultation outside of the *uchi* ('in-group/inside') context of family talk. As discussed in Chapter 3, the self-presentational stance as a display of politeness is a more salient interpretation in the *soto* ('out-group/outside') context because the speaker's polite behavior (showing a good side) is expected in this context. Thus, these instances of the *masu* form are more likely to be interpreted as a marker of politeness. In the homestay context, both learners and host family members sometimes deviate from the norm of Japanese native speakers' family talk and employ these functions of the *masu* form. As these instances are deviations from the norm, they are considered to be marked uses.

This chapter investigates to what extent and why the learners and host family members choose the 'marked' style from the point of view of Japanese family conversation. In the homestay context, however, the situation is more complex than that in Japanese families. The learner who lives with a host family is expected to play the role of a family member. They are encouraged to call the host father and mother *otoosan* ('father') and *okaasan* ('mother'), respectively.[2] All the host families in the present data report that they consider their JFL learner a family member, not a foreign guest. In reality, however, the learner's identity in the host family is often ambiguous. It is unclear whether the learner is a member of the family or a foreign guest. For this reason, participants in this social context may at times maintain the *soto* ('out-group/outside')

107

relationship. In this regard, Iino (2006: 205) notes that, 'It is not an easy task to measure the distance or the intimacy level between the participants in the homestay situation.' In addition, there may be a discrepancy between the learner's expectation regarding their identity in the family and their pragmalinguistic competence in the target language. On the one hand, the learner may self-report that he or she plays the role of a son or daughter in the host family. On the other hand, due to a low proficiency level in the target language, the learner may not be able to make use of linguistic and pragmatic resources of the target language in an appropriate manner to discursively create the identity of a son or daughter. This chapter raises the following questions: to what extent, do JFL learners and host family members employ the marked choice (with respect to family talk in Japanese families) that discursively creates the *soto* context? If so, what are the reasons for this choice? The learners' marked choice may reflect a lack of sociolinguistic competence, resulting from a low proficiency in Japanese, and/or it may index the learner's identity as an outsider (e.g. a foreign guest). As the host family members in this study are native speakers of standard Tokyo Japanese, they tacitly know what types of *masu* usages are marked choices in family conversation.[3] If they deviate from the unmarked usages, are they treating the learner as an outsider (e.g. a foreign guest) rather than as a member of the family? Or are there any other reasons why the host families employ marked uses of the *masu* form? Are there individual differences among the host families with respect to the *masu* form usages?

## *Masu* Form Uses that Index the *Soto* Context

In this section, I describe uses of the *masu* form that are marked from the perspective of Japanese family conversation. While these uses are rare in family conversation, they are common in many social situations, such as formal interviews (Ikuta, 1983, 2002; Nazikian, 2007), academic consultations between professor and student (Cook, 2006b) and conversations between participants with a different social status (Megumi, 2002). They help constitute the *soto* ('out-group') context. In this sense, they are unmarked for social situations outside the family setting but are marked in family talk.

The *masu* form in reactive tokens, short replies and fillers mostly occurs outside family conversation. A reactive token is 'a short utterance produced by an interlocutor who is playing a listener's role during the other interlocutor's speakership' (Clancy *et al.*, 1996: 355). In Japanese, expressions such as *soo (desu) ne*, *soo (desu) ka* and *soo (desu) yo* are used as reactive tokens as well as short replies.[4] They are used as short replies when uttered as an answer to a question. They function as a reactive token when they are uttered by the listener during the other interlocutor's speakership. Fillers are short expressions that typically occur at the utterance-initial position. They serve to keep the current speaker's turn while he or she is searching for the next word. Expressions such as *ano (desu) ne* and *eeto (desu) ne* are fillers. Short replies, reactive tokens and fillers can either be in the plain or *masu* form, as shown in (1).

(1)

| Plain form | *Masu* form |
|------------|-------------|
| Soo (da) ne | Soo desu ne |
| Soo ka | Soo desu ka |
| Soo (da) yo | Soo desu yo |
| Ano (ne) | Ano desu ne |
| Eeto (ne) | Eeto desu ne |

In a study of the shift pattern of the *masu* and plain forms in talk among two Japanese teaching assistants and a Japanese exchange student in an American university, Megumi (2002) reports that the exchange student (lower in rank) talks to the teaching assistants (higher in rank), shifting between the two forms; but his short replies and reactive tokens, such as *soo desu ne* ('that's right'), are all in the *masu* form. Similarly, in formal interviews, both interviewer and interviewee speak in the *masu* form; but when they express affect, they sometimes shift to the plain form (Ikuta, 1983). However, their short replies, reactive tokens and fillers are typically in the *masu* form. Examples (2a) and (2b), which are taken from a TV interview program called 'men's cooking', illustrate such uses of the *masu* form.[5]

(2a) (NHK TV interview program, *otoko no ryoori* ('men's cooking'))

1 I: soija mainichi shiire ni ja asa    hayaku okite iku wake **desu** ne.
then everyday stock to uh morning early rise  go  Nom Cop FP
'Then every day you get up early and go to buy chicken?'

2 C: ma: shichiji    goro **desu** yo ne
well 7 o'clock    about Cop  FP FP
'Well, at about seven o'clock.'

3 → I: aa soo **desu** ka.
oh so  Cop Q
'Oh, is that right?'

(2b)  (NHK TV interview program, *otoko no ryoori* 'men's cooking")

1 I: ichinichi kore kushi nanbon      gurai utsu wake **desu** ka?
    one day this skewer how many about stick Nom Cop Q
    'How many skewers do you make per day?'

2 → C: soo **desu** ne:. daitai senbon          gurai **desu** ne.
      so  Cop FP about one thousand about Cop  FP
      'Well, about one thousand.'

In (2a) and (2b) a male interviewer interviews a male *yakitori* chef in a *yakitori* restaurant.[6] Both participants for the most part speak in the *masu* form and never fail to use it in short replies, reactive tokens and fillers. In (2a) the interviewer produces a reactive token (*aa soo desu ka*) and in (2b) the chef prefaces his response with a filler (*soo desu ne:*), both of which are in the *masu* form. In contrast, in Japanese family conversation, short replies, reactive tokens or fillers are in the plain form. These observations indicate that the *masu* form in short replies, reactive tokens and fillers indexes politeness to the addressee. These uses of the *masu* form highlight a *soto* ('out-group/outside') context because politeness is expected in *soto*. Because in the homestay context the learner is, as a rule, incorporated in the host family as a family member, the expected speaking norm is that of the *uchi* context. From this perspective, the occurrence of the *masu* form in short replies, reactive tokens or fillers is marked.

In the *soto* context, the speaker's questions, answers and statements are not necessarily linked to the responsibility or authority of his or her social identity relevant to a given social context, for a display of the self-presentational stance is expected as the norm of this context. For example, the *masu* form may foreground the speaker's polite attitude toward the addressee. Consider (3), which is an example of the *soto* context, where a non-reciprocal exchange of the two forms indicates a hierarchical social relationship between B's mother and N. Here N is a college friend of Rick's host brother, B. He is visiting B's house and talking to B's mother. He uses the *masu* form when he responds to questions posed by B's mother in the plain form. N's use of non-reciprocal *masu* indexes politeness to B's mother.

(3) Rick012002

N (a male college student), B (N's close college friend, Rick's host brother), and M (B's mother)

1 M: tsuchiura toka ja nakute edogawa ja nakute tonegawa no?
     Tsuchiura etc. Neg      Edogawa  Neg       Tonegawa LK
     'It's not Tsuchiura nor Edogawa, but Tonegawa?'

2 → N: tonegawa no    hoo **desu**.
Tonegawa LK    way Cop
'It's Tonegawa.'

3 M: <u>chikaku</u>?
close
'Close to it?'

4 N: hai
yes
'Yes.'

5 M: huun    soko ni nani? ryooshin- goryooshin wa <u>sunderu</u> no?[7]
huhuh there in what parents    parents    Top live    FP
'Hu huh there, you mean? Your parents, your parents live there?'

6 B: <u>jikka</u> =
family home
'his family home'

7 → N: = jikka    **desu**.
family home Cop
'It's my family home.'

((13 lines omitted))

8 M: shuushoku wa?
getting job Top
'How about your job hunting?'

9 → N: aa **kimarimashita**.
uh decided
'uh, I got one.'

10 M: a- honto aa <u>yokatta</u> ne de ne:
uh really uh good    FP and FP
'uh- really? uh, it's great and'

11 N: nantoka
somehow
'Somehow (I managed).'

12 M: uun taihen    <u>datta</u>? yappari
uh    difficult Cop    after all
'uh, was it difficult? after all.'

13  → N: taihen **deshita** ne.
      difficult Cop    FP
      'It was difficult.'

In lines 2, 7, 9 and 13, using the *masu* form, N responds to B's mother's questions. B's mother asks N about the location of his parents' house and his job-hunting situation. None of N's responses are linked to his responsibility or authority as a guest and friend at B's house.[8] In this sense, these uses of the *masu* form differ from those related to the speaker's responsibility or authority (e.g. the *masu* form used by a parent when teaching a child about social etiquette). N is indexing through these uses of the *masu* form not only politeness to B's mother but also his *soto* ('out-group/outside') relationship with her. As this type of *masu* form use indexes the *soto* identity of the speaker, it rarely occurs in conversation between immediate family members. It is a highly marked usage among immediate family members in the homestay context as well.

## Marked Uses of the *Masu* Form in the Homestay Context

Both JFL learners and host family members at times deviate from the norm of Japanese native speakers (i.e. unmarked uses). They use the *masu* form in short replies, reactive tokens, fillers and questions/answers/statements expressed when they do not display their authority or responsibility directly related to their social role in the host family. To examine in more detail how the learners and the host families in this study use the *masu* forms typically used to index the *soto* context, I tabulated both unmarked and marked instances of the *masu* form. The following categories are used to distinguish the unmarked from the marked uses of the *masu* form in the *uchi* ('in-group/inside') context of the homestay situation:

- *Masu* forms that occur in the following situations are unmarked uses in the *uchi* context:
  1. set formulas (e.g. *itadakimasu* 'I am going to receive'),
  2. utterances that express authority/responsibility of the learner or host family members,
  3. utterances that express that the speaker is in charge (of the activity at hand),
  4. direct quotation and
  5. utterances that express playfulness.

- *Masu* forms that occur in the following are marked uses in the *uchi* context:
  1. questions, answers or statements not related to items (1) to (5) above and
  2. reactive tokens, short replies or fillers.

For example, when the host family members talk to the learner about Japanese culture, social customs or the Japanese language using the *masu* form, they are speaking with authority. Similarly, when the learner talks about social customs of their home country or English, they are also speaking with authority. These instances are considered unmarked uses in the *uchi* context. As I mentioned in Chapter 4, there are other topics that may be related to the authority and responsibility of the host family. However, only clear cases (i.e. statements, questions and answers about the speakers' own language, culture and social customs, or when a speaker is in charge of an activity at hand) are counted as unmarked uses of the *masu* form.

Figure 5.1 shows the frequencies of the marked and unmarked choices that learners made when they spoke in the *masu* form; Figure 5.2 shows the frequencies of the host families' marked and unmarked choices of the *masu* form per 2000 words.

Figure 5.1 indicates that more than half of the *masu* uses of the novice- and intermediate-level learners (Alice, Tom, Kate, Rick and Greg) are marked choices, while more than half of the *masu* uses of the advanced-level learners (Skip, Pete, Mary and Ellen) are unmarked choices. In particular, Skip's use of *masu* completely conforms to the Japanese native speakers' norm. The frequency of the marked choice becomes much lower when the learner reaches the advanced level. In contrast, Figure 5.2 shows that most of the host families' *masu* uses are unmarked except for those of the host families of Kate and Greg. For example, Rick's host family uses the *masu* form only in the unmarked manner. Kate's host family has the

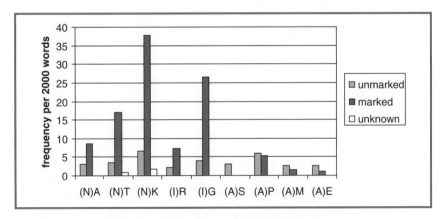

**Figure 5.1** Learners' frequencies of unmarked and marked uses of *masu**
* N, 'novice-level learner'; I, 'intermediate-level learner'; A, 'advanced-level learner.' For example, (N)A stands for 'novice-level learner, Alice'.

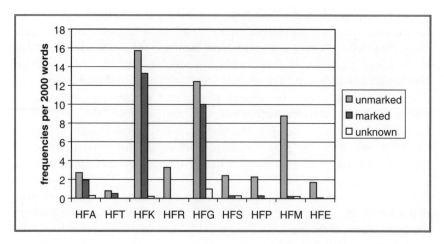

**Figure 5.2** Host families' frequencies of unmarked and marked uses of *masu*\*
\* HF, 'host family'. For example, HFA stands for 'host family of Alice'.

highest percentage of marked choices among the host families, but Kate's
family makes marked choices less than half of the time.

The following examples illustrate the participants' marked uses, which
index the *soto* context. Example (4) shows a *masu* form used in the learner's
reactive token and the host mother's filler. Here Greg's host mother is
explaining to him the meaning of the word *mukatsuku* ('to feel upset').

(4) Greg 012702

1 HM: a- bujoku sareta     yoo na?
       uh insult was done like Cop
       'uh like being insulted?'

2 G: ha:i
      yes
      'ye:s'

3 HM: un. sore de bujoku sareta hito      ga mukatsukutte [yuu wake
       uh so      insult was done person S feel sick      say   FP
       'uh so the fact is that a person who is insulted feels upset.'

4 →G:                                               [soo **desu**
                                                    so   Cop
                                                    'that's right.'

5 HM: bujoku shita      hito    wa mukatsuku n ja na kutte
        insult was done person Top feel sick Mom Neg
        'It's not that the person who insults someone feel upset.'

6 → G: soo **desu** yo. soo **desu** yo?
        So  Cop FP  so Cop  FP
        'That's right, that's right.'

7 HM: un
        uh huh
        'uh huh'

8 G: anata wa?
        you  Top
        'How about you?'

9 → HM: soo **desu** ne:, soo yuu yoo ni tsukatteru yoo ni watashi mo
        So  Cop  FP  so say  like  use        like I              also
        <u>omotteru</u>.
        think
        'Well, I think I also use (the word *mukatsuku*) in this manner.'

In lines 4 and 5, Greg gives reactive tokens (*soo **desu**, soo **desu** yo*).[9]
When asked about her own usage of the word *mukatsuku* ('to feel sick'),
the host mother in line 9 starts with *soo **desu** ne* ('well'). This expression is
a filler because it occurs at the utterance-initial position in her response to
Greg's question. Through the use of *masu* forms in reactive tokens and in a
filler, both participants jointly construct a distant relationship (*soto*). In
addition, Greg's choice of the address term *anata* ('you') to the host
mother indexes the identity of Greg as a foreigner as in Japanese the
pronoun *anata* ('you') is not normally used to address someone older than
the speaker.

In Example (5), Rick provides a reactive token in the *masu* form when
his host brother is telling him about a region in northern Japan called
Mito and its regional delicacy *natto* ('fermented soybeans'). Note that the
host brother speaks in the plain form. Rick's reactive token in line 4 is in
the *masu* form, which indexes that Rick is an outsider and may be lower
in status. One may argue that his use of the *masu* form in a reactive token
is simply a reflection of his lack of proficiency in Japanese.[10] Even if
Rick's use of the *masu* form here is due to his lack of proficiency in
Japanese, or he intends to use it as a marker of politeness, the *masu* form
in a reactive token indexes the *soto* context from the perspective of native
speaker norms.[11]

(5)  Rick011602

1 HB: Mito tte ne (0.5)  <u>Ibaraki-ken</u>
       Mito QT FP        Ibaraki Prefecture
       'Mito is (0.5) in   Ibaraki Prefecture.'

2 R: un
     uh huh
     'uh huh'

3 HB: chikai n kedo ichijikan han <u>gurai</u> kana (1.0) soko wa nattoo ga
      near   Nom but 1 hour half about wonder there Top nattoo S
      yuumee <u>na</u>   no
      famous  Cop FP
'It's near. It takes about an hour and a half, I think. It's famous for its
*natto*.'

4 → R: a:  soo [**desu** ka
        oh so  Cop  Q
        'Oh is that so?'

5 HB:              [uun       dakara ne suupaa      ni itte mo  ne
                   uhm        so     FP supermarket to go also FP
                   'uhm       so if you go to a supermarket'

Examples (4) and (5) portrayed the participants' uses of the *masu* form
in reactive tokens and fillers, which index the *soto* relationship.
   The *soto* relationship is created in another way. Questions, answers
and statements in the *masu* form, not directly linked to the speaker's
authority or responsibility in the homestay context, also index the *soto*
identity of the speaker from the perspective on Japanese native speaker
norms. Example (6) is an instance of this. Here the learner, Kate, provides
a short reply, and her host brother asks a question, both of which are in
the *masu* form.

(6)  Kate 060804

1 HM: doo yatte  <u>oboeru</u>     no?
      how do     memorize    FP
      'How do you memorize?'

2 K: [u:n
     uhm
     'uhm'

3 HM: [nooto mite?
       notebook look
       'looking at the notebook?'

4 → K: soo **desu** ne:
       so   Cop FP
       'That's right.'

5 → HB: nooto ni **kakimasu** ka?
        notebook on write   Q
        'Do you write in a notebook?'

6 K: un
     uh huh
     'uh huh'

In this example, Kate and her host family are talking about how to memorize dates when studying history. Kate provides a short reply to the host mother's question in the *masu* form. Then the host brother asks a question in the *masu* form. Here he is not teaching Kate how to memorize historical dates but is asking what she usually does. His question does not concern the authority or responsibility of his role as a host brother to Kate. Both Kate's short reply in line 4 and the host brother's question in line 5 index the *soto* identity of the speakers.

In a similar case, Example (7) shows the learner's use of the *masu* form in a statement in which she has no authority related to her social identity in the host family.

(7) Mary 020402

1 M: kondo =
     this time
     'This time'

2 HM: = un
      uh huh
      'uh huh'

3 → M: tai ni **ikimasu** sorede [kenburijji no]  okane  zenbu tsukatte
       Thailand to go so     Cambridge LK money all      use
       **shimaimasu** ga =
       end up    but
       'I will go to Thailand so I will end up using all the Cambridge money.'

4 HM:                            [un un]
                                 uh huh uh huh
                                 'uh huh uh huh'

5 HF:                            [((laughs))]

6 M: = soo yuu kakko       <u>warui</u> koto =
       so say  appearance bad    thing
       'Not a cool thing'

7 HM: = unn
       mhmm
       'mhmm'

Mary, who received a scholarship from Cambridge University to study in Japan, is telling her host parents that she will take a trip to Thailand and will spend money she received for the scholarship for this trip. In this statement she shifts to the *masu* form, which is not related to Mary's authority or responsibility as a foreign student or as 'daughter' in the host family.[12] The *masu* form in this example momentarily positions Mary as someone who has a *soto* identity in the host family.[13]

## Socialization Effects on the Learners

Marked and unmarked uses of the *masu* form in the *uchi* ('in-group/inside') context are linked to the speaker's expected responsibilities and authority associated with their social identity in this context. As typically Japanese language textbooks explain that the *masu* form is a polite or formal speech marker and that it is not used among family members and people in close relationships (see Chapter 7), it is in informal routine interactions with native speakers of Japanese that learners are socialized into unmarked uses of the *masu* form in the *uchi* context. With the learners in this study (except for Mary and Ellen whose mothers are Japanese) such socialization must have begun after the learners arrived in Japan. A low frequency of marked uses indicates that a learner has been socialized into the native speaker norm as a family member. A learner's marked *masu* usage may indicate his or her lack of linguistic and/or pragmatic competence in Japanese. Or it may mean that a learner prefers to keep distance and remains as a foreign guest in the host family. Although it is not always clear why learners make a marked choice, native speakers of Japanese perceive marked uses of the *masu* form as an index of a *soto* relationship.

As mentioned in Chapter 4, the average frequency of the *masu* form for the learners is 15.7 per 2000 words, and that for the host families is 8.6. The fact that most of the conversations between the JFL learner and the host family are carried out in the plain form indicates that they discursively construct a close *uchi* ('in-group/inside') relationship most of the time. The participants, however, at times create a *soto* identity when they shift to the *masu* form in a marked manner. Do the learners intentionally make marked choices to index the *soto* ('out-group/ outside') identity, or do they do so due to their lower proficiency in Japanese? If the former case applies, we would expect a higher percentage of marked uses if the learner feels that he or she is a foreign student rather than a son or daughter in the family. On the other hand, if it is the latter case, we would expect a decrease of marked uses as the learners become more proficient in Japanese. To answer these questions, we need to look at relationships (1) between the frequency and percentage of the marked uses and the learners' Japanese proficiency level and (2) between the frequency and percentage of marked uses and the learners' self-evaluation of their social identity in the host family.

Table 5.1 lists the learners' Japanese proficiency level, frequency of use of the *masu* form per 2000 words, percentage and frequency of marked uses of *masu* and the learners' self-reported social identity in the host family. The frequency of marked uses is calculated by multiplying the frequency of *masu* form usage that occurred in each learner's speech by the percentage of marked uses. We see that Table 5.1 does not show a clear relationship between the learners' self-reported social identity in the host family and the percentage of marked uses of the *masu* form. Tom, Kate and Greg, who are novice- and intermediate-level learners, feel that they are college-age children in the host family, but almost 80% or more of their *masu* usage is a marked choice, resulting in much higher frequencies of the marked choice per 2000 words. Such choices index that they are outsiders from the perspective of the Japanese native speaker norm.[14] Although the present data sample is too small to conclusively answer the above questions, they do suggest that at least in the present data, the novice- and intermediate-level learners' marked choice of the *masu* form is attributed to their lack of sociolinguistic competence. In response to two questions in the questionnaire, 'What do you learn most in speaking in Japanese with your host family?' and 'What is most difficult when you speak in Japanese with your host family?', no learner except for Pete mentions the use of the *masu* and/or plain forms. Only Pete briefly mentions speaking in 'casual language' with his host family, which, he reports, makes him feel that he is treated like a college-age son. The learners' self-reports suggest that when speaking with the host family, they are rather unaware of the speech style they employ.

It may be the case that a higher percentage of the marked choice is related to a higher frequency of the *masu* form. Table 5.1 indicates that

**Table 5.1** JFL learners' proficiency-level, percentage and frequency of the marked use of *masu* and self-reports of their social identity in the host family

| JFL learner | Japanese Proficiency-level | Frequency of masu per 2000 words | Frequency of marked uses per 2000 words (%) | Learner's self-report on their social identity in their host family |
|---|---|---|---|---|
| Alice | Novice | 11.9 | 8.7 (72.7%) | Unknown |
| Tom | Novice | 21.5 | 17.0 (79.2%) | college age son |
| Kate | Novice/high | 46.1 | 37.8 (82.1%) | college age daughter |
| Rick | Intermediate/low | 9.5 | 7.4 (78%) | college age son, young child, and foreign student |
| Greg | Intermediate | 30.6 | 26.6 (87%) | college age son |
| Skip | Advanced/low | 3.0 | 0 (0%) | college age son |
| Pete | Advanced | 1.1 | 5.3 (47.4%) | college age son (80%), foreign student (20%) |
| Mary | Advanced | 4.3 | 1.5 (35.3%) | foreign student |
| Ellen | Advanced | 3.7 | 1.0 (27.3%) | college age daughter |

the frequency of the *masu* form per 2000 words is not necessarily in proportion to the percentage of its marked use. For example, although the frequencies of the *masu* form used by Rick and Pete are similar (Rick's 9.5 and Pete's 11.1), Rick's percentage of marked use is much higher (78%) than Pete's (47%). What Table 5.1 shows is that in the present data, the percentage of marked *masu* choices is related to the learner's Japanese proficiency-level. The advanced-level learners' percentage of marked uses is much lower than those of the novice- and intermediate-level learners. The percentages of marked uses by advanced-level learners do not exceed 47%, whereas those of the novice- and intermediate-level learners range between 70% and 87%. This finding suggests the possibility that the advanced-level learners use the *masu* form in an appropriate fashion (i.e. in the unmarked manner) in the *uchi* ('inside/in-group') context more frequently in conversation with their host family. As the learners become more proficient in Japanese, their use of the marked *masu* form decreases. A larger set of data will have to be examined to definitively conclude that a higher proficiency of Japanese correlates with more unmarked uses of the *masu* form in the *uchi* ('inside/in-group'). As unmarked use of the *masu* form is probably not taught in Japanese language classes and thus perhaps only acquired through interactions with host family members or close friends, the advanced learners' lower frequencies of marked uses may be attributed to socialization effects.

Socialization effects can also be measured by the acquisition of a wider range of *masu* functions as well. As these indexical functions are typically acquired through interaction with native speakers of Japanese, we would expect that the more advanced the learners become in Japanese through participation in talk with the host family or close friends who are native speakers of Japanese, the more diverse their unmarked use of the *masu* form will become. Table 5.2 shows the distribution of types of the learners' unmarked *masu* forms in family conversation.

In Table 5.2, it is obvious that all but one learner uses the *masu* form in set formulas, e.g. *itadakimasu. Itadakimasu* literally means 'I am going to receive' and is always in the *masu* form.[15] As data were collected during mealtime, most of the participants used the set formula *itadakimasu* before they started eating dinner. Table 5.2 suggests that the advanced-level learners can use the *masu* form appropriately in a wider range of functions. Three advanced-level learners (Pete, Mary and Ellen) can use the *masu* form when they take charge of a task at hand. Similarly, three advanced learners (Skip, Pete and Mary) skillfully shift to the *masu* form when quoting other people (see Examples (19) and (20) in Chapter 4). Such shifts suggest that they have acquired the communicative competence of linking a particular social identity to a particular speech style. One advanced-level learner, Skip, uses the *masu* form in an

**Table 5.2** Distribution of types of the learners' unmarked uses of the *masu* form

| Appropriate masu uses | Alice (N) | Tom (N) | Kate (N/ high) | Rick (II low) | Greg (I) | Skip (A/ low) | Pete (A) | Mary (A) | Ellen (A) |
|---|---|---|---|---|---|---|---|---|---|
| Set formula | ● | ● | ● | ● | ● | | ● | ● | ● |
| In charge | | | | | | | ● | ● | ● |
| Authority | | ● | | | ● | | | | |
| Presenter | | | | | | | | ● | |
| Playfulness | | | | | | | | ● | |
| Quotation | | | | | | ● | ● | ● | |

N = Novice, I = Intermediate and A = Advanced

unmarked manner only in one type of function (i.e. direct quotation), which may be due to his low frequency of *masu* (3.0 per 2000 words, respectively) as well as the shorter length of data.[16] Two novice-level and one intermediate (low)-level learner (Alice, Kate and Rick) use it only in set formulas. We can say that at least in the present study, the advanced-level learners can use a wider range of functions of unmarked uses of the *masu* form in conversation with their host family. However, as the data are from naturally occurring conversation and topics are not controlled, the absence of a certain function in a learner's speech does not necessarily mean that he or she has not acquired it. For example, even novice- and intermediate-level learners such as Greg index their authority in teaching English or American culture to their host family by shifting to the *masu* form (see Example (9) in Chapter 4).

At least in the present study, the frequency of the advanced-level learners' marked choice of the *masu* form is much lower, which suggests that compared with novice and intermediate-level learners, advanced-level learners are socialized further into the unmarked uses (i.e. the Japanese native speaker norm) of the *masu* form in conversation with the host family. The advanced-level learners have spent a longer period in Japan and/or have a longer experience speaking with native speakers of Japanese. Skip and Pete, both advanced-level learners, stayed in Japan prior to the current study abroad experience and spent a total of more than 9 months in Japan. Mary and Ellen, also advanced learners, grew up hearing their mothers talk in Japanese even though they spoke with their mothers only in English. While research on L2 pragmatics shows that the length of stay in a foreign community does not always correlate with learners' pragmatic development (Kasper & Rose, 2002), the present study suggests that the more time learners spend with a host family or other native speakers of Japanese, the more they will be socialized into unmarked uses of the *masu* form in the *uchi* ('inside/in-group') context.

## Variations of Interactional Styles Among Host Families

Host families also sometimes make a marked choice when they shift to the *masu* form. Is it the case that an increased frequency of the *masu* form entails a higher frequency of marked choices? Does this mean that they are treating the learner as an outsider? Figure 5.2 clearly indicates that the host families of Kate and Greg use the *masu* form including its marked uses far more frequently than other host families. In Kate's host family's speech, the *masu* form occurs 29.2 times per 2000 words with 13.3 marked uses. Greg's host family uses the *masu* form 23.4 times per 2000 words with 10 marked uses. In contrast, the host families of Tom, Rick, Skip, Pete and Ellen are infrequent users of the *masu* form. Their frequency of *masu* form usage is 3 per 2000 words or less, and their marked uses are less than 0.5 per 2000 words. In fact, Rick's host family never makes a marked choice. For the most part, marked uses increase as the overall frequency of the *masu* form increases. The host families' frequencies of the *masu* form usage are linked to different interactional styles, as are their frequencies of marked uses.

In what follows, I will discuss different interactional styles found among the host families, namely teaching, non-teaching and accommodating styles. The three types of interactional style, which are grouped together based on frequencies of the *masu* form, shed light on the questions of why there are differences in frequency of *masu* usage among the host families, and why some host families make more marked choices than others.[17]

### Host families with a teaching voice

As noted above, the host families of Kate and Greg use the *masu* form more frequently than the other families, and their marked uses number more than 10 per 2000 words.

Figure 5.3 shows that two functions of the unmarked uses of the *masu* form, displaying authority (i.e. teaching voice) and quoting others, stand out in both host families. It is also noted that they do not use *masu* to be playful. In both families, more than 40% of the unmarked instances of *masu* occur when the family members display their authority in telling the learner about Japanese culture and language. When talking about Japanese culture and language to the learner, the host families of Kate and Greg are more likely to speak to the learner in the voice of a teacher by shifting to the *masu* form. Examples (8) and (9) illustrate this. In these examples, the host mothers are telling the learner about an aspect of Japanese culture. In so doing, they mix *masu* and plain forms. In Example (8), Kate's host mother is telling Kate about a Japanese summer festival called *Tanabata*, which is celebrated on July 7. According to the legend, if the sky is clear on that evening, the male and female stars can meet once a year. Children decorate a bamboo tree with colorful *tanzaku* ('strips of fancy paper') expressing their wishes.

(8) Kate 061004

1 → HM: keito wa tanabata tte **shittemasu** ka?
          Kate Top Tanabata QT know       Q
          'Kate, do you know about Tanabata?'

2   K: shirimasen
          know  Neg
          'I don't know about it.'

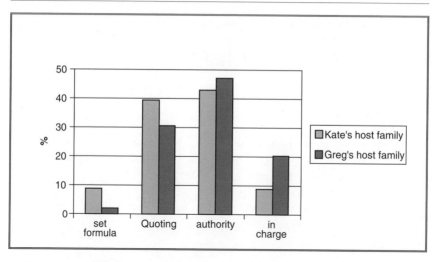

**Figure 5.3** Distribution of unmarked uses of *masu*.

3 HM: ano: chuugoku no: hito ni:   (0.5) tabun chuugoku: no (0.7)
     uh   China      LK people from   perhaps China   LK
     'uh from Chinese people, perhaps Chinese'

4      sora no amanogawa to itte (0.7) sora no hoshi ni kawa ga <u>aru</u> (.)
      sky LK Milky way QT say      sky LK star in river    S exist
      'There's what is called the Milky Way, a river among the stars in
      the sky.'

5      de soko de onna   no ko   to otoko no ko   ga: deau no ga ichi
      and there at female LK child and male LK child S meet Nom S one
      nen ni <u>ichido</u>
      year in once
      'And a girl and a boy up there meet once a year.'

      (0.5)

6      kawa no kochira gawa to kochira gawa ni tte iu   no   wa
      river LK this     side   and this   side in QT say Nom Top
      'In other words, one side and the other side,'

7      hoshi ga chikaku naru   n     da  to <u>omou</u> no ne (.)
      star  S close    become Nom Cop QT think  FP FP
      'I think, the stars get closer'

8        [ichi- ichi nen ni ikkai <u>dake</u> (.)
         one one year in once only
         'once- only once a year.'

9     K: [hu:n
         uh huh
         'uh huh'

10 →HM: so- shite au koto ga dekiru to iu   tanabata matsuri
         an- and meet Nom S able   QT say Tanabata festival
         to iu   no   ga   aru   n     **desu** kedo:
         QT say Nom S     exist Nom Cop   but
         'An- and we have the Tanabata festival when they can meet.'

11    K: tanabata
         'Tanabata'

12   HM: tanabata (1.0)
         'Tanabata'

13    K: hun
         uhm
         'uhm'

14  HM: un sore wa ne: u:n konaida       no takenoko no anna ookina
         uh that Top FP uh the other day LK bamboo LK that  big
         banbuu ja nakute
         bamboo    Neg
         'uh it's not such a big bamboo like the one we saw the other day.'

15    →  motto hosoi banbuu    na    n     **desu** [kedo
         more thin   bamboo Cop Nom    Cop   but
         'it's a thinner bamboo.'

16    K:                                   [un
                                           uhm
                                           'uhm'

17 HM: kore ni iron na kazari      mono o choodo kurisumasu tsurii
        this to various decorating thing O   just    Christmas  tree
        mitaku kazatte (.)
        like      decolate
        'We decorate it with various ornaments like a Christmas tree'

18   K: ((laughs))

19 HM: de  ano:  kamakura ja nai ya enoshima no (1.0)
         and uh   Kamakuar Neg  FP Enoshima LK
         'And uh Kamakura, no, Enoshima's'

20       futari        ga nakayoku **naremasu** yoo ni toka tte
         two people S good terms become   like     etc.   QT
         'wishing the two will become closer'

21       yatteru tokoro aru desho (.) aa yuu onegai goto to iu ne
         do      place  exist Cop       that say wish thing QT say FP
         'some people do that.   This sort of thing is called *onegai goto*'

22       watashi no kiboo tte yuu koto  o ne: tanzaku to itte:
         I         LK wish QT say Nom O FP *tanzaku* QT say
         'Things I wish for are put on a *tanzaku* (strip of fancy paper),'

23   → ko shikakui kami ni kaku  n      **desu** yo ne:
         this square paper on write Nom Cop  FP FP
         'a square piece of paper we write on.'

Kate's host mother shifts to the *masu* form when she asks if Kate knows about the festival. This is a 'pre-sequence', which provides the hearer with what type of telling will follow (Schegloff, 1980; Ten Have, 1999). Kate responds negatively saying *shirimasen* ('I do not know') in the *masu* form, which is a marked use in the *uchi* context. With her marked choice of the *masu* form, Kate indexes her *soto* identity in relation to her host mother.[18] In lines 4 and 5, the host mother tells the story of *Tanabata* and shifts back to the plain form. She continues the plain form when she expresses her opinion in line 7, but in line 10 she summarizes the story, shifting back to the *masu* form. She maintains the *masu* form to describe the bamboo used in the festival in line 17. In line 20 she quotes a voice that wishes good luck to the stars using the *masu* form. She concludes the explanation about *tanzaku* ('strip of fancy paper'), continuing to speak with the *masu* form. Kate's host mother's use of *masu* here indexes her identity as someone who is knowledgeable about the Japanese festival of *Tanabata*. It indexes the voice of a teacher telling a story associated with a Japanese festival to a learner.[19]

In a similar example, Greg and his host mother are sitting at the table getting ready to eat dinner. In this example, the host mother is explaining to him the Japanese food she has prepared. Then she explains to him about the Japanese custom of eating *kamaboko* ('fish cake') during the New Year's celebration.

(9) Greg 011302

1    HM: kore wa <u>tsukemono</u> (.) ne =
          this Top pickles          FP
          'These are pickles'

2       G: = un
             yeah
             'yeah'

3 → HM: tsukemono to kore  wa ano: (.) <u>kamaboko</u>. (0.5) tabeta koto
          pickles      and this Top uh      kamaboko        ate    Nom
          **arimasu** ka? =
          exist    Q
          'Pickles, and this is uh fish cake.    Have you ever eaten this?'

4       G: = sakana de dekite dekiteru desho =
             fish     by made made      Cop
             'It's made of fish, isn't it?'

5 → HM: = un (0.5) sakana de <u>dekiteru</u> no. yoku **shittemasu** ne:
          yeah      fish     by made      FP well   know        FP
          'yeah, it's made of fish. You are really knowledgeable,
          aren't you?'
(1.0)

6  → HM: ano oshoogatsu ni ne: kore wa ano kono kamaboko tte iu
          uh New Year on FP this Top uh this kamaboko    QT say
          no taberu n  [**desu** yo.
          Nom eat Nom Cop FP
          'uh on New Year's Day, this is the fish cake we eat.'

7       G:                    [un
                              uh huh
                              'uh huh'

    In line 3 after a half-second pause, the host mother points to the fish
cake ('*kamaboko*') and asks, using the *masu* form, if Greg has ever eaten it.
This is a pre-sequence to her telling of a Japanese New Year's custom. In
line 2, he guesses that *kamaboko* ('fish cake') is made of fish, and asks for a
confirmation. She confirms his utterance, shifting back to the plain
form and then produces an 'assessment' (Goodwin, 1986) in line 5
(i.e. *yoku shittemasu ne:*).[20] It is here in her assessment that the host
mother shifts back again to the *masu* form. Her use of the *masu* form in
the pre-sequence and assessment indexes her authority with respect to
Japanese food and her position that allows her to evaluate Greg's

knowledge of it. Then in line 6 she continues to use the *masu* form as she tells Greg about this New Year's custom of eating *kamaboko* ('fish cake'). These instances of *masu* construct her identity as an authority on Japanese food and New Year's custom.

When they talk about Japanese social customs, food and language, both Kate and Greg's host families often shift to the *masu* form to index their authority on the subject matter. The teacher's voice presupposes a student who does not have relevant knowledge. Thus, it discursively positions learners as 'foreigners who lack knowledge of Japan', creating distance between the host family and the learner.

The host families' tendency to use the teacher's voice correlates with increased marked uses of the *masu* form, which also positions the learner as an outsider, creating distance between the learner and the host family. As Figure 5.2 above indicates, the host families of Kate and Greg use the *masu* form in a marked manner more than 10 times per 2000 words, compared with other host families whose marked use is less than 1.9 times per 2000 words. Kate and Greg's host families tend to index the *soto* ('outside/out-group') identity in interaction with the learner more frequently than the rest of the host families. They are more likely to use the *masu* form when they give reactive tokens and fillers, ask and answer questions, and make statements concerning topics outside their areas of authority and responsibility. Consider Examples (10) and (11). In Example (10), Kate is trying to tell her host mother about a friend who lives in Tsukimino, an area not far from Kate's host family's house. Kate's host mother shifts to the *masu* form when she gives a reactive token and asks for confirmation.

(10) Kate060904.

1    K: denentoshi  line de tonari no stop wa? nan to iu
        denentoshi line  on next  LK stop Top what QT say
        'What is the next station on the Denentoshi Line called?'[21]

2 HM: suzukakedaira (.) sore wa dochira gawa? chuuoorinkan  no hoo?
        Suzukakedaira    that Top which side     Chuuoorinkan LK way
        'Suzukakedaira. Which side is it? Is it toward Chuuoorinkan?'[22]

3    K: e:to tsuki:
        well Tsuki
        'Well, Tsuki'

4 HM: tsukimino? un
        Tsukimino? Uhm
        'Tsukimino? Uhm'

5    K: tsukimino (.) ga ne: hajimete tomodachi wa: e:to nani
       Tsukimino    S FP   first time friend      Top well what
       'Tsukimino is the place where my friend first um:'

6  HM: tsukimino
       'Tsukimino'

7    K: tsukimino ni sunde <u>iru</u>
       Tsukimino in live    exist
       'He lives in Tsukimino.'

8  HM: a- <u>soo</u>. ano k daigaku no?
       oh so  uh  K university LK
       'Oh- is that so? uh one from K University.'

9    K: so so so hoku to <u>iu</u>
       so so so Hoku QT say
       'Right right right. His name is Hoku.'

10 HM: hoku
       'Hoku'

11   K: namae wa
       name Top
       'his name is'

12 → HM: hu:n     soo **desu** ka. Tsukimino ni **sundemasu**?
       uh huh  so   Cop Q  Tsukimino in live
       'uh huh, is that so?    He lives in Tsukimino?'

13   K: u:n (1.0)
       yeah
       'yeah.'

   The conversation is carried out in the plain form up to line 11, but in line 12 the host mother shifts to the *masu* form when she gives a reactive token (*soo **desu** ka*) and asks for confirmation (*Tsukimino ni **sundemasu**?*). These uses of the *masu* form do not co-occur with a topic over which the host mother has some authority. Thus, they are marked uses in family conversation and index the *soto* identity of the speaker in relationship to the addressee.

   Another example of a host mother marking a *soto* identity in relationship to the learner occurs when his host mother tells Greg that it is all right for him to prepare some food he likes to eat. In this example, the host mother shifts to the *masu* form when she expresses her feelings. Typically in the *uchi* context, a speaker's feelings are expressed in the plain form, so the *masu* form in the host mother's utterance in line 7 indexes her *soto* identity.

(11) Greg 012802.

1   HM: demo Gureggu-san wa  nanka        tabetai mono  ga attara =
         but    Greg          Top something eat want thing S exist
         'But if there's something you want to eat'

2     G: = aa aa sonna koto ja nakute [anata
           uh uh this thing Neg          you
           'uh uh it's not anything like that, you'

3     HM:                              [tsukutte morau to
                                    make      receive if
                                    '(it's good) to have you cook it'

4     G: ana- ana- anata no tame ni =
           yo  yo   you  LK for
           'for yu- yu- you'

5   HM: = aa watashi no tame ni? =
           uh I          LK for
           'uh for me?'

6     G: hai =
           yes
           'yes'

7 → HM: = a  ureshii **desu**
           uh happy Cop
           'uh I'm happy.'

8     G: ((laughs))

Just prior to this segment, the host mother told Greg that in Japan usually the host or hostess cooks for the guest and that the guest does not cook. Thus, the host mother's utterance in lines 1 and 3 implies either that even if Greg is a house guest, it is all right for him to cook or that as he is not a house guest, it is all right for him to cook. But in line 4 Greg tries to make the point that he will cook for her, not for himself. In line 5, the host mother asks for confirmation of what he has just said. Up to this point, the utterances of Greg and the host mother are fragments that do not end either with the *masu* or plain form. After his confirmation, in line 7 she expresses that she is happy, shifting to the *masu* form. As this statement in the *masu* form is not related to her authority or responsibility as a host mother and a speaker's feelings are usually expressed in the plain form in the *uchi* ('inside/in-group') context, the host mother's *masu* form indexes the *soto* ('outside/out-group') identity of the speaker.

The above examples illustrate that compared with the rest of the host families in this study, Kate's and Greg's host families are *masu* users, who tend to create a distance by positioning the learner as 'other' not only with the content of talk but also discursively by shifting to the *masu* form. The identity of 'other' is discursively created by the marked uses of the *masu* form as well as by the unmarked use of the *masu* form, which indexes the voice of a teacher. It is also noteworthy that the frequencies of the *masu* form used by Kate and Greg are much higher than those of the rest of the learners. Kate and Greg also tend to co-create the *soto* relationship with their host family by the frequent marked uses of the *masu* form. The host families' authoritative stance on Japanese culture and language is also reflected in the fact that they are the only host families who give lengthy lectures on the use of the Japanese language.[23]

## Host families with a non-teaching voice

In contrast to Kate and Greg's host families, the host families of Tom, Rick, Skip, Pete and Ellen are infrequent *masu* users. They use the *masu* form less than 3 times per 2000 words; accordingly, the frequencies of their marked uses are much lower as well. Although these families infrequently shift from the plain form to the *masu* form, when they do so, they do not use it to index their authority on Japanese culture and language. Table 5.3 illustrates the distribution of their unmarked uses.

Table 5.3 shows that the host families of Tom, Rick, Skip, Pete and Ellen use the *masu* form in set formulas, when quoting others, displaying playfulness and taking charge of an activity. A striking contrast with the host families of Kate and Greg is that they do not shift to the *masu* form to index their authority when discussing topics related to Japanese culture and language.[24] The absence of indexing authority, however, does not mean that they do not talk to the learner about Japanese culture and language. They simply do so without shifting to the *masu* form. Consider Examples (12) and (13). In (12), Tom's host family is talking to him about *kaiseki* cuisine, one of the traditional cuisines in Japan. Tom and his host family went to eat *kaiseki* cuisine at a restaurant the day before. The host father is telling Tom about it in the plain form. In other words, his authority on the topic of traditional Japanese cuisine is not foregrounded. Discursively he does not focus on the positioning of himself as the teacher/host father, and Tom as a foreign student.

**Table 5.3** Distribution of types of the unmarked *masu* form by host families that use a non-teaching voice

| *Appropriate masu uses* | *Tom's HF* | *Rick's HF* | *Skip's HF* | *Pete's HF* | *Ellen's HF* |
|---|---|---|---|---|---|
| Set formula | ● | ● | ● |  | ● |
| Quotation |  | ● | ● | ● | ● |
| Playfulness | ● |  | ● | ● | ● |
| Authority |  |  |  |  |  |
| In charge |  |  |  | ● |  |

(12) Tom 012802

1    HF: kinoo tabeta  ano: resutoran de tabeta shokuji wa =
         yesterday ate uh   restaurant at ate     meal Top
         'The meal we had yesterday in the restaurant'

2     T: = un =
         uh huh
         'uh huh'

3 → HF: = Nihon no (.) kotenteki na shokuji =
         Japan LK    classical    meal
         'Japanese classical meal.'

4     T: = un =
         uh huh
         'uh huh'

5 → HF: = shitteru? (.)    kaiseki ryoori tte
         know             Kaisek cuisine QT
         'Do you know Kaiseki cuisine?'

6     T: sono =
         that
         'uh'

7    HF: = mukashi ka- kara toradisshonaru =
          old time fr   from traditional
          'Fro- from old time, traditional'

8       T: = nn [soo soo soo soo
             uhm  so  so  so  so
             'uhm yeah, yeah, yeah, yeah.'


9 → HF:          [Japaniizu fuudo un (0.5)
                 Japanese food uhm
                 'Japanese food uhm'


By using the plain form when talking about *kaiseiki* cuisine, Tom's host
father keeps a close relationship with Tom.

Similarly, in Example (13), Pete's host mother is trying to explain the
meaning of the Japanese proverb *hana yori dango*, but she does not shift to
the *masu* form. The proverb *hana yori dango* literally means that one
prefers eating sweet dumplings to viewing cherry blossoms when one
goes to flower viewing: it describes someone who prefers material gains
to artistic values.

(13) Pete010503


1       P: nn:: (1.0) ohanami ne?
             uhm        flower viewing
             'uhm        flower viewing'


2   HM: nn ((laughs))
             mh mh
             'mh mh'


3       P: ikitai
             go want
             'I want to go.'


4 → HM: ohanami (1.0)    hana   yori dango      tte shitteru?
             Flower viewing flower than dumpling QT know
             'flower viewing. Do you know the saying 'dumplings are better
             than flowers'?'


5       P: shitteru shitteru =
             know    know
             'I know, I know.'


6 HM: = ((laughs))

7 →HF: doko ga kiree     tte chuuga kooen <u>da</u> ne
        where S beautiful QT Chuuga Park <u>Cop</u> FP
        'Talking about where (cherry blossoms) are beautiful, it's
        Chuuga Park.'

     (1.0)

8 →HM: hana    yori dango      tte hana   tte sono hana    tte
        flower than dumpling QT flower QT that flower QT

9         sakura no   hana    no koto    <u>na</u>   no ne? =
        cherry LK flower LK thing <u>Cop</u> FP FP
        '"Dumplings are better than flowers," the flowers mean, the
        flowers refer to cherry blossoms, you know.'

10     P: = ne
        FP
        'yeah.'

11 HM: soide (0.5) hana yori (.) oishii mono   no hoo ni me ga
        and        flower than    delicious thing LK    to eye S
        itte shimau koto o
        go   end up Nom O
        'and to set an eye on something more delicious than
        cherry blossoms'

12    → hana    yori dango      tte <u>yuu</u> no ne
        flower than dumpling QT say FP FP
        'is the meaning of "dumplings are better than flowers".'

13   P: nn
        uh huh
        'uh huh'

Telling a Japanese proverb to the learner without shifting to the *masu* form does not highlight the learner's identity as 'other', someone who does not know Japanese culture, at least in terms of discursive practice.[25] Also, the non-teaching voice does not index the host mother as someone who has authority with respect to the topic of talk.

A comparison of a pre-sequence between the host families who use a teaching voice and those that do not further illustrates differences between the two groups. A pre-sequence indicates that the telling of the Japanese language or customs will follow. It allows the speaker to narrate his or her story. Examples (8), (9), (12) and (13) all contain such a pre-sequence, which takes the form of a question as to whether the learner is familiar with the topic. I reproduce below part of these examples with the pre-sequence indicated by an arrow. In (8), (12) and (13), the pre-sequence is 'Do you know X?' and in (9), 'Have you ever eaten X?' In all the examples, X is a Japanese custom or aspect of Japanese culture.

(8) Kate 061004

1  → HM: Keito wa tanabata tte **shittemasu** ka?
        Kate Top Tanabata QT know        Q
        'Kate, do you know about Tanabata?'

2      K: **shirimasen**
          know Neg
          'I don't know about it.'

(9) Greg 011302

3 → HM: tsukemono to  kore wa  ano: (.) <u>kamaboko</u>. (0.5) tabeta
        pickles     and this  Top uh       kamaboko        ate
        koto **arimasu** ka? =
        Nom exist     Q
        'Pickles, and this is uh fish cake.      Have you ever eaten this?'

4      G: = sakana de dekite dekiteru desho
            fish   by made   made     Cop
            'It's made of fish, isn't it?'

(12) Tom 012802

5 → HF: <u>shitteru</u>? (.) kaiseki ryoori tte
        know          Kaisek cuisine QT
        'Do you know Kaiseki cuisine?'

6      T: sono =
          that
          'uh'

(13) Pete 010503

4 → HM: ohanami (1.0)   hana  yori dango    tte <u>shitteru</u>?
        Flower viewing flower than dumpling QT know
        'flower viewing. Do you know the saying "dumplings are
        better than flowers"?'

5       P: shitteru shitteru =
          know    know
          'I know, I know.'

Note that while the host families of Kate and Greg use the *masu* form in uttering a pre-sequence, those of Tom and Pete use the plain form. The host families that use a teaching voice tend to produce the pre-sequence in the *masu* form. In addition, it is interesting to observe in (8) and (13) that the speech style of the pre-sequence produced by the host family member and the response given by the learner are in the same form.

The host families that do not use a teaching voice use the *masu* form to be playful. For example, Ellen's host mother, who is a very infrequent user of the *masu* form, shifts to *masu* when she asserts her knowledge in English in a playful manner. Tom's host sister teases him shifting to the *masu* form. In the present data, such use does not occur in the speech of the host families that use a teaching voice.

As discussed above, all the host families speak in the plain form most of the time. However, when they shift to the *masu* form, there are differences in interactional style between the families that use a teaching voice and those that do not. The following lists summarize the co-occurring linguistic characteristics that constitute two types of voice in the speech of host families in this study:

In host families that use a teaching voice, we note:

- higher frequencies of the *masu* form (more than 23 times per 2000 words),
- frequent shifts to the *masu* form when telling the learner about Japanese culture and language,
- absence of the *masu* form in playful display and
- higher frequencies of marked uses of the *masu* form (more than 10 times per 2000 words).

In host families that do not use a teaching voice:

- lower frequencies of the *masu* form (3 times per 2000 words or less),
- use of the *masu* form when displaying playfulness,
- absence of the *masu* form when telling the learner about Japanese culture and language and
- lower frequencies of marked uses of the *masu* form (0.5 times per 2000 words or less).

In sum, two types of interactional styles used by the host families can be characterized as negative and positive politeness (Brown & Levinson, 1978, 1987). Brown and Levinson's politeness theory (1978, 1987) explains that politeness is a face-saving strategy. Speakers use negative or positive politeness strategies to mitigate acts that potentially threaten the addressee's negative or positive face. 'Negative face' is the desire to be unimpeded by others and 'positive face' is the desire to gain the approval of others. Thus, negative politeness strategies are those which create distance between the interlocutors while positive politeness strategies are those which create a close and intimate relationship. In Brown and Levinson's terms, the host families with the teaching voice have a preference for 'negative politeness' strategies. They tend to interactionally position the learner as an outsider by (1) frequent shifts to the *masu* form when teaching about Japanese culture and language and (2) higher frequencies of the marked use of *masu*. These uses of the *masu* form create a distance between the host families and the learner. With respect to their speech style, they also avoid a positive politeness strategy by not using the *masu* form in a playful way. In contrast, the speech style of the host families which do not use a teaching voice can be characterized as exhibiting 'positive politeness'. The absence of the *masu* form in telling the learner about Japanese culture and language as well as low frequencies of the marked use do not foreground the learner as 'other'. These families shift to the *masu* form rather infrequently and speak in the plain form almost all the time, which discursively indexes their identity as the learner's close 'friend/family member' rather than as a 'teacher' or 'host mother/father' who has the responsibility to teach the learner.

## A host family with accommodating strategies

In the speech of Alice's host mother, the marked use of *masu* often occurs as an accommodating strategy, which one could term 'foreigner talk' (Ferguson, 1975, 1981; Freed, 1981; Gass & Varonis, 1985; Snow *et al.*, 1981). Foreigner talk is a type of register 'used primarily to address foreigners, i.e. people who do not have full native competence (or possibly any competence at all) in one's language' (Ferguson, 1981: 10). One of the major functions of foreigner talk is to accommodate a foreign language speaker.

The characteristics of Japanese foreigner talk include: (1) the overuse of pronouns, (2) the use of the *masu* form, (3) frequent occurrence of grammatical particles such as the subject marker *ga* and the object marker *o* and subject, object and/or oblique NPs, (4) Western loan words and (5) avoidance of sentence-final particles (Iino, 1996; Richardson, 1997; Skoutarides, 1980). As in Japanese the pronouns are in general omitted in conversation, overuse of the pronouns such as *watakushi* 'I' and *anata* 'you' is generally marked. In addition, it is also considered awkward in conversation if all the potential NPs including pronouns are overtly encoded. Example (14a) is an example of typical Japanese foreigner talk.

(14a) Watakushi wa  ashita      toshokan de anata ni hon  o agemasu.[26]
      I         Top tomorrow library   in you  to book O give
      'I will give you a book in the library tomorrow.'

In (14a) all the potentially encoded NPs are overtly expressed. In conversation between native speakers, however, the pronouns *I* and *you* are most likely omitted, and if the location is understood, it is also not expressed either, as in (14b).

(14b) Ashita       hon  o agemasu.
      tomorrow  book O give
      '(I) will give (you) a book (in the library) tomorrow.'

In the present data, foreigner talk occurs only in Alice's host mother's speech. Alice is a novice-level learner and often does not understand what the host family members are talking about. Her poor comprehension and production of Japanese gives an impression that she is the least proficient in Japanese among the nine learners. The occurrence of foreigner talk in Alice's host mother's speech may be attributed to Alice's low proficiency of Japanese. Alice's host mother paraphrases, juxtaposes two sentences, one in the plain and the other in the *masu* form, and even ventriloquizes the learner's voice in order to answer for her when she does not understand questions. Consider Example (15), in which Alice's host mother is thanking Alice's real mother for the training she gave Alice. Prior to (15) the host mother comments that among the foreign students whom she has hosted, Alice is the only one who helps her with the dishes after a meal. She attributes it to the good training that Alice's mother provided. She uses the *masu* form as well as the pronouns *watashi* 'I' and *anata no* 'your'.

(15) Alice 012102

1 →HM: *Watashi wa anata no* okaasan ni kansha **shimasu**.
         I      TOP your   mother  to thank   do
         '*I* am thankful to *your* mother.'

2     A: ((laughs))

3 →HM: *anata no* okaasan ni
         your      mother to
         'to *your*  mother.'

Juxtaposition of the *masu* and plain forms often occur in the speech of Alice's host mother, in particular when Alice has difficulty understanding Japanese. Host family members' juxtaposition of the two forms is also reported in McMeekin's studies (2003, 2007). She finds that while the host family members in her studies speak to the learners in the plain form most of the time, they tend to shift to the *masu* form when comprehension becomes more difficult. The shift pattern of Alice's host mother is consistent with that reported in McMeekin's studies. In Example (16), the host mother juxtaposes two forms when Alice does not understand the expression, *oto mo hairu*, which is equivalent to *the sound is also being recorded*. Here the 10-year-old host brother naively asks Alice if the video camera placed near the dinner table records sound as well.

(16) Alice 012102

1    HB: kore tte oto      mo hairu no?
          this QT sound also enter FP
          'This records sound as well?

2     A: oto mo?
          sound also
          'the sound, too?'

3  →HM: oto mo      rekoodo **saremasu** ka? oto   mo  hairu?
          sound also record   done       Q sound also enter
          'Is the sound also being recorded? Is the sound also
          being recorded?'

4     A: hairu (.) oto     mo hairu? wakaranai
          enter      sound also enter understand Neg
          'hairu oto mo hairu? I don't understand.'

5   HM: rekoodo rekoodo
          record    record
          'record, record'

6     A: [oto mo
          sound also
          'the sound, too'

7   HM: [(  )

8     A: oh aa
          oh uh
          'Oh uh'.

9 → HM: oto mo     **hairimasu** ka?
      sound also enter     Q
      'Is the sound being recorded as well?'.

10 → A: **hairimasu** ka?
      enter     Q
      'Being recorded?'.

11 → HM: hai **hairimasu**
      yes enter
      'Yes, it is.'.

12   A: oh hh uun
      'Oh uh huh'.

13 HM: ((laughs)).

14   A: moo (.) teepu
      already tape
      'The tape is already'

15 HM: nai      owatta?
      exist Neg finish
      'You mean it's finished?'

16   A: un
      yeah
      'yeah'

In line 1, the 10-year-old host brother uses the expression *oto mo hairu* ('sound enters (in the video-recorder) too'). Alice's partial repetition of this expression with a rising intonation in line 2 is understood by the host mother as a sign of Alice's incomprehension. So in line 3 the host mother juxtaposes two similar questions, one in the *masu* form and the other in the plain form. She paraphrases in the *masu* form the host brother's initial question (*oto mo rekoodo saremasu ka* 'Is the sound also being recorded too?'), replacing the Japanese verb *hairu* ('to enter') with an expression that uses an English loan word *rekoodo sareru* ('to be recorded'). Then, immediately after the first question, shifting to the plain form, she partially repeats the host brother's utterance, *oto mo hairu?* ('Is the sound also being recorded?'). In line 4, Alice says that she does not understand. In line 9, the host mother repeats the host brother's original question, this time in the *masu* form. Hearing Alice's partial repetition of the question in line 10, which indicates her continued difficulty in understanding this expression, in line 11, the host mother plays Alice's part and answers the question for Alice using the *masu* form. Although the utterances in the *masu* form in Example (16) do not co-occur with pronouns, the question and answer pair of lines 9 and 11 (*Oto mo hairimasu ka? Hai, hairimasu*) has the flavor of a model dialogue in a textbook (cf. Hiraike-Okawara & Sakamoto, 1990). Furthermore, the act of speaking for the novice is one of the typical accommodation strategies found in L1 language socialization (Ochs & Schieffelin, 1984). The occurrences of paraphrasing, juxtaposing two sentences, one in the plain and the other in the *masu* form, are also reported in studies of Japanese children's language socialization (Clancy, 1986) as well as in studies of JFL learners and their host families (Iino, 1996; McMeekin, 2003, 2007). In sum, Alice's host mother's marked choices of the *masu* form are partly attributed to her accommodation to the novice-level learner, Alice.

## Limits of Awareness of Speech Style

Speech style is one of the linguistic resources that index the identity of the speaker as *uchi* ('in-group/inside') or *soto* ('out-group/outside').[27] In particular, marked uses of the *masu* form in the *uchi* context index the *soto* identity. Is there any correlation between the host families' subjective perception of the learner's identity in the family and their discursive practice with respect to marked uses of the *masu* form? In other words, do the host families that have a high frequency of marked uses (i.e. the host families which use a teaching voice) consider the learner as a guest or someone who is more distant than a family member, and do those with low frequencies of marked uses (i.e. the host families that do not use a teaching voice) regard the learner as a family member? Table 5.4 shows the host families' frequency of the marked uses of the *masu* form and their self-reported evaluations of their relationship with their exchange students.

Table 5.4 shows that there is no clear correlation between the host families' interactional style with respect to the *masu* form and their self-reported evaluations of their relationship with the learner. All the host mothers responded to the questionnaire stating that they consider the learner to be a member of the family, rather than a guest. However, when they were asked specifically if the family treats the learner as their own son or daughter, not every host mother responded positively. The host families of Kate and Greg, who discursively keep more distance from the learner, report that they treat the learners as their own daughter or son. In contrast, the host families of Tom, Rick, Pete and Alice, who use few marked instances of the *masu* form, state that they are a little more distant with the learner than they are with their own family members. A correlation between the frequency of the marked use of the *masu* form and self-reported evaluation of the relationship with the learner is observed only in the host families of Skip, Ellen and Mary. Mary's

**Table 5.4** Host Families' *Masu* Uses and Self-reported Evaluation of Social Relationship

| Host family | HF's frequency of masu form per 2000 words | HF's frequency of marked use/2000 words (%) | HF's evaluation of relationship to learner | Learner's evaluation of relationship to HF |
|---|---|---|---|---|
| **HF with teaching voice** | | | | |
| Kate's HF | 29.2 | 13.3 (45.6%) | Treat the learner as their own daughter | College age daughter |
| Greg's HF | 23.4 | 10.0 (42.6%) | Try to treat the learner as their own son | College age son |
| **HF with accommodating strategies** | | | | |
| Alice's HF | 4.9 | 1.9 (38.7%) | Keep a little more distance than their own family | Unknown |

**Table 5.4** (*Continued*)

| Host family | HF's frequency of masu form per 2000 words | HF's frequency of marked use/2000 words (%) | HF's evaluation of relationship to learner | Learner's evaluation of relationship to HF |
|---|---|---|---|---|
| **HF with non-teaching voice** | | | | |
| Tom's HF | 1.3 | 0.5 (40%) | Treat him as someone a little more distant than their own son | College age son |
| Rick's HF | 2.1 | 0 (0%) | Treat him as someone a little more distant than their own son | College age son, young child, foreign student |
| Skip's HF | 3.0 | 0.27 (10%) | Treat the learner as their own son | College age son |
| Pete's HF | 2.6 | 0.3 (12.5%) | Try to treat the learner as their own son but may treat him as someone a little more distant | College age son (80%), foreign student (20%) |
| Ellen's HF | 1.8 | 0.1 (6.7%) | Treat the learner as their own daughter | College age daughter |
| **Other HF** | | | | |
| Mary's HF | 9.2 | 0.2 (2.3%) | Treat the learner as their own daughter | Foreign student |

self-report, however, does not concur with that of the host mother. As the questionnaire was filled out by the host mothers, the views expressed in the questionnaire are most likely to reflect how the host mother feels about the relationship with her JFL learner. However, in all the host families, the host mother is the center of conversation, the main caregiver for the learner and the one who talks to the learner more than any other member of the host family. In the entire corpus for this study, the host mother is always present at every dinner and plays a central role in serving dinner and carrying out dinnertime conversation with the learner and family members. Thus, the host mother's perception about the relationship with the learner more or less represents the host family's view.

As discussed in 'Socialization Effects on the Learners', not all learners feel that they are treated as a college-age daughter or son in the host family. Table 5.4 also shows that there is no clear correlation between the host families' interactional style with respect to the *masu* form and the learners' perception of their position in the host family. For example, Rick feels that he is treated like a college-age son, young child and a foreign student, and his host family has an interactional style which does not foreground a teaching voice. On the other hand, Kate and Greg report that they feel that they are treated like a daughter or son of the host family, and their host families' interactional style is that of a teacher. Perhaps these discrepancies stem from the learners' inability to notice the speech styles employed in conversation with the host family (cf. Cook, 2001, 2002a).

The present study finds that the frequency of the marked uses of the *masu* form does not necessarily reflect the host families' subjective evaluation of their relationship with the learner. There are other linguistic and non-linguistic features that indicate interpersonal closeness or distance other than the *masu* and plain forms, such as pronouns and kinship terms.[28] Perhaps the host families of Tom, Rick and Pete employ other linguistic and non-linguistic resources to index distance from the learner. In response to the questions in the questionnaire, however, no host family mentioned the style shift of the *masu* and plain forms as a linguistic item to which they pay attention in conversation with the learner. This indicates that the native speakers of Japanese are not aware of their style shift patterns in daily conversation.

## Conclusion

Types of *masu* form usage that rarely occur in Japanese family conversation are those (e.g. reactive tokens, fillers, short replies, as well as use in questions, answers or statements) that are not linked to the authority or responsibility of the speaker's social role. I call these uses marked uses in the *uchi* ('in-group/inside') context. These marked uses index the speaker's *soto* ('out-group/outside') relationship with the addressee. In this study, both the learners and host families sometimes make marked choices, but for different reasons. The less proficient learners employ marked uses more frequently (more than 70% of the total tokens of *masu*) than the advanced-level learners (less than 50%). This suggests that the more socialized learners become, through interactions with host families and other native speakers of Japanese, the less frequently they make marked choices when speaking with their host family. In other words, JFL learners learn appropriate uses of the *masu* form through the process of socialization. However, the data size of the present study is small. Future research using a larger body of data will need to investigate the correlation between learners' proficiency level and their marked uses of the *masu* form.

The percentages of the host families' marked use are lower (less than 46% of the total tokens of *masu*) than those of the learners. The frequency with which the host families use the marked choice is more or less in proportion to their use of the *masu* form. Three different types of host families' interactional style have been identified: a teaching voice, non-teaching voice and accommodating. The host families that use a teaching voice are frequent *masu* users and also tend to make marked choices more frequently. Furthermore, when they use the *masu* form in an unmarked fashion in family talk, they usually use it while talking about the Japanese culture and language. They speak in the voice of a teacher who is responsible for teaching something Japanese. Their higher frequency in using *masu* in marked fashion and their use of a teacher's voice discursively position the learner as 'other' or 'outsider'. In contrast, the host families with a non-teaching voice are infrequent *masu* users who maintain the plain form when teaching the learner about the language and culture. Their frequency of marked uses is also low. In this sense, they do not display a teacher's voice. At the same time, their unmarked *masu* uses include a display of playfulness. With respect to *masu* usage, their speech style indexes that they are a close friend, rather than a teacher. In sum, host families that use a teaching voice prefer a somewhat distant interactional style, or what Brown and Levinson (1987) refer to as 'negative politeness'. In contrast, host families that use a non-teaching voice prefer an interactional style emphasizing 'positive politeness'.

Another reason why a host family may choose the marked use of the *masu* form when talking to the learner is accommodation. In the present data, only Alice's host mother employs this strategy when Alice has difficulty understanding Japanese. Alice's host mother's strategies include foreigner talk, paraphrasing, juxtaposing two sentences, one in the plain and the other in the *masu* form, and answering for the learner, all of which accommodate the learner and have the goal of helping her understand what is being said. These strategies are common when novice learners (1st and 2nd language learners) show difficulty in understanding.

The marked use of the *masu* form at least temporarily foregrounds a *soto* ('out-group/outside') identity in family conversation. In this sense, an increased frequency of the marked use of the *masu* form in family conversation can discursively index distance between interlocutors. However, a higher frequency of the *masu* use does not necessarily correlate with the host families' self-report on their relationship with their learner. This fact suggests that the choice of speech style and its social meaning in a given social context are beyond the limits of awareness of the average Japanese speakers (cf. Silverstein, 2001).

## Notes

1. If such a usage of the *masu* form occurs in conversation among family members, who are native speakers of Japanese, it sounds as if they are talking as outsiders. In my own Japanese family conversation data, there was no instance of this type of *masu* use.
2. In the present data, only Ellen and Mary call their host parents *otoosan* ('father') and *okaasan* ('mother'). Greg and Tom call them *anata* ('you'). The rest of the learners never address their host parents. On the other hand, the host mothers of Ellen, Kate, Alice and Pete refer to themselves as *okaasan* ('mother') as in *okaasan ga soo itta no* ('the mother (I) said so'). A parent's reference of her/himself as *okaasan* ('mother') or *otoosan* ('father') in talking with children is a common practice in Japanese society.
3. Among the members of all the Japanese host families, only Pete's host father is not a speaker of Tokyo standard Japanese. He is a speaker of Kansai dialect.
4. These examples incorporate both plain and *masu* form versions. Exclusion of the word in parentheses (e.g. *soo ne*) denotes the plain form, and the inclusion of the word in parentheses (e.g. *soo desu ne*) indicates the *masu* form.
5. In this interview program, both the interviewer and interviewee speak in the *masu* form except for one specific context. The interviewer sometimes uses the naked plain form (i.e. the plain form without an affect key such as a sentence-final particle) in the summary turn in order to clearly convey the content of the interviewee's statement to the TV audience (see Cook, 2002b). This is attributed to the function of the naked plain form, which points to the content of talk.
6. *Yakitori* is roasted chicken on a skewer.
7. The mother repairs to *goryooshin* ('honorable-parents') even though she is using plain forms. *Go-* is an honorific prefix to a noun. When it is prefixed to nouns denoting an interpersonal relation or the action of the addressee and/or the third party, it indicates respect to the addressee and/or the third party. The co-occurrence of the plain form and the prefix *go-* indicates that the speaker is talking in a spontaneous and informal manner while she expresses respect to the addressee and/or the third party.
8. Responsibility or authority is linked to the speaker's situational identity. In this sense, the responsibility and authority differ from Kamio's (1991) notion of 'territory of information'. N's utterances in lines 2, 7, 9, and 13 fall in the

speaker's territory of information according to Kamio's (1991) theory of territory of information (i.e. his information rather than B's mother's).

9.  The more appropriate expression is *soo desu* plus the sentence-final particle *ne* as in *soo desu ne* instead of *soo desu* or *soo desu yo*.

10. Sawyer's study (1992), in which he investigated JFL learners' acquisition of the sentence-final particle *ne*, suggests that some JFL learners learn the use of the particle *ne* as in a chunk such as *soo desu ne*. His finding partly explains why learners tend to give reactive tokens in the *masu* form, in particular learners with lower proficiency.

11. L2 norms can be different in that L2 speakers might use the *masu* form here to simply index politeness.

12. As a student on a scholarship, Mary is not an in-group member of the family. Her use of the *masu* form could be interpreted as very skillful.

13. Although it is not clear whether learners are intentionally marking a *soto* position or simply marking themselves as non-native speakers, native speakers of Japanese interpret their uses of the *masu* form in Examples (4–7) as an index of a *soto* identity.

14. There are other linguistic features that index the outside identity of the speaker such as pronouns. However, here I focus on the *masu* form.

15. The plain form *itadaku* is not a set formula.

16. Skip recorded dinnertime conversation only once while the rest of the learners did so three times. His dinnertime conversation with the host family members lasted over 90 minutes.

17. Mary's host family does not belong to any of the three groups.

18. In this instance, one might argue that Kate is simply responding to the cue in order to express politeness. However, at least from the perspective of Japanese native speaker norm, Kate's *masu* form here co-constructs the *soto* context.

19. At the same time, shifts into the plain form index informality and intimacy. The contrast between the two forms here makes the use of the plain form more salient and meaningful.

20. An 'assessment' is defined as 'an interactive activity which involves the expressed evaluation of some entity, event, situation, or state' (Strauss, 1995: 177).

21. The Denentoshi Line is a private train that runs near Kate's host family's house.

22. Suzukakedaira, Chuuoorinkan and Tsukimino are the names of stations on the Denentoshi Line.

23. Some examples are discussed in Chapter 6.

24. This does not mean that the host families with a non-teaching voice do not construct the social identity of a teacher at all. In the present data, they do so by the use of the tentative form of the copula *deshoo*. All the nine host families use *deshoo* in the present data with an average frequency of 14.1 per 2000 words.

25. Eton Churchill (personal communication) points out that the host mother's behavior (i.e. her telling of the proverb even though Pete says he knows it) possibly positions Pete as someone who does not know the proverb (a *soto* position).

26. (14a) and (14b) are sentences made up by the researcher.

27. My proposal that the plain and *masu* forms are the linguistic resources that index the identity of the speaker as *uchi* ('in-group/inside') or *soto* ('out-group/outside') differs from Sukle's claim. Sukle maintains that the plain form is a marker of *uchi* and the *masu* form is a marker of *soto*. In contrast, my

proposal does not directly link the linguistic forms and the contextual dimensions of *uchi* and *soto*. What I propose is that the plain and *masu* forms indirectly index the identity of the speaker as *uchi* or *soto*. In my analysis, the contextual dimensions of *uchi* and *soto* are not direct indexes of linguistic forms.

28. The address terms used by the learner and host family members also reveal their relationship. A discussion on address terms is beyond the scope of this book, but it is interesting to investigate in future research how the address terms are used between and/or among the learner and the host family members and how the address terms change over the course of the homestay program.

## Chapter 6
# Explicit Language Socialization: Socialization to Use Polite Language

The previous chapters have discussed how the host family members and the learners construct their social identities through the use of the *masu* form and how this practice implicitly socializes the learners into appropriate uses of the *masu* form. In contrast, this chapter discusses explicit language socialization to use polite language including the *masu* form, which is typically used in contexts outside the host family. Explicit language socialization is 'the most salient and most widely described' (Ochs, 1990: 290) form of language socialization. It is an explicit way to teach novices appropriate language behavior in society. Modeling is a type of explicit language socialization practice in which a member of a speech community presents a model of a language expression for a novice and prompts him or her to repeat it. In the context of first language socialization, modeling by caregivers for young children is observed in a wide range of cultures. Modeling has been documented in different social groups in the USA including the white working class (Miller, 1986), black working class (Heath, 1986), black and white middle class (Snow *et al.*, 1990), and Mexican Americans (Eisenberg, 1986). It is also observed in southern Africa (Demuth, 1986), Papua New Guinea (Schieffelin, 1990) and Solomon Islands (Watson-Gegeo & Gegeo, 1986). Japanese mothers also actively take every opportunity to teach children polite expressions by modeling (Burdelski, 2006; Clancy, 1986; Nakamura, 1996). As discussed in Chapter 4, in the context of interactions between the JFL learner and host family, the modeling of polite expressions sometimes occurs when the host family members speak using the voices of other people (i.e. reported speech). This is a context where the host family members often shift to the *masu* form. In many cases, as polite expressions in Japanese often include a combination of the *masu* form and referent honorifics (i.e. exalting the addressee and humbling the speaker), modeling provides a good opportunity for the learner to learn referent honorifics as well, which occur very rarely in family conversation except for a few set formulas such as *itadakimasu*.

Explicit socialization also takes the form of instruction on social norms in many cultures as well (Clancy, 1986; Ochs, 1988). Through explicit instruction on what to do and what not to do, novices learn not only the appropriate behaviors but also beliefs of society. For example, the instruction 'Boys do not cry' can teach young boys not to cry as well as a tacit assumption about gender inequality in society. Although Japanese host family members neither correct inappropriate usages of the *masu* form nor tell the learner when and how to use the *masu* form, they talk about Japanese social customs, including polite language behavior, that they consider unique in Japan or different from those of the learner's home country. The explicit explanations about polite language socialize the learner into the discourse of Japanese polite language and the culturally meaningful distinction between *uchi* ('in-group/inside') and *soto* ('out-group/outside').

## Socialization to Speak in a Formal Setting

### Modeling an appropriate voice

Modeling is an effective way of teaching novices social norms of the target language and culture, for it can easily demonstrate the manner in which information should be conveyed. Through modeling, Japanese families provide children with examples of how to talk to certain categories of people outside the family (cf. Burdelski, 2006; Clancy, 1986; Nakamura, 1996). Also in certain social situations, modeling can provide examples of genre-specific ways of writing. Example (1) shows that a father is telling his son how to write a *sakubun* ('composition') through modeling. A *sakubun* is an elementary school child's composition, in which children are taught to describe daily events and express their feelings toward the events and people involved in them. Typically a *sakubun* is written in the *masu* form. Note the contrast between the plain and *masu* form used in this excerpt. The family members talk to each other in the plain form, but the father shifts to the *masu* form when modeling for his son, K, how to write a *sakubun* ('composition'). In Example (1), seven-year-old K fell and injured his knee when he went out with his bother H and his mother. The children and the mother are reporting this event to the father. At the same time, the father is instructing K on how to write his *sakubun* about the event.

(1) [Family O] (Cook, 1997)

1 K: <u>mitenakatta</u> mon, hiro. saki itchatta n    <u>da</u>   mon.
   look Neg   FP   Hiro before went Nom Cop FP
   'Hiro did not look at me. He went before me.'

2 M: hiro saki  itteta kara <u>shiranakatta</u> no   ne.
   Hiro before went so   know Neg   Nom FP
   'Hiro went before K so he did not know (about K's falling)'

3 →F: otooto          wa saki    **itchaimashita** tte.
     young brother Top before went          QT
     '(Write), 'my younger brother went ahead of me.'

4   M: isoide ano   iremono ga  tonda n de
     hurry uh    container S   flew Nom Cop
     'In a hurry, uh the container flew away and'

5   K: (                    )

6   F: un
     uh huh
     'uh huh'

7   M: <u>wakatta</u> no ne.  Isoide iremon o totta no wa hiro =
     found Nom FP  hurry container O caught Nom Top Hiro
     'found out (K's falling). Hiro was the one who caught
     the container.'

8   K: oto de
     noise by
     'By noise.'

9   H: un
     uh huh
     'uh huh'

10  K: [oto de wakatta n de
     noise by found Nom and
     'By noise (H) found out (my falling) and'

11  H: [un (   ) guni tte <u>nachatta</u> (   )
     yeah       flat   QT became
     'yeah (     ) became flat.'

12 →F: oto  de wakatta soo    **desu** tte.
     noise by found appear Cop  QT
     '(Wirte), 'by noise (H) found out (that I fell).'

13 (  ) sore kara tochuu kaerimichi ne,
     then       on the way back  FP

14 →okaasan ga ano kusuriyasan yotte akachin          o  nutte
     mother  S  uh pharmacy      stop Mercurochrome O apply
     **kuremashita** tte.
     give            QT
     '(Write), "on the way back, my mother stopped at a pharmacy and
     applied Mercurochrome (to my wound)."'

15 → Moo  ima wa itaku **arimasen**
more now Top hurt exist Neg
'It does not hurt any more now.'

16  H: akachin ja <u>nai</u> yo maakiro maakiro
akachin Neg  FP Mercurochrome Mercurochrome
'It's not akachin. It's Mercro, Mercro.'

17  F: maakiro
Mercurochrome
'Mercuro'

18  K: boku sukoshi shika otoofu haitte <u>nai</u>
I      little    only  tofu    enter Neg
'There's only a little tofu (in my miso soup).'

19 → F: moo ima  wa  itaku **arimasen**.
More now Top hurt  exist Neg
'It does not hurt any more now.'

As K and the mother report this event to the father, the father models for K by providing the appropriate expressions for K's *sakubun* ('composition'). He uses the *masu* form so that K will be able to write his experience of injuring his knee in a proper manner in the *sakubun*. As the rest of the conversation is carried out in the plain form, the father's shifts to the *masu* form while modeling are salient. As this example illustrates, modeling is an efficient way of teaching novices not only what to say but also how to say it.

When the learner does not know how to say an expression properly, host family members provide the learner with a model of how to say the polite expression. Modeling informs the learner of the appropriate speech style for a given social context. In many cases, this may be a form with which the learner is not familiar. In the example below, Kate's host mother is modeling for Kate. Shifting to the *masu* form, she takes on the voice of a model speaker who calls a restaurant to make reservations.

(2) Kate 060904

1  HM: sa: nihongo de gambatte yoyaku    shite ((laughs))
well Japanese in do best  reservation do
'Well, do your best and make reservations in Japanese.'

2      demo sonna ni muzukashiku <u>nai</u> yo
but    that    difficult        Neg FP
'But it's not that difficult.'

3     K: [doo yuu fuu      ni kakeru no
         how say manner in call      Nom
         'How do I call them (the pub)?'

4 HM → [ne 'nannichi no  nanji kara nanmei         onegai **shimasu'**
        FP what day Nom what time from how many request do
        tte itte
        QT say
        'Say, 'I'd like to make a reservation on such and such a day
        from such and such a time for this number of people.'

5  HM: e: tabun ne  menyuu toka kikareru no kana (2.0)
         uh maybe FP menu   etc. be asked FP FP
         'uh maybe, I wonder if you will be asked what food you'd
         like to order.'

6     K: tabehoodai ni suru kara:
         eat all      into do so
         'I'll make it "all you can eat".'

7  HM: a  sore dattara moo tabehoodai nomihoodai de:
         oh that Cop if then eat all        drink all   and
         'Oh, if that's the case, then "all you can eat and drink"'

8 → e: 'nijuunin ikura       desu ka' tte 'hitori ikura  desu ka' tte
       uh 20 people how much Cop Q QT 1 prson how much Q QT
       'kikanai to   ne (.)
       ask      QT FP
       uh you need to ask, "How much does it cost for 20 people?"
       "How much does it cost for one person?"'

9 → 'nijuunin sono hi no toki no kaihi to shite **atsumemasu'** to iu toki ni:
      20 people that day LK time LK fee as   collect    QT say time at
      'When you say, "I will collect the money for 20 people for
      this event",'

10    ikura      ikura       tte kono hitotachi ni iwanakya ikenai
      how much how much QT these people to have to say
      desho, keito
      Cop   Kate
      'you need to tell these people how much it costs, right? Kate'

11    K: ee
         yes
         'Yes.'

12 HM: ((laughs)) (5.0)

13    K: OK

Speaking in the plain form, Kate's host mother encourages Kate to call an *izakaya*, a Japanese-style pub, and make reservations in Japanese. In line 3, Kate specifically asks how to call an *izakaya*. In line 4, the host mother overlaps with Kate. Here shifting to the *masu* form, she speaks with a model voice calling an *izakaya* on the phone. Then she wonders if the *izakaya* will ask Kate what she would like to order. When expressing her thoughts, she shifts back to the plain form. But in lines 8 and 9, as the host mother models someone talking to the *izakaya*, she shifts to the *masu* form again. The host mother's animated voice explicitly teaches Kate how to speak to an *izakaya* when she actually calls them.

Formal occasions that occur in the host family promote the modeling of polite expressions. While the *masu* form occasionally appears in family conversation, referent honorifics are normally not used except for a few set formulas such as *itadakimasu* ('I will receive + humble'), which is said before every meal.[1] Formal occasions in the host family provide an opportunity for learners to learn expressions involving referent honorifics beyond *itadakimasu*. For example, in the present data, Rick's host mother hosted a family gathering for a Japanese tea ceremony to which the host brother's college friend was invited. The Japanese tea ceremony is a very formal social occasion in which a sequence of ritual actions (e.g. the order in which guests drink tea) are coordinated with polite verbal and/or non-verbal fixed expressions (see Curley, 1998). In order to perfect the tea ceremony, it takes years of lessons. Many Japanese women take tea ceremony lessons for a number of years with a master teacher. In a tea ceremony, the host or hostess fixes tea and offers it to the guests one by one. In Rick's host family, the host mother played the role of the hostess of the ceremony with the rest of the host family members, Rick and a visitor as guests.

Although Rick's host family members are one of the most infrequent *masu* users during dinnertime family conversation among the nine host families in the present data, during the tea ceremony they frequently used honorifics, including the *masu* form.[2] In Example (3), after the first guest, who is the host father, drinks the tea, it is Rick's turn. The host family members model for Rick the polite, ritual expressions of the tea ceremony while they collaboratively teach him how to properly pick up the teacup and drink tea as a guest of the ceremony.

(3) Rick 012002

1 HM: hai kondo    rikku ne (.) hai doozo ((places a tea cup in front of
       Rick))
       yes this time Rick   FP     yes please
       'Yes, this time it's Rick. So, please go ahead.'

2          tara  otonari ni
           then next     to
           'then, (bow) to the person next to you.'

3     R: a-   hai ((bows to the guest next to him))
           uh  yes
           'uh yes'

 4   HM: a  ja   [ochawan o mannaka e  mo(.)te]
           uh then  teacup    O middle  to hold
           'uh then  hold the tea bowl in the middle.'

5    HF:          [muko        yoko e     soo soo soo]
                  over there   side to    so  so  so
                  'over there to the side    yes yes yes'

6    HB: aida    ni
           middle in
           'in the middle'

7     R: u   un
           uh huh
           'uh huh'

8    HF: [soo    soo soo]
           so     so  so
           'yes    yes yes'

9   → R: [nan da   te]
           what Cop QT
           'what (did you say)?'

10 → HM: osaki ni ((bows))
              first  in
              'Excuse me for going first.'

11  → HF: osaki ni ((bows))
              first  in
              'Excuse me for going first.'

12 → HM: osaki ni ((bows)) =
              first  in
              'Excuse me for going first.'

13   →  R: osaki ni ((bows))
              first  in
              'Excuse me for going first.'

14   HM: [doozo ((laughs))
            please
            'Please (drink the tea).'

15      All: [((laugh))

16      HS: okashi ((laughs))
            sweets
            'Sweets'

17      HF: koko e [oite
            here to put down
            'Put them down here'

18       R:              [a
                          uh
                          'uh'

  19  HF: a- koko e  oite
            uh here  to put down
            'uh put them down here.'

20       R: oh  hai  hai ((puts the sweets on the table))
            oh   yes  yes
            'Oh yes yes'

21      HF: un sore de [( )
            yeah then
            'yeah then (   )'

22 → HM:                [a- sore de watashi ni ita- **ita[dakimasu** tte
                         uh then     I    to re-  receive        QT
                         'uh, then you say to me "I'll receive".'

23       R:                                    [aa
                                               uh
                                               'uh'

24 → HS: otemae choodai **itashimasu**
            artistry  receive  do
            'I'll receive the tea you've made.'

25   HM: un
            yeah
            'yeah'

26      →  otemae choodai **itashimasu**
            artistry receive  do
            'I'll receive the tea that you've made'

27  → R: otemae o choodai **itashi[masu**
      artistry O receive do
      'I'll receive the tea that you've made'

28  HF:                              [@hai@
                                yes
                                'yes'

29  HM: doozo
      please
      'Please go ahead'

30  R: hai      ((picks up the tea cup))
     yes
     'Yes'

Just before Example (2), the host mother, as the hostess, fixed tea for the first guest, the host father. Rick is the second guest. In line 1, the host mother announces to Rick that it is his turn to receive tea as she places the teacup in front of him. Then in line 2, she tells him to bow to the guest next to him. In lines 4 through 8, the host mother, host father and host brother collaboratively instruct Rick exactly where the teacup should be placed. In line 9, instead of asking *nan to iu n desu ka* ('what do I say?'), Rick mistakenly says, *nan da te*, which is an informal expression to ask what the addressee was saying (i.e. what did you say?). The host parents have apparently figured out what Rick intended to say and interpret his utterance as a request for the proper thing to say (i.e. what do I say?). So in lines 10–13, both the host mother and father model what to say for Rick. In line 10, the host mother starts to tell Rick what to say before he drinks the tea. She says *Osaki ni* ('Excuse me for going first') as she bows. The host father repeats the host mother's expression and gesture. The host mother then repeats these actions once again after the host father. In line 13, finally it is Rick's turn to say the phrase while bowing. He successfully models the actions of the host mother and father. The host mother's *doozo* ('please (drink the tea)') acknowledges Rick's proper actions. However, Rick is eating some sweets and still has some left in his hand. In lines 16 and 17, the host sister and host father tell him to put the sweets on the table. In line 22, the host mother models for Rick by saying *Itadakimasu* ('I will receive'), which is a set formula used before eating or drinking. Then in line 24, the host sister repairs the host mother's phrase to a more formal expression specific to the tea ceremony, *Otemae choodai itashimasu* ('I will receive the tea that you have made'). This expression includes not only the *masu* form but also the referent honorific form *itasu* (the humble form of *suru* 'do'). The host mother repeats this for Rick. The host parents and host siblings all collaboratively model polite expressions and gestures for Rick during the tea ceremony so that Rick can fully participate in the tea ceremony in a proper manner. With the scaffolding from the host family, Rick – a novice of *sadoo* ('the way of tea') – succeeds in properly performing the role of a guest in a tea ceremony. In line 27, Rick utters the proper phrase used in a tea ceremony and simultaneously bows before drinking tea. Although Rick's Japanese proficiency is at the novice level, the host family members' models help Rick successfully perform both the proper linguistic and non-linguistic actions during the tea ceremony.

Another factor that promotes the host mother's modeling of polite expressions is the presence of a small child or children in the host family. While the child is the 'addressed recipient' of the host mother's modeling, the learner can benefit from it as an 'unaddressed recipient' (Goffman, 1981: 133). For example, in Alice's host family there are three small children; the host mother's modeling provide not only the child but also the learner with a good example of when and how to express politeness.[3] In Example (4) the host mother's utterance is directly addressed to the child, but Alice as a participant is given an opportunity to learn the appropriate speech style for a formal self-introduction. The pattern of introduction X *desu* ('I am X') is not a difficult expression and may be one of the first expressions that JFL learners learn in the classroom. However, in the homestay context, in which most conversation is carried out in the plain form, the host mother's modeling of this expression reminds the learner when to use it appropriately. Here Alice's host mother is talking to her five-year-old daughter, Sae. Sae just got up from a nap and came to the dinner table where Alice and the host mother were eating dinner. As the video camera is recording their conversation, the host mother tells Sae that the video will be shown to a professor in Hawaii, and she starts to model a proper self-introduction for Sae.

(4) Alice 012102

1 HM: ((pointing to the video camera and talking to Sae))
    Sae-chan are Hawai no daigaku    no sensee ni miseru
    Sae    that Hawaii LK university LK teacher to show
    n    da    tte
    Nom Cop QT
    'Sae, they say that this will be shown to a professor from Hawaii University.'

    ((turning Sae toward the video camera))

2    Sae-chan no kao mo misetoite hora (.)
    Sae    LK face also show    see
    'Sae, show your face (to the video camera), see.'

3  → 'Sae **desu**' tte (.) 'Sae **desu**' (.)
    Sae Cop   QT    Sae Cop
    'Say 'I am Sae,' 'I am Sae.''

4     hai <u>oshimai</u>
    yes end
    'That's all.'

As this is an example of a formal self-introduction, the host mother naturally shifts to the *masu* form when modeling for Sae how to introduce herself to a high-status stranger. The host mother's modeling directed to Sae provides an opportunity for Alice to learn the appropriate speech style for a formal self-introduction.

Modeling is one of the explicit socialization practices that brings formal settings into the intimacy of the home setting. Polite expressions for formal occasions such as the tea ceremony and self-introductions are salient due to the fact that they occur in ritualized contexts. As a result, the host family members have clear metapragmatic awareness of the form-context correlation. So they have no trouble modeling the appropriate polite expressions for such occasions. Although referent honorifics do not usually occur in family conversation, special occasions such as a tea ceremony held at the host family's house provide opportunities for the host family to explicitly socialize the learner into the use of honorifics through modeling.

## Indexing the 'On-stage' Presentational Frame Through the *Masu* Form

The sociolinguistic competence to shift appropriately between the 'on-stage' presentational and 'off-stage' non-presentational frames (Goffman, 1974; Tannen, 1993) is an important aspect of pragmatic competence in Japanese. Japanese children are socialized into the presentation of self through the use of the *masu* form in daily interaction with caregivers. As they become older, the social contexts in which they appropriately display the self-presentational stance expand. They have more opportunities to participate in culturally organized activities outside of the home (*soto* contexts). One of the cultural activities organized for children salient outside of the family is *happyoo*, a class presentation common in elementary schools (Anderson, 1995; Cook, 1996b). Through *happyoo* activities, Japanese children learn to engage further in an appropriate display of the self-presentational stance. However, family conversation socializes children earlier in life to the point that they are able to shift between the 'on-stage' presentational frame and 'off-stage' non-presentational frames long before they go to elementary school (e.g. Cook, 1996a).

Similarly, the experience of staying with a host family provides JFL learners with opportunities for implicit as well as explicit language socialization. In the present study, by the time learners have reached the advanced level, they have been socialized to move in and out of the 'on-stage' and 'off-stage' frames without the host family's assistance. In this section, I illustrate similarities between style shifts found in the *happyoo* activity in an elementary school classroom and those in a spontaneous cooking lesson given by a learner at a host family's house. Both require appropriate shifts between the *masu* and plain forms to index the on-stage presentational and off-stage non-presentational frames. I argue that the underlying sociolinguistic competence to move in and out of these two frames involves the judgment of whether or not it is appropriate to be on stage. This competence is acquired through *masu* form uses in family talk and is the basis for appropriate use of the *masu* form as a so-called 'polite speech marker' in the *soto* context. As we see below, both nine-year-old Japanese children and advanced-level learners can move between the two frames, which indicates that they have acquired the sociolinguistic competence as to when it is appropriate to be on stage and off stage.

The *happyoo* activity takes place in elementary schools in Japan (Anderson, 1995; Cook, 1996b). In the *happyoo* activity, students stand up and present their opinions or answers to the class. It is similar to the English show-and-tell activity. When students participate in this activity, they typically shift to the *masu* form and sustain it while they are engaged in the activity.[4] They are literally, or figuratively (depending upon the physical arrangement of the classroom), on stage making a presentation. The participants in the *happyoo* activity also include the rest of the students in the class. They ask the presenters questions regarding their presentation by using the *masu* form. The participants, however, sometimes shift to the plain form when they speak to the teacher who is not a participant in the activity. In Example (5), students in Ms. A's class are engaged in a *happyoo* activity. Abe-kun, the student who is presiding over the activity, is standing in front of the class. The teacher, who is standing to the side of the class, is an observer but not an active participant in the activity. The other students participate in the *happyoo* activity by asking questions or offering comments to the presenter. Here Abe-kun speaks in the *masu* form, but shifts to the plain form to talk to the teacher (Cook, 1996b: 76).

(5) Ms. A' class [4th grade]

1   Abe: de shitsumon san wa eeto shitsumon ni to onaji de
           and   question 3 Top uh    question   2 with same Cop
           'And question 3 is    the same as question 2, and'

           toomee no fukuro ni gomi- toomee no fukuro o- gomibukuro ni
           clear LK bag     in garb   clear LK bag     O garbage bag in

zembu matomete dashite **imasu**.
all       together   put out exist
'clear bags, garbage- clear bags- are all put out together in clear
garbage bags.'

2 Ms. A: kore wa bunbetsu shite <u>aru</u> wake?
this Top separate  do    exist FP
'Is this sorted?'

moeru   no to    moenai    no tte
burnable one and unburnable one QT
'one that is burnable and one that is unburnable?'

3   Abe: <u>shitenai</u> ((low voice))
do Neg
'It is not.'

4 Ms. A: koko wa bunbetsu <u>shinai</u>
here Top separate  do Neg
'Here (they) do not sort it.'

5   Abe: bunbetsu <u>shinai</u>
separate  do Neg
'(They) do not sort out.'

6       moo matomete zembu <u>dashichau</u>.
all   together  all      put ou
'(They) put it all out.'

7 Ms. A: (not clear)

8   Abe: ((turns to the whole class))
ii       **desu** ka::
good  Cop  Q
'Is it OK?'

9 Children: ha:i
yes
'Yes'

In this example, the student, Abe-kun, who is the presenter in the
*happyoo* activity, is speaking in the *masu* form. In line 2, the teacher, who is
off stage observing the students' *happyoo* activity, asks a clarifying
question, using the plain form. Abe-kun answers the teacher's question
shifting to the plain form. Then the teacher asks another question in the
plain form, which Abe-kun also responds to in the plain form. In line 8,
turning to the students, Abe-kun resumes the *happyoo* activity. Here he
shifts back to the *masu* form. This activity illustrates the *masu* form being
used as a marker of the self-presentational stance. Speaking in the plain

form to the teacher does not mean that the students are impolite. Rather the shift to the plain form indexes the off-stage frame. The *happyoo* activity reinforces the claim that there is a direct indexical relation between the *masu* form and the self-presentational stance. The way in which Japanese children are exposed to the *masu* form at early ages at home and the way in which they continue to use it in the *happyoo* activity in the elementary school suggest that the direct indexical connection between the *masu* form and the self-presentational stance is first acquired at home. Then children can develop uses of the *masu* form in a wide range of social contexts in which the self-presentational stance is appropriate in Japanese society.

In a similar manner, advanced-level learners can move in and out of the on-stage presentational and off-stage non-presentational frames. In the cooking demonstration below, Mary shifts to the *masu* form when she makes a formal demonstration and shifts back to the plain form when she moves out of the on-stage presentational frame. In Example (6), Mary is conducting a cooking demonstration for her guests and host parents. Mary has invited her American and Irish classmates, Julia and Sally, to her host family's house for dinner. After the host mother shows them how to cook vegetables and meat in a pot on the table, Mary decides to do a mini-cooking demonstration for her guests and host parents in front of the video camera.

(6) Mary 012902

((Mary is standing at the table and acts as a hostess. She is about to demonstrate how to prepare a *nabe* dish by putting vegetables in the pot))[5]

1 HF: sutanbai de　ii　　no kana = ((talking about the video camera))
　　　standby Cop good FP FP
　　　'Is the standby mode all right?'

2　M: = aa [tsuita tsuita
　　　　oh turned on turned on
　　　　'Oh, it's on, it's on.'

3 HF:　　[aa okkee
　　　　oh OK
　　　　'Oh, OK.'

4 M: → [yasai　　de gozaimasu ((starts her cooking demonstration
　　　　in front of the camera.))
　　　　vegetable Cop
　　　　'These are vegetables.'

5 HF: [a- yasai　　desu ka = ((laughs))
　　　　oh vegetable Cop Q
　　　　'Oh- are they vegetables?''

6    M: = kore kara onabe o **tsukurimasu** =
         this from pot   O make
         'I am going to cook a *nabe* dish now.'

7    HF: hai
         yes
         'yes.'

8  → M: kore o **desu** ne: [ano happa ni nita kanji na   n  da kedo =
         this O Cop FP   uh leaf   similar feel  Cop Nom Cop but
         'This, uh this looks like a leaf but'

9    HF:                 [hai
                         yes
                         'yes'

10   HF: = seri    **desu** yo =
         parsley Cop  FP
         'It's parsley.'

11    M: = nani? =
         what
         'What?'

12 → HF: = seri seri =
         parsley, parsley
         'Parsley, parsley.'

13    M: = seri =
         parsley
         'Parsley.'

14   HF: = un =
         yeah
         'yeah'

15 → M: = kore ga seri   **desu** ne: kono naka ni irete =
         this S parsley  Cop  FP this  inside in put in
         'This is parsley. We put it inside of this.'

16    J: = kore wa nan **desu** ka
         this Top what Cop Q
         'What is this?'

17    M: kore wa- kore wa seri    [**desu** ne: =
         this Top  this Top parsley Cop   FP
         'This is- this is parsley.'

18   HF:                          [@ seri **desu** ne:@
                              parsley Cop FP
                              'It's parsley.'

19   J: a- seri aa ja: kore- sore [wa
        oh parsley oh well this that Top
        'Oh, parsley oh, well, this- that is'

20   HF:                          [((laughs))

21   M: = sore wa- sore a- a- kore wa (0.5) enoki **desu** =
        that Top that uh uh this Top       enoki Cop
        'That is- that uh- uh- this is an enoki mushroom.'

22   HF: = soo **desu** atari **desu** ((laughs))
         so   Cop right Cop
         'That's right. You're right.'

23   M: shiitake ni nite       **imasu** kedomo yahari enoki de **gozaimasu**
        shiitake to similar exist   but      still    enoki Cop
        'It's like a shiitake mushroom but it is actually an enoki
        mushroom.'

In lines 1 through 3, Mary and her host father are checking to see if the
video camera is working. As the cooking demonstration has not started
yet, both are still in the off-stage frame and speak in the plain form. Once
Mary starts her cooking demonstration in line 4, she shifts to the *masu*
form. The frame shifts here from the off-stage, informal conversation
frame to the on-stage, formal frame of the cooking demonstration. Mary
even uses the 'super polite' *gozaimasu* form (lines 4 and 23), which
indicates the formal nature of her demonstration. In line 6, Mary
announces what she is going to cook, continuing with the *masu* form.
The host father also shifts to the *masu* form in line 5 indexing that he too
is a participant in Mary's cooking demonstration. He is no longer an off-
stage observer of Mary's demonstration like the teacher in Example (5).
In other words, both Mary and the host father are jointly constructing the
on-stage frame, acting in role in front of the video camera and engaging
in the activity of cooking demonstration.

In lines 8 through 14, Mary and her host father are momentarily
stepping out of the on-stage cooking demonstration frame and shifting to
the off-stage frame. In line 8, Mary is not sure of the name of the vegetable
that looks like a leaf. Here Mary starts out with *kore desu ne* ('this one *ne*').
She is using *desu*, the *masu* form of the copula, which indexes that she is
still in the demonstration frame. But she cannot come up with the name of
the vegetable she is going to present to the audience. As she describes the
shape of the vegetable, she shifts back to the plain form, which indexes that

she is stepping out of the demonstration frame. In line 10, the host father offers the name of the vegetable by saying that it is *seri* ('parsley'). He still maintains the on-stage presentational stance by using the *masu* form here. Mary apparently has trouble hearing him and produces a repair initiator *nani?* ('what?') in the plain form. The host father tells her again that it is *seri* ('parsley'), but this time he too steps out of the on-stage demonstration frame by speaking in the plain form. His 'off-stage' non-presentational stance is also indexed by the informal acknowledgment token *un* ('yeah') in line 14. Once the trouble is resolved, in line 15 Mary resumes the formal cooking demonstration by shifting back to the *masu* form and maintains this form as she continues. Thus, Example (6) illustrates Mary's tacit sociolinguistic knowledge concerning how a change in the frames is indexed by the *masu* and plain forms. This example suggests that advanced-level learners usually acquire the necessary knowledge to give a formal presentation using the *masu* form. The formal presentation is similar to the *happyoo* activity in the elementary school classroom in that the presenter moves in and out of the on-stage presentational frame by manipulating the *masu* and plain forms as resources.

## Explicit Accounts of Sociolinguistic Rules

Socialization can also occur when social norms – what is an appropriate behavior in a given social situation – are explicitly taught. In many cultures, parents explicitly teach children polite behavior. For example, American mothers teach children to say 'please' when making a request, and to say 'thank you' when a request is accepted (Snow *et al.*, 1990). Japanese parents tell children to say set formulas such as *itadakimasu* ('I will receive') and *gochisoosama* ('thank you for the meal') before and after a meal (Burdelski, 2006; Clancy, 1986) and instruct children how to behave properly (e.g. not to leave food on the plate) (Cook, 1997). In the homestay context, instead of correcting learners' inappropriate usages, host families sometimes explicitly teach their exchange students about the social norms and customs of the target society including polite language behavior (Cook, 2006a; DuFon, 2006; Iino, 1996). In the present data, the host mothers of Greg and Kate (i.e. the host mothers who use a teaching voice) give lengthy explicit accounts of sociolinguistic rules, such as how gendered language or honorifics are used. These accounts often reflect folk beliefs about how polite language is used in Japanese society. Typical host families' beliefs found in this study are, for example, that women speak more softly and politely than men, and that *sonkeigo* ('respect forms') are used to addressees of a higher status.

These folk beliefs are not always consistent with actual practice in Japanese society, as recent research on language and gender in Japanese society (cf. Okamoto & Smith, 2004) has demonstrated. For example, not all Japanese women use so-called 'female language'. Women in farm villages and young women, in particular, rarely use this speech style. As for honorifics, in actual practice in Japanese society, out-group member-ship takes precedence over status/rank in determining whether or not the speaker uses honorifics. For example, *sonkeigo* ('respect forms') are not necessarily used when speaking to someone with higher status. Rather, the primary use of *sonkeigo* is to address or refer to an addressee who belongs to the realm of *soto* ('out-group/outside') (Niyekawa, 1991). Therefore, instead of exalting her boss (a higher status person), a secretary usually uses humble language to refer to him when talking to a customer (i.e. an outsider or person in a *soto* relationship). On the other hand, the speaker may refer to the child of the addressee with *sonkeigo* ('respect form') if the speaker and the addressee are in a *soto* ('out-group') relationship. The point here is that by participating in the host mothers' discussion about gendered language or honorifics, the learners are socialized into the discourse of Japanese folk beliefs concerning polite language.

While Greg and Kate's host mothers do not specifically give metalinguistic explanations about the *masu* form, they include examples of both the plain and *masu* forms as they discuss gendered language or honorifics in Japanese. The host mothers' narratives reflect folk notions of language use in Japanese society. Below I illustrate the learner's socialization into the Japanese discourse of gendered speech. In this example, use of the *masu* form is not the focus of the talk, but is included in the discussion.

## Gendered language

The example below shows that the host mother's narrative on gendered speech influences choices the learner makes in his words and that it also socializes the learner into the Japanese discourse of gendered speech. In Example (7), Greg's host mother's comments on the *masu* form and the sentence-final particles *ne*, *yo* and *wa* reflect her view on how Japanese men and women should speak. As discussed in earlier chapters, the *masu* form is described as *teineitai* ('polite style') in Japanese grammar. However, in Example (7), in relation to gendered speech in Japanese, Greg's host mother describes the *masu* form as *kitsui* ('harsh'). She goes on to explain that the harshness of the *masu* form can be softened with the sentence-final particle *ne*, which she says is suitable for women's speech.[6] We note that the learner, Greg, only uses reactive tokens that the host mother describes as male speech and does not use what the host mother refers to as female speech or harsh speech. Furthermore, his choice of linguistic forms becomes more masculine as the host mother's narrative unfolds. Although it is not clear whether

Greg consciously avoided what the host mother calls female and harsh speech, it is observed that Greg's linguistic behavior is in line with the host mother's descriptions. In this sense, the host mother's narrative on gendered speech provides Greg with an opportunity to speak like an ideal 'male' in Japanese society.

To illustrate gendered speech, Greg's host mother uses as an example the expression, *soo (da/desu)* ('that's right'). In Japanese this expression has several variants because it can be said either in the *masu* (*soo desu*) or plain (*soo* or *soo da*) form, and can be followed by the sentence final-particles *ne(ne:)*, *yo*, *yo ne* or *wa*.[7] In Example (7), the host mother explains which variants should be used by women and which ones should be used by men. It is noted that as the host mother explains different connotations of the expression, Greg's reactive token changes from *soo* (lines 5 and 17) to *soo da yo* (lines 24 and 35). Although both of the expressions are described by the host mother as male forms, the latter (*soo da yo*) sounds strongly masculine (cf. Okamoto, 1995).

(7) Greg 012802

1 HM: otoko no hito    wa daitai    'soo **desu** soo **desu'** tte yuu koto o
        male LK person Top generally so Cop   so   Cop   QT say Nom O
        'In stead of saying 'soo desu, soo desu,' men generally say,
        'soo da ne:'

2       'soo da ne:' tte yuu kedo, onna no hito    wa 'soo yo ne:' toka =
        so Cop FP QT say but female LK person Top so  FP FP   etc.
        'but women say things like 'soo yo ne:'

3   G:  = a::: =
        oh
        'Oh'

4 HM:  = 'a- soo ne:'
        oh so  FP
        'and "a- soo ne:."'

5  → G: a  soo
        oh so
        'Oh is that right?'

6 HM: un =
        uh huh
        'uh huh'

7   G:  = uhm =
        hum
        'hum'

8 HM: = otoko no hito wa   'soo' to mo yuu shi onna   no hito   mo
           male  LK person Top so QT also say and female LK person also
           'soo' mo      yuu- yuu kedo (1.0)
           so   also   say say but
           'Men also say "soo" and women also say, "soo" but'

9         nn   yappari ne josee   kotoba   na   no ne:? =
           uhm after all FP female language Cop FP FP
           'uhm it is after all women's language.'

10    G:  = [nn
                 uhm
                 'uhm'

11    HM:     [josee  kotoba    da     to omou =
                 Female language Cop QT think
                 'I think it's women's language'

12    G:  = nn
               uhm
               'uhm'

13    HM: 'soo yo ne:' toka   'soo **desu** yo ne:' ma- 'soo **desu** yo ne:'
            so  FP FP  etc.   so  Cop  FP FP well  so  Cop  FP FP
            wa otoko mo yuu ne
            Top male also say FP
            'soo yo ne:' or 'soo desu yo ne:' Well, men also say, 'soo
            desu yo ne:'

            (2.0)

14→HM: 'ne:' o tsukeru n      **desu** yo, saigo ni ne: nihon no baai =
            FP O add       Nom Cop FP last   at FP Japanese LK case
            'In Japan, we place "ne:" at the end (of a sentence).'

15    G:  = nn =
               uhm
               'uhm'

16    HM: = toku       ni josee?
               particular in female
               'In particular, women do so.'

17   →G: nn   soo
            uhm so
            'uhm is that so?'

18  HM: 'soo yo' mo yuu kedo. 'soo **desu**' to mo yuu kedo.
        so FP    also say but    so   Cop  QT also say but
        'We say, "soo yo" and also "soo desu" but'

19  → chotto '**desu**' tte yuu to  chotto kitsui desho? iikata ga
        little   Cop  QT say QT little   harsh  Cop    say way S
        'when we say, "desu," it's a little harsh, that way of speaking.'

20  → G: kitsui?
        harsh
        'harsh'

21  HM: un
        uh huh
        'uh huh'

        (2.0)

22    G: nn (1.0) [nn nn
        uhm       uhm uhm
        'uhm      uhm uhm'

23 → HM:        [chotto  kitsui iikata    na no 'soo **desu**' tte yuu to
        little   harsh say way Cop FP so  Cop   QT say QT
        'It's a slightly harsh way of saying things when
        you say "soo desu."'

24  → G:  = aa soo da yo
        oh so Cop FP
        'Oh, that is right.'

25  HM: 'hai **wakarimashita**' tte koo yuu fuu ni ne?
        yes understood        QT this way     in FP
        '(the addressee responds) by saying "I understand."
        This is how'

26   G: a:  = ((laughs))
        oh
        'Oh'

27  HM:  = naru no =
        become FP
        'it becomes.'

28    G:  = hu:n =
        uh huh
        'uh huh'

29  HM:  = de =
        and
        'and'

30    G:  = dakara  'ne:' o tsukattara [motto =
          therefore FP  O use   if  more
          'So if you use "ne:" more'

31  HM:                    [nn
                     uhm
                     'uhm'

32  HM:  = 'soo ne:, soo **desu** yo ne:' ttara 'hai **wakarimashita**'
          So  FP  so  Cop FP FP   then yes understood
          ni wa  naranai    de
          to Top  beeomd Neg and
          'if you say, "soo ne:" or "soo desu yo ne:," then they
          won't respond by saying "yes, I understand."'

33    G: nn =
        uhm
        'uhm'

34 HM:  = nn   'a soo ne:' nante mata koo chotto yawarakai?
          uhm oh so  FP  like  again this little  soft
          [yawarakai kotoba? ga =
          soft          word  S
          'uhm, when you say, "a soo ne:" A little soft, it's a soft word'

35  →G:  [aa soo da yo
          oh so Cop FP
          'Oh, that is right'

36    G:  = nn =
        uhm
        'uhm'

37 HM:  = ano (1.0) onna no  hito   no baai wa tsukau  kara saigo
          well      female LK person LK case   Top use so  last
          ni gobi tte yuu no ne
          at end QT say FP FP
          'in the case of women, they use "wa," so at the end,
          the end of a sentence,'

38      saigo gobi- gobi na  n     da kedo kotoba no gobi ni 'ne:'
      last  end  end Cop Nom Cop but word  LK end at  FP
      toka 'yo ne:' toka =
      etc. FP FP   etc.

'the sentence-final, at the sentence-final position they use
"ne:" or "yo ne:"'

39   G: = nn =
       uhm
       'uhm'

40 HM: = soo <u>da</u> wa ne:. ['ne:' **desu** ne:, yappari ne:.
        so Cop FP FP   FP   Cop FP   after all FP
        'That's right. It is 'ne:' after all.'

41   G:                       [((laughs))

42   G: ((laughs)) yappari
                 after all
                 'after all'

The host mother's point in this example is that, as the *masu* form alone sounds harsh, it is advisable for women to use sentence-final particles such as *ne* or *yo ne* to soften the expression. Table 6.1 summarizes the host mother's development of the argument and Greg's reactive tokens.

In lines 1 and 2, contrasting the expressions *soo da ne* (*soo* + plain form coupula + FP) and *soo yo ne* (*soo* + FP + FP), the host mother comments that the former is male speech and the latter is female speech. In line 4, she continues to say that 'a soo ne' is also female speech. In line 5 Greg gives a reactive token *a soo* 'Oh, is that right?'. In line 8, the host mother makes a version of the reactive token just produced by Greg (i.e. a *soo*) as an object of metalinguistic comment and starts to talk about the usage of *soo*. She first mentions that *soo* is used by men and adds that it is also used by women. Then, in line 13, the host mother begins to talk about the *masu* form and sentence-final particle *ne*. In lines 14 and 16 she makes a point that in particular women use the sentence-final particle *ne*. In line 19, the host mother comments that *soo desu* (without *ne*) sounds *kitsui* ('harsh'). In line 20, Greg repeats the word *kitsui* ('harsh') with a rising intonation, suggesting that he is possibly questioning the host mother's assertion. There may be a discrepancy between the host mother's explanation and what he probably learned in his Japanese language classes (i.e. the *masu* form is a marker of politeness). In line 23, the host mother repeats that *soo desu* is a harsh expression and provides a reason why it is harsh. She explains that one would respond *hai, wakarimashita* ('yes, I understand') to the expression *soo desu*. In other words, she is implying that *soo desu* is so deterministic that the hearer is forced to accept the speaker's opinion. She continues to assert that the harsh sound of *soo desu* can be softened by adding the sentence-final particle *ne*. The host mother's explanation that the *masu* form sounds harsh may reflect a certain interpretation of the self-presentational stance, the image of the

**Table 6.1** The host mother's development of the argument and Greg's reactive tokens

| Line | Linguistic expressions discussed by the host mother | The host mother's metalinguistic comments | Greg's actual practice (i.e. his reactive tokens) |
|---|---|---|---|
| 1–2 | Soo <u>da</u> ne | Male language | |
| 2 | <u>Soo</u> yo ne | Female language | |
| 4 | A soo ne | Female language | |
| 5 | | | A <u>soo</u> |
| 8 | Soo | Male language | |
| 8, 9, 11 | Soo | Women use it too | |
| 13 | Soo **desu** yo ne | Men use it too | |
| 14, 16 | ne | In particular, women use *ne* | |
| 17 | | | Nn <u>soo</u> |
| 19 | Soo **desu** | Sounds harsh | |
| 23 | Soo **desu** | Sounds a little harsh | |
| 24 | | | Aa soo <u>da</u> yo |
| 32 | <u>Soo</u> ne | Sounds soft | |
| 32 | Soo **desu** yo ne | Sounds soft | |
| 35 | | | Aa soo <u>da</u> yo |
| 37, 38 | Ne, yo ne | Female language | |

upright posture (*shisei o tadasu*), which is the opposite of that of relaxed posture indexed by the plain form. In line 24, right after the host mother's explanation that the *masu* form sounds harsh, Greg changes his reactive token to a more masculine version, *aa soo da yo* 'Oh, is that right?' (cf. Okamoto, 1995).[8] *Soo da* (*soo* + the plain form copula *da*) is a variation that the host mother calls male language. He repeats *aa soo da yo* in line 35 right after the host mother describes *soo ne* and *soo desu yo ne* as soft expressions. It seems that he gives *soo da yo* (male language) in reaction to the host mother's explanations of *soo desu* (harsh expression) and *soo ne* (female language) and *soo desu yo ne* (soft expression). In other words, he avoids what the host mother refers to as a harsh expression, female language and soft expression, and marks his speech masculine by using the more masculine version, *soo da yo.*[9]

Furthermore, the host mother's narrative on gendered speech possibly socializes the learner into the Japanese discourse of gender ideology. Three points raised by the host mother in Example (7) are: (1) the *masu* form is a harsh expression (lines 19 and 23); (2) the sentence-final particle *ne* is primarily a female particle (lines 14 and 16); and (3) the sentence-final particle *wa* is also a female particle (line 37). These points do not necessarily reflect actual practice of Japanese speakers. As this book has claimed, the *masu* form is not a marker of harsh speech. Sociolinguistic literature on Japanese discourse documents that the sentence-final particle *ne* is used by both men and women (e.g. Cook, 1992, in press; Maynard, 1993). The sentence-final particle *wa* is occasionally used by men, in particular when it occurs with a falling intonation. Throughout the host mother's lengthy presentation of her ideas on how women and men talk, Greg produces reactive tokens, which gradually become more masculine. In line 42, Greg repeats the host mother's expression *yappari* ('after all') with a laugh. It is not clear whether he agrees with the host mother, but interactionally he orients to her view by giving reactive tokens, repeating the host mother's expressions and laughing. Through participation in the host mother's talk, Greg is being socialized into the Japanese discourse of gendered speech.

## Absence of explicit socialization to use the *masu* form

The present study suggests that the host families neither explicitly teach appropriate uses of the *masu* form (e.g. when talking to the teacher, you should use the *masu* form) nor correct the learners' inappropriate uses of it. These facts suggest that the *masu* form is not a focus of attention. Furthermore, in the questionnaires that I distributed to the host families and the learners, one of the questions was 'what are the most difficult aspects of speaking in Japanese with the JFL learner/the host family?' None of the participants commented on style shifts as a difficult aspect of speaking Japanese. Most of the learners were concerned about vocabulary and whether they could make themselves understood in Japanese. Most host families responded that they sometimes worry about whether the learners understood what they said. Both the learners and the host families focused on the referential content of conversation, rather than on the pragmatic aspect of their talk (i.e. the manner in which their talk is delivered). Mary's host family was the only host family who said that sometimes they corrected the learner's incorrect *keigo* ('honorifics'). However, no correction of *keigo* ('honorifics') occurred in the speech of Mary's host family in the data. In the present study, the questionnaire responses of the learners and the host families seem to indicate that during dinnertime talk, the speech style (i.e. the choice between the *masu* and plain forms) is beyond their conscious choice, and yet it is a part of the tacit sociolinguistic knowledge of native speakers of Japanese and functions as a tool by which they construct various social identities, as seen in earlier chapters. For the learners, the speech style is something that they do not consciously manipulate during conversation with the host family, but they learn to speak appropriately through routine participation in daily activities.

## Conclusion

In the present data, explicit language socialization about how polite language is used occurs in two ways. One is the host family members' modeling of polite expressions, and the other is an explicit explanation of sociolinguistic rules. A host family member, in particular the host mother, models appropriate expressions for different formal occasions, which are utterances in the *masu* form. During some special occasions such as the tea ceremony, the modeling includes not only the *masu* form but also referent honorifics, which rarely appear in dinnertime talk between the learner and host family. During formal occasions such as the tea ceremony, learners are given an opportunity to encounter referent honorific expressions other than the limited set formulas that are often used in family conversation (e.g. *itadakimasu*, a set formula said before eating). With the host family's help, even a novice-level learner such as Rick can participate in a formal occasion (e.g. a tea ceremony) that calls for appropriate linguistic and non-linguistic behavior. The learner's accomplishment is jointly constructed with the host family members. By the time learners reach the advanced level, they often have acquired the sociolinguistic competence to use the *masu* and plain forms as resources to create the on-stage presentational and off-stage non-presentational frames, just as Japanese elementary school children do when they engage in the *happyoo* ('presentation') activity. By participating in a variety of culturally organized activities outside the home, Japanese children expand their knowledge of where, when and with whom the self-presentational stance is appropriate (Cook, 1996a, 1996b). In a similar manner, as JFL learners become more proficient in Japanese, they expand the range of contexts in which they appropriately take a self-presentational stance.

The host families' explicit metalinguistic explanations may provide opportunities for learners to index an 'ideal social identity' through the use of linguistic features prescribed for those identities (e.g. gender identities). At the same time, the host families socialize learners into the discourse of folk notions of gendered speech and polite language. In the present data, only the host mothers of Greg and Kate offer lengthy accounts of sociolinguistic rules. It is also noted that the host mothers' explanations are based on folk beliefs and do not necessarily reflect actual practice. For example, Kate's host mother's explanation about the use of honorifics discussed only vertical social relations, and the *uchi/soto* ('in/out-group') relationship is left uncovered. In sum, the host mothers' discussion about gendered language or honorifics socializes the learners into the discourse of Japanese folk beliefs concerning polite language.

## Notes

1.  Another frequently used set formula at home that contains a referent honorific form is *itte mairimasu* ('I am going'), which is said every time someone leaves home.
2.  The conversation from tea ceremony gathering held in Rick's host family is not included in the tabulation of tokens of the *masu* form because it involves a visitor to the family (the host brother's friend).
3.  I am not saying that Alice's Japanese proficiency is too low to be able to use a polite expression in front of a camera. She probably knows how to say *Alice desu* 'I am Alice'. What I am arguing is that the more learners have opportunities to hear polite expressions said in an appropriate context, the easier it becomes for learners to use these expressions appropriately.
4.  In some classes I observed, students used the plain form without any 'affect keys' (Ochs, 1996) (a detached style) to focus on the content.
5.  The *nabe* dish is a dish which is cooked in a pot placed on the table. For example, *Sukiyaki* and *Shabu shabu* are typical *nabe* dishes.
6.  *Ne:* is a variant of the sentence-final particle *ne*. It sounds more emphatic because of the prolonged vowel [e]. Greg's host mother uses *ne* and *ne:* interchangeably in her discussion.
7.  The particle *yo* is an emphatic particle used to emphasize the speaker's point, and the particle *wa*, which softens the pragmatic force of a sentence, is considered as a typical female particle (Cook, in press).
8.  Greg's use of *yo* in *soo da yo* is not as polite as polite as *soo da ne*. *Ne* creates a shared perspective with the host mother. Instead, *yo* in *soo da yo* gives an impresson that Greg is the authority of Japanese gendered speech.
9.  Elsewhere, Greg uses as reactive tokens *soo desu* and *soo desu yo*. For example, in Example (4) in Chapter 5, he gives reactive tokens *soo desu* and *soo desu yo* in lines 4 and 6, respectively.

## Chapter 7
# *Implications of the Study for L2 Pragmatics and Pedagogy*

It has been pointed out that effective instruction of pragmatics in the foreign language classroom requires the analysis of not only the native speakers' norm of behavior but also that of learners as well (Kasper, 1997). This book has analyzed in detail how the JFL learners and their host families index various social identities using the *masu* form as a resource and how the learners are socialized into appropriate uses of the *masu* form. All the learners in this study studied Japanese at a university in their home country prior to arriving in Japan. This means that when they started to live with their host families, their experience of learning Japanese shifted from classroom instruction centered on textbooks to daily interactions with their host family members. This chapter explores (1) how the homestay context has impacted their pragmatic development of speech style and (2) how the explanations about Japanese speech styles given in the Japanese language classes in their home institutions possibly differed from their experiences with style shifts in the homestay context. To investigate the second point, I will examine the descriptions of the *masu* and plain forms in the major Japanese language textbooks widely used in North America and other regions in the world. First, I will discuss the strength of the homestay context. I will argue that the study abroad experience, in particular the experience of staying with a host family, plays an important role in the acquisition of speech styles, and I will discuss the importance of the learner's agency in this process. Second, I will investigate if there are any discrepancies between L2 textbook descriptions of the *masu* form and the actual usages that are described in the present book. I will examine seven beginning-level Japanese language textbooks widely used in North America and other regions in the world, and present the results of the survey of these textbooks. What is found is that language textbook descriptions are permeated with prescriptivism rather than observations of actual interactions. Finally, the chapter suggests a way to introduce an indexical approach to language instruction.

## Contributions of Study Abroad Experiences to Learners' Acquisition of Speech Styles

### Interaction with the host family

Native speakers do not always have awareness of the different social meanings associated with a given linguistic index due to its semantic ambiguity deriving from its context dependency. As the number of contexts is unlimited, it is nearly impossible to list all the shades of the social meaning of a given index. This means that it is beyond native speakers' ability to describe to learners all the uses of an index in the target language. Discussing contextualization cues, which are a type of index, Gumperz (1996: 383) also points out that indexes are difficult to teach through direct instruction:

> Because of the complexity of the inferential processes involved and their inherent ambiguity, contextualization cues are not readily learned, and certainly not through direct instruction.

While indexical meanings of linguistic forms are difficult to teach by direct instructions, they are learned through participation in language-mediated activities. Family conversations provide rich interactional contexts that help novices acquire indexes. Study abroad experiences, in particular the experience of staying with a host family, play an important role in providing opportunities to fully participate in activities with native speakers of the target language. The learner is typically the center of attention during dinnertime and topics of conversation are often tailored to the learner. Host family members tell the learners about the host country's culture and social customs and ask about the learner's life both in the target community and in his or her home country (Cook, 2006a; DuFon, 2006; Iino, 1996, 2006; McMeekin, 2003, 2006). Further-more, interactionally they co-construct conversation with learners. Therefore, even when the learner's proficiency in the target language is low, the learner can be a participant in the talk. In this sense, homestay experiences provide an ideal context for learning the target language, in particular the social meanings of linguistic structures.

In the present data, the host family members provide learners with contexts in which the self-presentational stance indexes various social identities and relationships. It was found that the advanced-level learners in this study were able to index the self-presentational stance when playing the teacher role, taking charge of a task at hand, giving a presentation and speaking with the voice of other people. Two of the advanced-level learners, Ellen and Mary, have a mother who is a native speaker of Japanese. Although both Ellen and Mary report that they grew up speaking English at home, it is possible that they were socialized to use the *masu* form by participating as non-ratified participants in Japanese conversations that their mother engaged in with other native speakers of Japanese. What is remarkable is the case of Pete, who studied Japanese for only two and a half years prior to coming to Japan and spent a total of nine months with Japanese host families at the time of the data collection. His skillful shifts to the *masu* form in an appropriate manner suggest that it is possible for some JFL learners to become competent users of the *masu* form after staying in the country nine months on study-in-Japan programs. The novice learners also at times speak in the *masu* form in an appropriate fashion even if such a shift is made inadvertently.

In contrast to JFL learners in a homestay context, those who are in a foreign language classroom seem to have more difficulty learning style shifts in Japanese (i.e. appropriate shifts between the *masu* and plain forms). How the contexts of homestay and JFL classroom differ with respect to L2 language acquisition has not been fully investigated. McMeekin's (2003) study, which compares how JFL learners negotiate and use communication strategies in the two contexts, found that the homestay provides JFL learners with more opportunities for 'negotiation of meaning' (Gass & Varonis, 1985; Long, 1996). The term 'negotiation of meaning' is defined as an 'exchange in which there is some overt indication that understanding between participants has not been complete and there is a resultant attempt to clarify the non-under-standing' (Gass & Varonis, 1985: 39). The assumption about 'negotiation of meaning' in SLA research is that learners receive an increased amount of native speakers' input in the target language if they ask clarification questions when they do not comprehend. McMeekin (2003) concludes that in contrast to the context of the classroom, in which the time constraint to finish the instructional goals within the class period limits the amount of negotiation between the teacher and students, in the host family context, the family members are not constrained by time and thus provide more accommodation. They spend a longer time talking about various topics. In this process, learners have more opportunity to negotiate the meaning of linguistic expressions in the target language with host family members. Through negotiation, learners not only resolve difficulties in comprehension, but also gain more opportunities to receive input from native speakers. The findings of the present study are in line with those of McMeekin and suggest the important role homestay experiences play in the process of acquiring appropriate uses of the *masu* and plain forms.

## Learners' shift of dominant speech style

The present study finds that all the learners in this study usually speak with their host family members in the plain form. This finding is in line with those of studies in L2 pragmatics, which indicate that in general during a study abroad, learners acquire informal speech styles (cf. Kasper & Rose, 2002). Marriott (1993) also reports that all 11 Australian high school students who had spent a year with a Japanese host family predominantly used the plain form in the interview conducted soon after they returned from Japan. Her study hypothesized that students who had studied Japanese in their home institutions longer before the departure to Japan would use more *masu* forms. In her study, the students' prior study of Japanese ranged from two weeks to six years, but during the interview with native speakers of Japanese, all the students, regardless of the length of their Japanese study prior to the departure to Japan, spoke mostly in the plain form. These findings indicate that staying with a host family contributed to a shift in learners' dominant speech style.

As discussed later, most of the dialogues presented in beginning-level Japanese language textbooks widely used in North America are written in the *masu* form (cf. Matsumoto & Okamoto, 2003).[1] In the present data, all the JFL learners studied Japanese at a university in their home country for at least two years prior to going to Japan.[2] It is very likely that in the Japanese language classes they took in their home institution, the dominant speech style used was the *masu* form. They most likely learned to speak Japanese using the *masu* form in their textbooks.[3] This means that when they first arrived in Japan, they were *masu*-dominant speakers. In fact, all five learners in McMeekin's study (2007) chose the *masu* form as a dominant speech style when they first arrived at the home of their host family. In her study, the first recordings of their conversation with the host family members show that more than 90% of the intermediate-level learners' final predicate forms were in the *masu* form and that more than 56% of the advanced-level learners' final predicate forms were also in the *masu* form. The third recordings of the conversation, which took place at the end of the eight-week program, reveal that all except for one learner showed some increase in plain form uses and decrease in *masu* form uses. McMeekin's study suggests that as JFL learners become more integrated in the host family as in-group members, they gradually learn to shift to the plain form. At the time of data collection, all the learners in this study had spent four months or more with the host family. The fact that the learners in McMeekin's study are *masu*-form dominant speakers and the learners in this study are plain-form dominant speakers indicates that sometime between the second and fourth months while living with their host family, learners shift from *masu*-form dominance to plain-form dominance.

When asked on the questionnaire about difficult aspects of speaking Japanese, Pete was the only learner to mention speech style, which suggests that most learners are not aware of their own speech style when speaking to the host family. If they shifted their speech style from *masu*-form dominance to plain-form dominance as they become more integrated in the host family as an in-group member, it is a result of language socialization through their interactions with the host family and other contacts in Japanese society. For instance, Alice and Tom, both novice learners, studied Japanese in their home institution for about two years prior to going to Japan. At the time of the data collection, they had been living with their host family for four months. Within four months, they shifted to the plain form as their dominant speech style, at least in the homestay context.[4] This fact suggests that daily routine interactions with host family members and other contacts (e.g. Japanese peers) have a strong impact on learners' acquisition of the plain form. Furthermore, as discussed in Chapter 3, the predominant use of the plain form with occasional shifts to the *masu* form is the expected norm in Japanese family conversation. In this sense, the learners in this study demonstrated their competence to use the normative style shift pattern in Japanese family conversation at least some of the time. The advanced-level learners in this study also displayed their ability to shift to the *masu* form when they engaged in a demonstration, took on the voice of another person, and talked to outsiders. This fact suggests that they may be able to shift to the *masu* form when they assess a given social situation as the *soto* context, such as an interview. In sum, the strong suggestion put forward here is that homestay experience is a powerful language socialization resource, in which learners acquire speech styles appropriate to social context.

### The role of learners' agency in the acquisition of speech style

Many studies on L2 pragmatics indicate that learners' study abroad experiences do not guarantee their pragmatic development. Summarizing a wide variety of literature on L2 pragmatics, Kasper and Rose (2002: 220) claim that learners' agency within the host context is one of the important factors in learning L2 pragmatics. They state:

> ...residence in the host country alone holds no guarantee for successful pragmatic learning but...such learning depends on a range of societal and local conditions as well as the learners' agency within the host contexts.

The comment above is echoed by Siegal's (1994, 1996) findings that what is important is how language is used around the learner and how learners are actively involved in interactions with native speakers of the target language. Dewey (2005) too points out that greater individual differences are found among learners who studied abroad than among those who are studying the target language at-home in the classroom. The study abroad experience exposes learners to a variety of social contexts, and the literature suggests that learners who actively engage in conversation with native speakers in the target language in a wider range of contexts have an advantage in learning L2 pragmatics.

The findings of the present study are consistent with those of the previous studies. There are individual differences in terms of socialization into the appropriate use of the *masu* and plain forms in the host family context. Learners who actively seek opportunities to interact with the host family seem to be more successful in acquiring appropriate style shifts. For example, Kate and Pete are similar in terms of the college Japanese courses they took at their home institutions and their length of stay in Japan, but they have reached different levels of proficiency and their use of *masu* shows some striking differences. Kate studied Japanese at a university in England for two years prior to going to Japan, and at the time of the data collection, she had been staying with her host family for eight months. Pete took Japanese courses at a university in the USA for two and a half years before going to Japan. He first joined a semester-in-Japan program in northern Japan and stayed with a host family there for six months before joining the study abroad program in the Tokyo area and moving to the present host family three months before the data was collected. At the time of the data collection, he had been staying with host families for a total of nine months. Despite the similarity in their Japanese learning, their level of proficiency is quite different. Kate is at the novice/high proficiency level while Pete's is at the advanced level. As we saw in Chapter 5, their percentage of marked uses of the *masu* form reflects their Japanese proficiency level. While Kate's percentage of marked uses is 82.1%, Pete's is only 47%.

The differences in Kate and Pete's proficiency and their use of the *masu* might be due to their motivation and the ways that they interact with the host family. As shown in Table 7.1, some differences can be observed between Kate and Pete in terms of motivation and the linguistic environment in their host family.

Table 7.1 suggests that Pete's integrative motivation to study Japanese is higher than Kate's. Pete's reason for going to Japan to study Japanese is to be in a total immersion program in Japanese, whereas for Kate, studying in Japan for a year is required for her college degree. Similarly,

**Table 7.1** Motivation and linguistic environment of Kate and Pete

|  | *Kate (a novice-level learner)* | *Pete (an advanced-level learner)* |
|---|---|---|
| Reason for going to Japan to study Japanese | 'This is actually a required year of study abroad for my degree'. | 'Immersion is the best possible way (I believe) to acquire a higher level of proficiency'. |
| Language used in conversation with the host family | Japanese (100%) with host mother, Japanese (50%) and English (50%) with host brother | Japanese (99.9%), English (0.1%) |

while Pete says that he speaks almost all the time (99%) with his host family in Japanese, Kate reports that she speaks English with her host brother half the time. As Kate's host mother does not speak English, Kate speaks in Japanese regularly with the host mother. With the host brother, who can speak English, she has a choice of language, and she speaks English with him at least half of the time. In contrast, although Pete's host mother can speak English fairly fluently, both Pete and his host mother choose to speak Japanese without using English. Evidently, Pete has more opportunities to speak Japanese with his host family members.[5]

Furthermore, as suggested by the data in Examples (1) and (2), Pete seems to participate more actively in conversation with his host family members. Pete can use the *masu* form far more appropriately than Kate when talking with his host family. He talks about a wide range of topics, from Japanese and American customs to politics. He presents his own opinions and seeks his host family members' reactions. In contrast, Kate is interactionally less active. It is almost always her host family members who initiate a topic and elaborate on it. In most interactions, Kate is a recipient of talk rather than an initiator of a topic. The following examples illustrate this difference between Pete and Kate. In both Examples (1) and (2), the host family initiates topics concerning the learners' home country, i.e. the geography of the learner's home country and the climate of the learner's home country. Both are topics with which the learners are familiar.

(1) Pete 010603

```
1 HF: tekisasu tekisasu tte darasu   kuukoo no chikaku?
      Texas    Texas   QT Dallas    airport LK near
      'Texas,   Texas, is (your home) near  Dallas airport?'
```

```
2 P: iya austin koo austin nanka ichiban mannaka no [shi kyaputen tte
     No  Austin this Austin uh   most    middle  LK city Captin   QT
     yuu yo ne? =
     say FP FP
     'No, Austin, Austin, a city sort of in the middle (of the state).
     It's called Captin'.
```

```
3 HM:                                              [a (  )
                                                   oh
                                                   'Oh (   )'
```

```
4 HF: = iya iya kuukoo wa doko   na  no?
        no  no  airport Top where Cop FP
        'No, no where is the airport?'
```

```
5 P: kuukoo kuukoo mo  austin mo   arushi santa fe  mo   arushi
     airport airport also Austin also exist  Santa Fe  also exist
     'There is an airport, airport in Austin, also one in Santa Fe'.
```

demo   ichiban ookii wa darasu <u>da</u>
but    most   big  Top Dallas Cop
'But the biggest one is in Dallas'.

6 HM: a: hai hai  tekisasu de
      oh yes yes  Texas    in
      'Oh yes, yes, in Texas'

7 P: darasu nihon kara  wa  darasu    [made ore wa <u>notta</u> yo ne
     Dallas Japan from  Top Dallas       to   I  Top ride FP FP
     'Dallas, from Japan to Dallas, I flew'.

8 HM:                                 [un  un   un
                                      yeah yeah yeah
                                      'yeah yeah yeah'

(2) Kate 060804

1 HM: tabun   igirisu   no natsu   wa  mijikai to omou n <u>da</u> kedo =
      perhaps England LK summer Top short  QT think  Nom Cop but
      'Summer in England must be short, I think'.

2 K: un    totemo <u>mijikai</u>.
     yeah very      short
     'Yeah, it's very short'.

3 HM: mijikai  desho:?
      short    Cop
      'It's short, isn't it?'

4 K: hachigatsu da  to   motto
     August      Cop QT think
     'In August, it is more'

5 HM: [u:n <u>soo</u> ne
      yeah so  Cop
      'yeah, it is true'.

6 HB: [u:n
      uh huh
      'uh huh'

7 HM: moo hachigatsu no owari da to(.) kekkoo samukattari <u>suru</u> no ne
      already August LK end Cop if   fairly  cold become do FP FP
      'At the end of August, it already becomes fairly cold'.

8 K: un:
     yeah
     'Yeah'

9 HB: nihon wa  kugatsu chuujun gurai made [ja nai   ne
      Japan Top September middle about till    Neg  FP
      'In Japan it's (warm) till the middle of September, isn't it?'

10 HM:                             [un
                                uh huh
                                'uh huh'

When asked by the host father about the location of his home in Texas, Pete explains that it is in the middle of the state, like Austin, and that the town is called Captin. When further asked by the host father about the location of the airport, Pete describes airports in different locations in Texas. He not only answers the host father's questions, but also offers his personal story that he flew from Japan to Dallas. In contrast, when the host mother asks if the summer in England is short, Kate provides a short reply by repeating the same predicate (*mijikai* 'short'). In line 4, Kate tries to say something about August. The host mother gives a reactive token anticipating what Kate was going to say. Kate does not continue her turn to elaborate on the August climate in England. In line 7, the host mother fills in for Kate. At this point she could say something about her own personal experience such as wearing a sweater at the end of August but does not add any personal story. Pete's more active participation in talk may have to do with his higher proficiency level in Japanese. It is speculated that his active agency in talk can create more opportunities for negotiation of meaning (Gass & Varonis, 1985; Long, 1996), which may have helped him attain a higher proficiency level. The present study suggests that active agency on the part of the learner is important for acquiring the sociolinguistic competence of style shifts. The topics of the learner's agency and individual differences in terms of acquisition of honorifics and speech style merits future investigation.

## Descriptions of Speech Styles in Japanese Language Textbooks

### Textbooks versus authentic interaction

Since the late 1970s, the communicative language teaching movement has stressed the importance of the use of authentic teaching materials (e.g. Bardovi-Harlig *et al.*, 1991; Frommer, 1992; Harmer, 1983; Herron & Seay, 1991; Myers-Scotton & Bernsten, 1998; Nostrand, 1989; Wong, 2002). By the term 'authentic teaching materials', most scholars mean textbook dialogues and descriptions that are not invented with pedagogic intent by the author of the textbook, but those taken from naturally occurring discourse.[6] In other words, textbook dialogues created by textbook writers often lack linguistic and interactional features that are present in naturally occurring discourse. For example, often textbook dialogues lack back-channeling, which would typically occur in natural conversation (cf. Ono & Jones, 2005). It is argued that the use of authentic teaching materials is essential because (1) they motivate learners, (2) they prepare learners for the real world, (3) they provide cultural context and (4) there is no other alternative (i.e. invented dialogues are not adequate). Those calling for authentic teaching material presuppose that any dialogues invented by textbook writers are tinted by the writers' belief about the language. In the field of ESL, the use of authentic teaching materials is now an established practice.

In the area of Japanese as a foreign language, however, the ramifications of using unauthentic materials have just begun to be considered. A few researchers have examined the authenticity of dialogues used in Japanese language textbooks (Matsumoto & Okamoto, 2003; Ono & Jones, 2005; Siegal & Okamoto, 2003; Takahashi *et al.*, 1995). By studying naturally occurring talk in various social contexts, these studies have found gaps between the Japanese language presented in textbooks and the Japanese language used in the real world. They have found that dialogues in Japanese language textbooks are, for the most part, simplified and prescriptive. Takahashi *et al.* (1995) compared the dialogues in two beginning textbooks (JSL and Yokoso) with naturally occurring informal conversations between two female speakers in terms of morphosyntactic and lexical features. They found that the textbook conversations contained less complex syntactic structures, and fewer loan words and affective words, but used a wider variety of polite expressions. However, it is not sufficient to compare textbook dialogues with any type of naturally occurring discourse in terms of the frequencies of linguistic features. For pedagogical reasons, textbook dialogues typically include more formal interactions. Takahashi *et al.*'s conclusion that the textbook dialogues contained more formal expressions may be skewed due to the comparison of textbook dialogues with informal conversations. A comparison needs to be made between or among discourses of the same type.

Studying textbook descriptions of gender classification of sentence-final forms in Japanese, Siegal and Okamoto (2003) report that textbook descriptions of gender classification emphasize a stereotype of gender speech and give the false impression that these classifications must be strictly observed. Matsumoto and Okamoto (2003), who examined the representations of indirect expressions, speech styles (i.e. the *masu* and plain forms) and dialects in five major Japanese textbooks widely used in the USA, found that the textbooks simplify complex features associated with naturally occurring discourse. With respect to speech style, they compared two conversations between college students (one from a textbook conversation and the other from naturally occurring conversation) and illustrated that the textbook version overused the *masu* form. Example (3) is from the textbook and (4) is from the authentic discourse, both of which are taken from Matsumoto and Okamoto (2003). Example (3) is written exclusively in the *masu* form, whereas Example (4) is in the plain form. For readers who have no knowledge of Japanese, I have added glosses to the original text and in accordance with the convention used throughout this book, I have underlined the plain form and put the *masu* form in bold.

(3) [quoted from Matsumoto & Okamoto (2003: 35)]

(Textbook: *Yokoso*, p. 123; conversation among classmates in a university)

Brow: Sumimasen. Denwa wa **arimasu** ka.
    Excuse      phone Top  exist  Qt
    'Excuse me. Is there a phone?'
Hayashi: Ee, soko ni **arimasu**.
      yes there at exist
      'Yes, there is one over there'.
Gibson: Hayashi-san wa **imasu** ka.
      Hayashi Mr. Top exist  Q
      'Is Mr. Hayashi here?'

(4) [quoted from Matsumoto & Okamoto (2003: 35)]

(Naturally occurring conversation between college students)

Aki: Emi, piano no renshuu <u>shiteru</u>?
    Emi piano LK practice do
    'Emi, have you been practicing the piano?'
Emi: Un, <u>shiteru</u> yo.
    yeah do    FP
    'Yeah, I have'.
Aki: Itsu <u>dakke</u>? <u>Juu-gatsu</u>?
    when  Cop October
    'When is it? October?'
Emi: Juu-gatsu no <u>juuyokka</u>.
    October LK 14th
    'October the 14th'.
Aki: <u>Juushi</u>?
    14th
    'The 14th?'
Emi: Un.
    right
    'Right'.
Aki: Moo sugu <u>jan</u>.
    more soon isn't it
    'That's very soon, isn't it?'

Emi: Nee, moo    <u>sugu</u>.
  FP  more soon
  'Right, very soon'.
Aki: Nishuu-kan <u>gurai</u>, ato?
  Two weeks about later
  'In about two more weeks?'
Emi: Soo <u>da</u>  nee.
  so  Cop FP
  'Yeah, that's right'.

It is clearly shown in Examples (3) and (4) that the textbook version consistently uses the *masu* form in a conversation between two college classmates whereas the naturally occurring conversation between two college classmates is conducted in the plain form. However, there is a difficulty with this comparison. While we know these two dialogues are between college classmates, we do not know the relevant contextual information, e.g. exactly in what setting the dialogue took place, whether the classmates are close friends or not, the goal of the interaction, whether there is a third party present, and if so, what the relationship is between the college students and the third party. As textbook dialogues are usually not accompanied by specific contextual information, it is difficult, if not impossible, to make an impartial comparison between naturally occurring discourse and textbook dialogues.

## Textbook descriptions of Japanese speech styles

Although studies by Takahashi *et al.* (1995) and Matsumoto and Okamoto (2003) include brief observations regarding the treatment of the *masu* and plain forms in textbooks, as far as I know, there has been no research that focuses on the treatments of these forms in Japanese language textbooks. Here I examine how the *masu* and plain forms are introduced in the seven beginning-level Japanese language textbooks widely used in North America and other English-speaking countries. The seven beginning-level textbooks are:

- *An Introduction to Modern Japanese* [IMJ] (Mizutani & Mizutani, 1995)
- *Japanese for Busy People 1* [JBP] (Association for Japanese Language Teaching, 1996)
- *Genki 1: An Integrated Course in Elementary Japanese* [GK] (Banno *et al.*, 1999)
- *Yokoso: An Invitation to Contemporary Japanese* [YK] (Tohsaku, 1994)
- *Nakama: Japanese Communication* [NK] (Makino *et al.*, 1998)
- *Situational Functional Japanese vol. 1* [SFJ] (Tsukuba Language Group, 1992)
- *Japanese: The Spoken Language Part 1* [JSL] (Jorden & Noda, 1987)

The textbooks examined reveal an overemphasis on the *masu* form. This tendency seems to be due to the belief that the *masu* form is the correct speech style and the speech style to be used by foreigners. Because in Japanese the *masu* form is called *teineitai* ('the polite style'), as opposed to the plain form, which is called *futsuutai* ('the ordinary style'), most native speakers of Japanese have a conscious understanding that the *masu* form is a polite or formal speech marker, whereas the plain form is a non-polite or informal speech marker. Many Japanese language textbooks also provide similar explanations on the *masu* and plain forms.

Among the beginning-level textbooks listed, there are three groups with respect to the treatment of the *masu* and plain forms. IMJ, JBP and GK do not provide any explanations on these forms, and the dialogues, drills and texts are written in the *masu* form throughout the textbook. The impression that IMJ, JBP and GK give is that the *masu* form is the only speech style in Japanese. JBP and GK come in two volumes. JBP introduces the plain form in Lesson 17 of the second volume. Similarly, GK first presents the plain form in Lesson 14 of the second volume. Learners who use IMJ, JBP or GK do not learn from these textbooks that there are stylistic differences marked by the *masu* and plain forms in Japanese at the beginning level.

In contrast, YK and NK provide descriptions of the *masu* and plain forms, but the dialogues and other texts are all written in the *masu* form. The following are the descriptions of the plain and *masu* forms given in YK and NK.

*Yokoso: An Invitation to Contemporary Japanese* (1994)

> The *plain form* is used when speakers address very familiar people on the same social level, such as close friends. It is also used in diaries and in newspaper articles...On the other hand, the *polite form* is used, for instance, to address people with whom one is not well acquainted or to speak impersonally with in-group people (such as one's superior). In addition, it is used to address most out-group people, in personal letters, TV news, and most public speeches. The polite form is the appropriate speech register among adult speakers who are getting to know each other. (p. 187)

*Nakama: Japanese Communication* (1998)

> The polite form is used among acquaintances, people of different age-groups, and strangers in public places. It is also used in television and radio broadcasts and letters. The plain form is used among family members, young children, and close friends of the same age as well as in newspaper and magazine articles. (p. 144)

Both YK and NK refer to the *masu* form as the 'polite form', which implies that the form is used to show politeness to the addressee(s). The plain form is mentioned as a form to use between or among people who are in a close relationship, such as family members and good friends of the same age. In its written form, it is associated with newspapers and magazines. JFL learners who use textbooks such as YK or NK subjectively experience first-year Japanese language classes as a polite encounter with their instructors and peer students, or they may be under the impression that it is not appropriate to speak in the plain form among classmates.

SFJ and JSL are different from the rest of the textbooks in that they provide explanations of Japanese speech styles at the beginning level and incorporate some dialogues that are mainly in the plain form. However, in both textbooks, the majority of the dialogues are in the *masu* form. In SFJ Volume 1, out of the dialogues in eight lessons, only three lessons incorporate a brief dialogue with some plain form exchanges. JSL Volume 1 contains 11 lessons, out of which only Lesson 9 focuses on the plain form and introduces informal dialogues between close friends. Both textbooks explain that the *masu* form is a marker of distance. SFJ explains:

*Situational Functional Japanese vol. 1* (1992)

> There are two speech styles in Japanese, casual ( = informal) and formal, from which you make a choice according to the relationship between yourself (the speaker) and the listener. The plain form is used in casual style sentences, while the polite form is used in formal style sentences. (p. 48)

> The casual style is used between people who are close, such as family members or good friends. The formal style is used between speakers whose relationship is rather distant and formal, such as between strangers or between a student and a teacher. When one speaker is perceived to be of lower social status than the other (for instance, a junior student at school, or a company employee of lower rank), styles often occur on a one-way basis: the Lower will normally use the formal style towards the Higher, while the Higher might use the casual style in return. (p. 52)

Similarly, JSL mentions that the *masu* form marks linguistic distance between interlocutors. Therefore, JSL refers to the *masu* form as the distal style. JSL promotes the *masu* form because it is safer and correct for foreigners.

*Japanese: The Spoken Language Part 1* (1987)

> This style [*masu*] indicates that the speaker is showing solicitude toward, and maintaining some linguistic distance from, the addressee, i.e. s/h is being less direct and more formal as a sign of deference to the person addressed (and/or the topic of discussion), rather than

talking directly, intimately, familiarly, abruptly, or carelessly. This variety of speech is most generally acceptable for foreign adults just beginning their study of the language. (p. 32)

The comment that the *masu* form is the acceptable form for foreign adult learners reflects the belief that the *masu* form is for foreigners. JSL (1987) emphasizes the difficulty of style choices for non-native speakers of Japanese. It further states:

This concept of style in Japanese is extremely complex and constitutes one of the most difficult features of the language for the foreigner to master...Of course every language reflects stylistic differences (consider English 'How do you do?' versus 'Hi!', which are certainly not interchangeable) but the pervasiveness of the differences in Japanese is overwhelming. Every use of the language requires a stylistic choice. We are starting out with the "safest" style for foreign adult speakers, but other styles will be introduced soon. (p. 32)

The assertion that the *masu* form is the safest speech style for foreigners arises from the belief that foreigners should speak politely, which is generally shared in L2 teaching. The motivation is that learners of a foreign language will not offend native speakers of the target language by showing politeness.

However, it is not possible to discuss the appropriateness of a particular speech style without knowing the participants, topic, activity, goal and setting of talk. The *masu* form may be safe if the learner talks with the addressee in a *soto* ('outside/out-group') relationship. On the other hand, if the learner is trying to establish a close relationship with his or her Japanese college classmates, continuing to speak only in the *masu* form may prevent him or her from attaining the goal of making close Japanese friends or being fully integrated into the host family. In this case, the *masu* form is not the safest speech style. The belief that the *masu* form is safe for foreigners can keep learners from getting in a close *uchi* ('inside/in-group') circle in Japanese society. Besides, the majority of verbal interactions in Japanese are mixed in speech style. Perhaps sustaining the *masu* form without shifting to the plain form in all social contexts marks one as a foreigner. Having said this, I am not rejecting the practice of introducing the *masu* form first in textbooks, for textbooks have to start somewhere. What I am advocating is that textbooks incorporate explanations closer to reality.

Another aspect of a curriculum that overemphasizes the *masu* form is the prescriptive aspect. Within this approach, learners of a foreign language are expected to speak the target language 'correctly'. This attitude has been noted in various studies on JFL learners. Iino's study (1996), which investigated dinnertime conversations between 33

American JFL learners and their Japanese host families, found that most of the host families in this study, speakers of the Kyoto dialect, shift to standard Japanese when talking to the learners. Ohta (1993) surveyed how Japanese people responded when four advanced learners of Japanese spoke to them in Japanese. She reports that one of the learners was told by his Japanese friends that he should speak proper Japanese and was discouraged from speaking in a rough male speech style, because a rough male speech style was not deemed appropriate for foreigners. These reports suggest that the overemphasis on the *masu* form in textbooks may be related to a pervasive belief that the use of the *masu* is the 'correct' speech style for foreigners.

An argument for emphasizing the *masu* form at the novice level is that it is confusing for foreigners to learn the *masu* and plain forms at the same time. However, Matsumoto and Okamoto (2003: 38) caution against overemphasizing the *masu* form at the beginning level:

> Although the complexity of choice between formal and informal expressions may be too difficult for beginning learners to fathom, we should also be aware that language learners are not best served by over-emphasizing one style or by an over-simplified explanation based on a stereotype of Japanese society.

As the plain form is grammatically required in subordinate clauses regardless of speech style, the argument that it is too confusing to teach learners both *masu* and plain forms early is not tenable.[7]

## An Indexical Approach to the Instruction of the *Masu* Form

From the foregoing discussion, it is clear that none of the listed textbooks adequately explains how the *masu* forms are actually used in Japanese society. None mentions that the core meaning of the *masu* form is the self-presentational stance. Perhaps one of the reasons why the style shift is difficult for JFL learners may be that they learn the *masu* form as a polite or formal marker, which is only one of its social meanings, and hence that they cannot use it to index various social identities. In order to learn to use the *masu* form appropriately, learners need to learn its direct indexical meaning and the cultural knowledge that connects various social identities with the direct indexical meaning. Moreover, textbooks do not mention that the *masu* form is used between or among people in a close relationship, such as one finds in the family. However, as discussed in this book, the reality is that it is used in family conversation. Also, the converse is true. The plain form appears with the *masu* form in interviews and academic talk (Cook, 2006b; Ikuta, 1983; Megumi, 2002; Nazikian, 2007; Okamoto, 1998). However, according to Japanese textbooks, only the *masu* form should be used in these social contexts. The one-to-one mapping found in textbooks between the linguistic form (the *masu* form) and social meaning (politeness) is not capable of accounting for the multiple social meanings of the *masu* form. As discussed in this book, use of the *masu* form in conversation between a professor and a student during the professor's office hours can be interpreted as a marker of politeness. At the same time, it indexes the professional relationship between the two. In the *happyoo* activity in elementary schools, the self-presentational stance of the *masu* form indexes the activity of *happyoo* as well as the identity of the speaker as a presenter. It does not necessarily indicate politeness to the addressees. Textbook descriptions of the *masu* form, however, give the impression that the social meaning of the *masu* form is limited to politeness and formality. Such descriptions are static and cannot capture the dynamic nature of the indexical functions.

While evaluating different approaches to teaching Japanese speech style is beyond the scope of this book, I would like to suggest that Japanese language instruction should incorporate an indexical approach to the *masu* form. What I mean by *indexical approach* is that language is context dependent and is a tool to accomplish interactional goals. As evidenced in the first language socialization of Japanese children, the direct indexical value of an index is the source of a variety of situational meanings. For example, applying the core meaning of the *masu* form (the self-presentational stance or *shisei o tadasu*) in different situations, caregivers index social identity of 'the mother', 'teacher' and 'playful person' among others. I propose that this core meaning of the *masu* form be introduced at the beginning-level of Japanese language instruction. Once the direct indexical value of the *masu* form is explained to learners, then they can have opportunities to apply it to a wider range of social contexts, as their knowledge of cultural practices of the target language develops. Learners do not have to memorize each and every social meaning that the *masu* form indexes in different social contexts. Rather, they need to know the unmarked cultural patterns of behavior. Once JFL learners have learned that the *masu* form is an index of the self-presentational stance (*shisei o tadasu*), they can develop the knowledge of where in Japanese society people typically display the self-presentational stance (*shisei o tadasu*).

The concepts of the *uchi* ('inside/ingroup') and *soto* ('outside/outgroup') contexts should be introduced as well. As discussed by researchers on Japanese language and culture (Bachnik & Quinn, 1994), the distinction between *uchi* and *soto* contexts has cultural significance in Japanese society. Although the *masu* form does not have a one-to-one indexical relation with *soto*, it can either evoke the *soto* context or its social meaning can be narrowed down by the framing of the *uchi* or *soto* context. The *soto* context is the one in which Japanese people are more likely to be concerned about being watched by others. Hence they tend to act in role on stage. In contrast, the *uchi* context is that in which Japanese people are off-stage and free from inhibition (Lebra, 1976; Maynard, 1993). The stance displayed on stage is the self-presentational stance the *masu* form indexes. Family conversation is a prototypical *uchi* context, where habitually the family members are off-stage, but at times they show the self-presentational stance when they are in charge of, responsible for or have authority over the matter related to their situational social identity or speak in another's voice. These patterns of verbal behavior are the norms of Japanese family conversation. However, as the speaker is a free agent who can choose how to speak, he or she may not always observe the normative patterns of verbal behavior in order to accomplish a certain communicative goal.

The above explanation from the point of view of the indexical approach has an advantage over the structural approach, which assumes a one-to-one mapping between a linguistic form and social meaning and social rules that govern language use. First, the indexical approach does not explain how language is used by external social rules (e.g. prescriptive rules) that the speaker has to observe. As we have seen in actual practice, speakers choose to observe or deviate from prescriptive rules (e.g. the *masu* form is a politeness marker). This approach conceptualizes the learner as an active participant in interaction. Also this approach explains individual variations among speakers. Failure to observe a normative usage is no longer seen as a violation of social rules. Thus, learners' deviation from the normative usage is not considered as an error. Rather, when learners do not choose the normative usage, they are understood to be indexing social meanings different from those of the norm. Socialization is a process in which learners acquire knowledge as to what is the normative pattern of usage associated with a given social context. It is this knowledge that enables learners to deviate from the normative pattern to successfully index their identities outside of the norm.

An indexical approach to teach speech styles requires a detailed analysis of social situations by instructors, but such an analysis can enhance the learners' awareness of the indexical values of speech styles. For example, if in a role-play the learner as a college student speaks to a professor in the plain form, the language instructor can point out that the student's use of the plain form indicates that he or she is off-stage and has acted toward the professor as if he or she is the learner's close friend. The instructor can then provide some instances in which the student may speak with the professor in the plain form. The instructor can add that the normative pattern is to speak in the *masu* form to index a mutual professional relationship as well as show politeness to the professor. The self-presentational stance indexed by the *masu* form can simultaneously accomplish these communicative goals. The instructor's comment on what social meanings are indexed in particular social contexts given the direct indexical meaning of the *masu* form may help make learners 'notice' the contextual features surrounding the *masu* form (Schmidt, 1993, 1995).

## The Importance of Analysis of Social Contexts

In order to teach Japanese speech styles from the point of view of the indexical approach, it is essential to investigate in detail how the *masu* and plain forms are employed in a wide range of social contexts. However, native speakers' intuition is often limited to prescriptive uses, and hence is not always reliable (cf. Silverstein, 2001). Research on speech styles using questionnaire surveys as a research method may find the subjects' beliefs about usage, but these beliefs do not necessarily reflect accurate descriptions of real use. Recently, a number of scholars have begun to explore the Japanese speech styles in various social contexts, which reveals the complexity and diverse nature of the phenomenon. They have investigated uses of the *masu* and plain forms in interviews (Cook, 1998; Ikuta, 1983, 2002; Nazikian, 2007), elementary school classroom interactions (Anderson, 1995; Cook, 1996a), family dinner talk (Cook, 1996b, 1997), talk in academic settings (Cook, 2006b; Megumi, 2002), sales talk (Okamoto, 1998) and written discourse (Makino, 2002; Maynard, 1993). These studies reveal that the *masu* form helps construct various social identities and activities, indexes affective dispositions, and helps organize discourse structures. They also inform us that the *masu* and plain forms are not used in the same way in every social context and that there are always individual variations. Future research needs to examine a wider range of social contexts and explore how style shifts are utilized as resources to construct aspects of context.

Research on a wider range of social contexts will contribute to L2 pragmatics and pedagogy. One of the current problems with L2 pragmatics is that the native speakers' norm is treated as a homogeneous entity. As discussed above, this attitude is reflected in textbooks. Findings from future research will make it possible to specify a particular native speaker norm in a given social context. For example, a non-reciprocal exchange of the *masu* and plain forms may index difference in status in institutional talk, or in contexts where the social status is foregrounded. In this case, the lower-status person may speak in the *masu* form and the higher-status person in the plain form. In contrast, a non-reciprocal exchange of the *masu* and plain forms may index the *masu* user's self-presentational stance, which is linked to their situational social identity. In a conversation between a mother and her child, the mother may speak in the *masu* form to index the voice of 'mother', while the child speaks in the plain form. Here, the non-reciprocal exchange does not foreground a status difference.

In future research, scholars and language instructors also need to qualitatively examine both native speakers' and learners' uses of the *masu* and plain forms, for any social interaction is a joint achievement of the participants. For example, to study how learners use the *masu* form in a formal interview with a native speaker of Japanese, it is important to qualitatively analyze interview data. Only qualitative data can inform us if the shifting pattern is in line with the native speaker's norm in the *soto* or *uchi* context. Researchers also need to investigate how native speakers use the *masu* and plain forms in such an interview, for the way learners use these forms will undoubtedly be affected by the ways in which the interviewers use them. In sum, the analysis of speech styles in various contexts from the perspective of joint construction of social interaction will help improve textbook descriptions of the *masu* and plain forms and help language instructors.

## Conclusion

In relation to the findings presented in the earlier chapters, this chapter has explored how study abroad experiences and descriptions in textbooks may influence learners' acquisition of the speech styles. It showed that the homestay experience provides learners with a good opportunity to carry on conversation in Japanese as a ratified conversational participant. However, learners' agency is important. To become a proficient user of style shifts, the learner needs to actively engage in conversation.

We have seen that the textbook descriptions of Japanese speech styles do not necessarily reflect attested usages. Textbooks describe the *masu* form as a marker of politeness or formality and encourage learners to use the *masu* form because it is a 'safe form' for foreigners. Typically, in the language classroom, learners are given instructions that are in line with textbook descriptions. However, most social interactions in Japanese are not carried out in a single speech style. In order to skillfully shift from one style to the other to attain a communicative goal, learners need to acquire the core indexical meaning of the *masu* form and the sociocultural knowledge as to when to display the self-presentational stance. This is a challenging goal for JFL learners, but the present study suggests that it is an attainable goal. The nine learners of this study had at least two years of Japanese instruction at their home institution before going to Japan. Perhaps they learned to use the *masu* form as a marker of politeness in the classroom. But four months after arriving in the host family's home, many of them have learned to speak with the host family members mostly in the plain form, and sometimes appropriately shift to the *masu* form. Even novice-level learners show some signs of accomplishment at times. What is noted in this study is that all the host families report that they consider the learner as a member of the family, and for the most part, they do not alter much the habitual speech style pattern of Japanese family conversation, by using foreigner talk for example. Although there are differences in interactional styles among the host families, in general, the family members do not speak to the learner in the same manner as they would speak to outside guests. Such discursive practice on the part of the families may help learners develop their sense of identity in the host family. Wade (2003: 12), who herself is a learner of Japanese and once studied in Japan, examined style shifts in classroom interactions in six schools both in Japan and the USA and makes the following comments:

> For a non-native speaker of Japanese . . . the exact social consequences associated with particular use of language may be unclear; thus, the linguistic place being expressed may be dissociated in the speaker's awareness from its possible consequences for social place.

Perhaps, while participating in a study abroad program, learners gradually develop a sense of their own identity in the host family, school, and community. In other words, learners need to be included in meaningful interaction with native speakers of the target language. Based on the present study and the previous studies that discuss L2 learner's social identities (Siegal, 1994, 1996; Wade, 2003), it is speculated that the most important factor for JFL learners to acquire appropriate uses of the *masu* form is to fully participate in Japanese life with a certain sense of who they are and what is expected of them.

## Notes

1. For example, in the production (speaking and writing) sections of the advanced placement (AP) Japanese Language and Culture Exam, which is designed for students who have taken 300 hours of instructions of Japanese at college level, students are expected to produce the *masu* form regardless of the social contexts given in the exam (Tohsaku, 2006, HATJ pre-workshop presentation).
2. Mary only studied Japanese in college for one year prior to going to Japan, but her mother is a native speaker of Japanese.
3. In the present study, the specific Japanese textbooks each learner used in the Japanese language course(s) are not identified. It would be interesting to investigate in a future study whether the type of textbook used in the classroom and the instructional style have a long-term effect on learners' style shifts in interaction with native speakers of Japanese.
4. Four learners in the present study had been staying with their host families for four months at the time of the data collection. The rest of the learners had been staying with their host families longer than four months.
5. There is no indication in the data that the host family of Pete insists on speaking Japanese.

6. Some scholars, however, question this definition and argue that textbook dialogues and descriptions are also 'authentic', because they are a form of language learner literature (see Day, 2005).
7. In fact, most beginning-level Japanese textbooks introduce the plain form as the form required in the subordinate clause and as a noun modifier.

# Chapter 8
## *Conclusion*

This chapter summarizes the main points presented in the book, briefly discusses contributions of the study, and proposes directions for future research.

### Summary of the Main Points

This book has explored how Japanese host families express their identity through the use of the so-called 'addressee honorific' *masu* form and how JFL learners are socialized through its use. This book distinguishes itself from other investigations of the *masu* form in its theoretical perspective and in its focus on informal social contexts, specifically conversation between learners of Japanese and their host families. Taking an indexical approach, this study has challenged the view that the *masu* form has a one-to-one relation with social meaning. Rather, adopting Ochs' (1996) two-step indexical model, it argued that the *masu* form has multiple social meanings. Because the *masu* form directly indexes an affective stance of self-presentation (i.e. *shisei o tadasu* 'to hold oneself up'), it evokes various social identities, politeness and/or formality in different social contexts. In this way, the indexical model can account for the fluidity of social meanings of the *masu* form. As an index, the social meaning of the *masu* form depends in part on the social context in which it occurs. Therefore, in the *uchi* ('in-group/inside') context, the *masu* form foregrounds various social identities. In contrast, in the *soto* ('out-group/outside') context, it indexes politeness because politeness is socially expected in this context.

The book also drew on a language socialization perspective (Ochs, 1988, 1990, 1996; Ochs & Schieffelin, 1995; Schieffelin & Ochs, 1986, 1996) to argue that in conversation with the host families, learners are socialized into the norms of *masu* form usage. They are socialized both explicitly to use language and implicitly through the use of language (Schieffelin & Ochs, 1986). Socialization to use language can be seen in the host families' explicit instructions on how to speak to different categories of people outside the home (Chapter 6). Socialization through the use of language is seen in the process of learning to associate direct index of the *masu* form (i.e. the self-presentational stance) with various social meanings (cf. Ochs, 1996) (Chapters 3–5).

Chapter 3 concentrated on the analysis of the *masu* form and its uses by Japanese families. Based on a critical review of the literature, it was argued that previous studies failed to capture the dynamic nature of the *masu* form because they assumed a direct one-to-one relationship between the *masu* form and politeness or formality. Then, Ochs' two-step model of indexical relation (Ochs, 1996) was introduced, and it was demonstrated that this model can explain various social meanings associated with the *masu* form. I also illustrated that the context of *uchi* ('inside/in-group') and *soto* ('outside/out-group') mediate interpretation of the *masu* form. Then the discussion turned to a qualitative analysis of *masu* form usage in Japanese family conversation. Drawing on previous studies (Clancy, 1985; Cook, 1996a, 1997, 1998; Nakamura, 2002; Takagi, 2002), it was shown that while Japanese family members speak mainly in the plain form, they occasionally shift to the *masu* form in predictable ways. The *masu* form used in Japanese family conversation most commonly occurs in (1) set formulas; (2) the display of various social identities linked to the responsibility or authority of the parent(s); and (3) reported speech. Even children as young as three years old can occasionally shift to the *masu* form appropriately when displaying that they are good children. It was illustrated that in Japanese family conversation, young Japanese children are first exposed to and learn the *masu* form as a direct index of the self-presentational stance. Because of the ways in which parents use the *masu* form, direct index of the *masu* form evokes the identity of a person with responsibility or authority in the household or of someone outside the family circle. Japanese families' shifting patterns discussed in this chapter were used as a basis in evaluating the shifting patterns found in the homestay context in Chapters 4 and 5.

Chapter 4 qualitatively analyzed dinnertime conversation between JFL learners and their host families, focusing on participants' identity construction through use of the *masu* form. It was found that both learners and host families speak in the plain form most of the time and that they also shift to the *masu* form in ways similar to Japanese families. In other words, they tend to shift to the *masu* form when (1) uttering set formulas, (2) highlighting various aspects of their social identities associated with the homestay context and (3) foregrounding identities of speakers in reported speech. In particular, the latter two uses provide them with tools to create a range of social identities both in and outside the family context. In this way, the social identities of host family members can be linked to their duties, responsibilities and/or authority in the immediate social context (e.g. host parent). Through the *masu* form, learners can also construct various social identities such as someone in charge, English teacher and presenter. Through the host family members' use of direct quotations, learners are given opportunities to learn how conversation with people outside the host family is carried out. In sum, Chapter 4 demonstrated that while the *masu* form occurs relatively infrequently in the homestay context, it is an important linguistic resource for expressing a variety of social identities and it can be used to socialize learners to become speakers who can competently display a range of social identities.

Whereas Chapter 4 explored unmarked uses of the *masu* form (i.e. *masu* usage normally found in Japanese family conversation), Chapter 5 investigated marked uses of the *masu* form (i.e. those that rarely occur in Japanese family conversation). The chapter examined the frequencies of marked choices made by the learners and host families, and attempted to explain why marked uses occur in the homestay context. In the present study, it was found that advanced learners made fewer marked choices in interaction with their host family. This finding suggests that the frequency of marked uses decreases as learners become more proficient in Japanese. While the data size of the present study is not large enough to make any generalization, this finding can serve as a hypothesis for future research.

In this study, the percentage of marked use of *masu* by the host families is much lower than that of the learners. Moreover, the host families' frequency of marked choice is more or less in proportion to their overall frequency of the *masu* form. It was found that the host families' frequency of the *masu* form is linked to different interactional styles (e.g. a teaching or non-teaching voice and accommodation). Host families that use a teaching voice exhibit relatively frequent *masu* uses, both marked and unmarked, and often use it in describing Japanese language and culture. In other words, they play the role of a teacher of Japanese language and culture. In contrast, host families that do not use a teaching voice are characterized by infrequent *masu* uses and the absence of the *masu* form when telling the learner about Japanese language and culture. Host families that use a teaching voice prefer a somewhat distant interactional style, or what Brown and Levinson (1987) refer to as 'negative politeness'. Of the families studied, two were identified as families who use a teaching voice; the other five were identified as families who use a non-teaching voice. Another marked use of *masu* occurred in instances of accommodation. This type was only found when the host mother of the least proficient learner used 'foreigner talk' (Ferguson, 1981).

Because an increased frequency of the *masu* form in family conversation – in particular, marked uses – discursively indexes a distant relationship between interlocutors, participants' perception of their social relationship is expected to be more distant in host families where a teaching voice is used. However, it was found that there was no clear association between higher frequencies of the *masu* form (both marked and unmarked) and the participants' perception of increased social distance. Perhaps other linguistic and non-linguistic factors affected the perception of closeness or distance. This finding suggests that social meanings of the *masu* form are beyond the limits of the average Japanese speakers' awareness (cf. Silverstein, 2001).

In contrast to Chapters 3–5, in which the focus was on 'implicit language socialization' (Schieffelin & Ochs, 1986), Chapter 6 explored ways in which host family members explicitly socialize learners into polite linguistic behavior. The chapter showed that explicit language socialization was used to teach novices through modeling and meta-linguistic explanations of sociolinguistic rules. For example, the host family members modeled appropriate expressions for different formal occasions outside the homestay context. In addition, during some special occasions – such as a tea ceremony – that took place in the home, modeling included both the *masu* form and referent honorifics. Such special occasions provided learners with a unique opportunity to learn to use referent honorific expressions, as these expressions are not normally used in dinnertime conversation.

In the present study, two host mothers who use a teaching voice explicitly explain their folk beliefs on sociolinguistic rules concerning gendered speech and polite language. While these explanations do not necessarily reflect actual practices of the Japanese people, they do seem to affect learners' choice of linguistic expressions, and thus socialize them into the Japanese discourse of gendered speech or polite language. In the present study, no instance of explicit socialization to use the *masu* form alone (e.g. You should use the *masu* form when talking to a higher status person) was found. Rather, when the *masu* form is used in the host mothers' sociolinguistic description, it is part of other features such as gendered speech or referent honorifics. Furthermore, in questionnaires I distributed to the host families and learners, none of the participants commented on style shifts as a difficult aspect of speaking Japanese. The participants focused on the referential content of conversation when talking to each other, and were not consciously aware of which form they were using. The chapter concluded that, due to the unconscious nature of speech style, the *masu* form alone is not treated as an object of metalinguistic description.

Chapter 7 examined the impact of the homestay context on learners' pragmatic development of speech style and compared *masu* usage in the host family with the presentation of the *masu* and plain forms in seven widely used beginning-level JFL textbooks. It was found that the experience of staying with a host family plays an important role in the acquisition of the normative style shift patterns in the *uchi* ('inside/ in-group') context. Given that most beginning-level Japanese language textbooks emphasize the *masu* form over the plain form, the learners must have learned to speak in the *masu* form in their Japanese classes before going to Japan. Therefore, the observed shift in the learners' speech from *masu*-form dominance to plain-form dominance must have occurred as a result of language socialization through participation in daily interactions with their host families and peers. Even novice-level learners could at times shift from the plain form to the *masu* form in an unmarked manner. These facts suggest that the study abroad experience socialized learners to shift from dominant use of the *masu* form to the plain form and to appropriately use the *masu* form in conversation with their host family.

The survey of JFL textbooks revealed that their descriptions are permeated with prescriptivism and overemphasize *masu* usage. Although idealized dialogues serve a pedagogical purpose, it was argued that dialogues in textbooks should reflect actual usage. To provide more effective instruction on Japanese speech style, teachers are encouraged to analyze social contexts and to introduce an indexical approach to language instruction.

## Contributions of the Study and Directions for Future Research

The analysis presented in this book contributes to our understanding of (1) indexicality, (2) language socialization and (3) L2 pragmatics, particularly in the study abroad context. First, focusing on speech style, this book illustrated ways in which indexicality operates in conversation. The analysis showed that Ochs' two-step model of indexical relations can account for how a semantic fluidity of an index is contextually determined. The account presented in this book enriches our understandings of indexicality in naturally occurring language. In particular, it contributes to research on affect markers (e.g. lexical items denoting affective dispositions, pragmatic particles and certain grammatical constructions) and epistemic markers (e.g. evidentials, and pragmatic particles). Secondly, this book contributes to the research agenda on language socialization. Ochs (1996, 2002) claims that indexical knowledge is at the core of linguistic and cultural competence and that language socialization is the process involved in acquiring this knowledge. While there have been a number of studies on language socialization, most of them have dealt with explicit socialization processes (e.g. Duff & Hornberger, 2008). Few studies have closely examined multiple social meanings of a linguistic index and the ways in which novices are implicitly socialized to connect the linguistic form with its various social meanings. In this way, this book substantiated Ochs' theoretical claim by investigating the processes by which JFL learners gain linguistic and cultural competence in using the *masu* form. Thirdly, this book contributes to our understanding of the acquisition of speech style in the study abroad context. In the study abroad context, previous investigations of pragmatics have examined the acquisition of routines

(DuFon, 1999, 2006), registers (Marriott, 1993, 1995), terms of address (DuFon, 1999; Siegal, 1994), speech acts (Barron, 2003; Churchill, 2002; Hoffman-Hicks, 1999; Kondo, 1997) and host family interaction (Cook, 2006a; Iino, 1996, 2006; Knight & Schmidt-Rinehart, 2002). This book is the first to focus solely on speech style in the homestay context and to document language socialization into and acquisition of appropriate uses of the *masu* form.

In terms of method, this book has demonstrated the importance of qualitative analysis of spoken data in order to study speech style, in particular the speech styles of JFL learners. Some studies on JFL learners' use of the *masu* and plain forms (e.g. Marriott, 1993) have not included a qualitative analysis of spoken data because they assume that the *masu* form is simply a polite form. This book showed that a deeper analysis is required to study style-shift phenomenon. Crucial questions revolve around when and in what ways speakers shift their styles. What type of activities are learners and host family members engaged in when they are most likely to shift to the *masu* form? Are learners' shifts random or in line with the normative shifting patterns of native speakers of Japanese? When and what types of marked use of the *masu* form do learners and host family members choose? What do marked uses index in a given context? Does a learner's failure to make an unmarked choice mean that they failed to appropriately assess the social context? How does the speech style used by the host family members affect the choice of the learners' speech style? Without qualitative analysis of spoken data, such as that used in this book, it is not possible to answer these questions.

While the qualitative analysis used in this book has its strengths, there are also limitations in this approach. Namely, only nine pairs of JFL learners and their host families were examined. Due to the small size of the study, there is insufficient data to draw conclusions based on statistical analysis. For example, it was found that the frequency of the learners' unmarked *masu* choices was proportionate to their proficiency. It remains to be seen whether this finding can be statistically substantiated in a larger study.

As the present study is a cross-sectional study, it does not address the issue of changes in speech style in the homestay context over a period of time. It is generally assumed that the longer the period of association, the closer a human relationship becomes. Thus, it is expected that the relationship between a learner and his or her host family will change over time. When a learner and host family meet for the first time, they are more likely to treat each other in a *soto* ('out-group/outside') relationship. But over time, the learner is more likely to be incorporated into his or her host family as an in-group member. Reflecting such changes in their relationship, do both learners and their host families change their speech style over a period of time (i.e. from dominant use of the *masu* form to use of the plain form)? If so, when and how does such a change occur? Or do they start to talk to each other mainly in the plain form even from their first encounter? Are there individual differences in speech style among learners as well as host family members? McMeekin's study (2007) indicates that learners predominantly use the *masu* form to speak with their host family members for the first two months with a gradual increase in the plain form. However, because of the short duration of the study-in-Japan program that she investigated, her study alone does not answer the question of how learners' speech style changes over a long period of time. Based on the findings of the present study and those of McMeekin, we can speculate that somewhere between the second and fourth months of staying with the host family, learners shift from *masu*-form dominance to plain-form dominance. An ethnographic study examining the speech style of several learners and their host families over the period of a study abroad program (about one academic year) could more accurately answer the above questions. Such studies can document ways in which learners and their host families change their relationship over the course of the homestay and how changes in their relationship are (or are not) reflected in speech style.

The present study discussed different interactional styles of the host families based on the frequency of their *masu* form. However, it is not clear to what extent these differences in interactional style affect learners' acquisition of appropriate uses of the *masu* form. A long-term ethnographic study could help determine if such differences have any impact on learners' acquisition of appropriate uses of the *masu* form. It is also important to document learners' contact in Japanese society outside of their host family. For example, learners' interactions with their Japanese peers are an important socialization resource as well. Clearly, more research needs to be conducted to investigate to what extent both host families and peers contribute to learners' language socialization.

## Appendix 1
# Questionnaire for JFL Learners

Name:
Univesity:
e-mail address:

List all Japanese language courses you have taken at any university, college or community collage, beginning with the most recent.

School     Course     Instructor     Semester/year     Grade

_____

_____

_____

_____

_____

_____

_____

List other Japanese instruction you have received.

School     Course     Instructor     Semester/year     Grade

_____

_____

_____

_____

_____

_____

_____

Your native language: _____ English _____ other (specify)_____

Check if either of your parents or anyone else with whom you have lived for a substantial length of time is a native speaker of Japanese:

_____ mother _____ father _____other (specify)_____

How many months/years have you lived in Japan?

TOTAL number of years of residence in Japan _____
From year_____ to year_____ (age_____to age_____)

Please answer the following:

1. What is the main reason why you are studying Japanese?

2. Why did you decide to come to Japan to study Japanese?

3. Do you feel you are accepted as a member of your host family?

4. Do you speak mostly in Japanese with your host family?

_____% speak in Japanese
_____% speak in English

5. Can the members of your host family speak English?

6. What do you learn most when you speak in Japanese with your host family?

7. What is the most difficult thing when you speak in Japanese with your host family?

8. When you speak with your host parents, you feel you are treated like
   _____a young child
   _____a college age son/daughter
   _____a foreign student
   _____other (specify)_____

9. How often do you eat meals with your host family?

10. What other activities do you do with your host family?

11. Do you feel that your host family tries to speak Japanese slowly to you?

12. Any other comments about speaking Japanese.

## Appendix 2
# Questionnaire for Host Families (English Translation)

Please answer the following questions:

Name:
Family members:
Name of JFL learner:

1. Average length of time you spend with the learner per day (week days)
1 hour____, 2 hours____, 3 hours____, more than 3 hours

2. Average length of time you spend with the learner per day (weekend)
1 hour____, 2 hours____, 3 hours____, more than 3 hours

3. What percent of the time do you and the learner speak in Japanese?
90% or more ____, 80% or more____, 70% or more____, 60% or more____,
50% or more____, 40% or more____, 30% or more____, 20% or more____

4. Whom does the learner speak to?
host father___, host mother___, host siblings___, Other___ (          )

5a. Reason for becoming a host family for JFL learners


5b. How many times have you hosted a JFL learner?


6. We feel our JFL learner is
   a. _____ a member of the family.
   b. _____ a guest.

7. If you answer that your JFL learner is a member of the family:
   a. _____ We treat him/her in the same manner as we treat our own son/daughter.

b. _____ We treat him/her in a manner a little more distant than we treat our own son/daughter.

8. What do you talk about with the learner in Japanese?

9. What concerns you most when you talk with the learner in Japanese?

10. What is the most difficult thing when you talk with the learner in Japanese?

11. If you have any additional information you would like to share, please provide it below.

# References

Agha, A. (1998) Stereotypes and registers of honorific language. *Language in Society* 27, 151–193.

Anderson, F. (1995) Classroom discourse and language socialization in a Japanese elementary-school setting: An ethnographic-linguistic study. Unpublished doctoral dissertation, University of Hawaii-Manoa.

Aoki, H. (1986) Evidentials in Japanese. In W. Chafe and J. Nichols (eds) *Evidentiality: The Linguistic Coding of Epistemology* (pp. 223–238). Norwood, NJ: Ablex.

Association for Japanese Language Teaching (1996) *Japanese for Busy People: New, Unique Approach to Effective Daily Communication in Japanese.* Tokyo: Kodansha International.

Austin, J. L. (1962) *How to Do Things with Words.* Oxford: Oxford University Press.

Bachnik, J. (1994) Introduction: *Uchi/soto*: Challenging our conceptualizations of self, social order, and language. In J. Bachnik and C. Quinn (eds) *Situated Meaning: Inside and Outside in Japanese Self, Society, and Language* (pp. 3–37). New Jersey: Princeton University Press.

Bachnik, J. and Quinn, C. (1994) *Situated Meaning: Inside and Outside in Japanese Self, Society, and Language.* New Jersey: Princeton University Press.

Bakhtin, M. (1981) *The Dialogic Imagination: Four Essays.* M. Holoquist (ed.). Austin, TX: University of Texas Press.

Banno, E., Ohno, Y., Sakane, Y., Shinagawa, C. and Tokashiki, K. (1999) *Genki: An Integrated Course in Elementary Japanese.* Tokyo: The Japan Times.

Bardovi-Harlig, K. and Hartford, B. (1990) Congruence in native and nonnative conversations: Status balance in the academic advising session. *Language Learning* 40 (4), 467–501.

Bardovi-Harlig, K., Hartford, B., Mahan-Taylor, R., Morgan, M.J. and Reynolds, D.W. (1991) Developing pragmatic awareness: Closing the conversation. *ELT Journal* 45, 4–15.

Barron, A. (2003) *Acquisition in Interlanguage Pragmatics. Learning How to do Things with Words in a Study Abroad Context.* Amsterdam: John Benjamins.

Bateson, G. (1972) *Steps to an Ecology of Mind.* New York: Ballantine Books.

Bayley, R. and Schecter, S. (2003) *Language Socialization in Bilingual and Multilingual Societies.* Clevedon: Multilingual Matters.

Besnier, N. (1990) Language and affect. *Annual Review of Anthropology* 19, 419–451.

Blum-Kulka, S. (1997) *Dinner Talk: Cultural Patterns of Sociability and Socialization in Family Discourse.* New Jersey: Lawrence Erlbaum.

Bourdieu, P. (1977) *Outline of a Theory of Practice* (R. Nice, trans.) Cambridge: Cambridge University Press.

Brown, P. and Levinson, S. (1978) Universals in language usage: Politeness phenomena. In E. Goody (ed.) *Questions and Politeness: Strategies in Social Interaction* (pp. 56–324). Cambridge: Cambridge University Press.

Brown, P. and Levinson, S. (1987) *Politeness: Some Universals in Language Usage.* Cambridge: Cambridge University Press.

Bucholtz, M. (1999) "Why be normal?": Language and identity practices in a community of nerd girls. *Language in Society* 28, 203–223.

Bucholtz, M. and Hall, K. (2004) Language and identity. In A. Duranti (ed.) *A Companion to Linguistic Anthropology* (pp. 369–394). Malden, MA: Blackwell.

Burdelski, M. J. (2006) Language socialization of two-year old children in Kansai, Japan: The family and beyond. Unpublished doctoral dissertation, University of California-Los Angeles.

Chafe, W. and Nichols, J. (1986) *Evidentiality: The Linguistic Coding of Epistemology.* Norwood: Ablex.

Chomsky, N. (1965) *Aspects of the Theory of Syntax.* Cambridge, MA: MIT Press.

Churchill, E. (2002) The effect of a short-term exchange program on request realizations by Japanese learners of English. *Kanagawa University Studies in Language* 24, 91–103.

Cicourel, A. (1973) *Cognitive Sociology.* Harmondsworth: Penguin.

Clancy, P. (1985) The acquisition of Japanese. In D. Slobin (ed.) *The Cross-linguistic Study of Language Acquisition, Vol. 1: The Data* (pp. 373–524). Hillsdale, NJ: Lawrence Erlbaum Associate.

Clancy, P. (1986) The acquisition of communicative style in Japanese. In B. Schieffelin and E. Ochs (eds) *Language Socialization across Cultures* (pp. 213–250). Cambridge: Cambridge University Press.

Clancy, P., Suzuki, R., Tao, H. and Thompson, S. (1996) The conversational use of reactive tokens in English, Japanese and Mandarin. *Journal of Pragmatics* 26, 355–387.

Cook, H.M. (1990a) The role of the Japanese sentence-final particle *no* in the socialization of children. *Multilingua* 9, 377–395.

Cook, H.M. (1990b) An indexical account of the Japanese sentence-final particle *no. Discourse Processes* 13, 401–439.

Cook, H.M. (1992) Meanings of non-referential indexes: A case of the Japanese particle *ne. Text* 12, 507–539.

Cook, H.M. (1996a) Japanese language socialization: Indexing the modes of self. *Discourse Processes* 22, 171–197.

Cook, H.M. (1996b) The use of addressee honorifics in Japanese elementary school classroom. In N. Akatsuka, S. Iwasaki and S. Strauss (eds) *Japanese/Korean Linguistics* (Vol. 5, pp. 67–81). Stanford, CA: Center for the Study of Language and Information.

Cook, H.M. (1997) The role of the Japanese *masu* form in caregiver-child conversation. *Journal of Pragmatics* 28, 695–718.

Cook, H.M. (1998) Situational meaning of the Japanese social deixis: The mixed use of the *masu* and plain form. *Journal of Linguistic Anthropology* 8 (1), 87–110.

Cook, H.M. (2001) Why can't learners of Japanese as a foreign language distinguish polite from impolite speech styles? In K.R. Rose and G. Kasper (eds) *Pragmatics in Language Teaching* (pp. 80–102). New York: Cambridge University Press.

Cook, H.M. (2002a) Pragmatic judgments on politeness: A case study of 400-level JFL students. Paper presented at the American Association of Applied Linguistics Salt Lake City, UT, 1998.

Cook, H.M. (2002b) The social meanings of the Japanese plain form. In N. Akatsuka and S. Strauss (eds) *Japanese/Korean Linguistics* (Vol. 10, pp. 150–163). Stanford, CA: Center for the Study of Language and Information.

Cook, H.M. (2006a) Joint construction of folk belief by JFL learners and Japanese host families. In M. Dufon and E. Churchill (eds) *Language Learners in Study Abroad Contexts* (pp. 152–193). Clevedon: Multilingual Matters.

Cook, H.M. (2006b) Japanese politeness as an interactional achievement: Academic consultation sessions in Japanese universities. *Multilingua* 25, 269–292.

Cook, H.M. (in press) The pragmatics of Japanese sentence-final forms. In P. Clancy (ed.) *Japanese/Korean Linguistics 13*. CA: Stanford Linguistics Association.

Comrie, B. (1976) *Linguistic politeness axes: Speaker-addressee, speaker-referent, speaker-bystander*. Pragmatics Microfiche 1.7:A3. Dept. of Linguistics, University of Cambridge.

Coulmas, F. (1986) Direct and indirect speech in Japanese. In F. Coulmas (ed.) *Direct and Indirect Speech* (pp. 161–178). Berlin and New York: Mouton de Gruyter.

Curley, C.A. (1998) Teaching the body to make tea within social interaction. *Issues in Applied Linguistics* 9 (2), 151–178.

Day, R. (2005) An expose of the use of authentic materials. Brown bag talk. Dept. of Second Language Studies, University of Hawaii at Manoa, March 3.

Demuth, K. (1986) Prompting routines as cultural influences upon language acquisition. In B. Schieffelin and E. Ochs (eds) *Language Socialization across Cultures* (pp. 51–79). Cambridge: Cambridge University Press.

Dewey, D. (2005) Maximizing learning during study abroad: Some research-based programmatic suggestions. *Occasional Papers, Association of Teachers of Japanese* 3–11.

Duff, P. (2002) The discursive co-construction of knowledge, identity and difference: An ethnography of communication in the high school mainstream. *Applied Linguistics* 23 (3), 289–322.

Duff, P. and Early, M. (1999) Language socialization in perspective: Classroom discourse in high school humanities courses. Paper presented at the American Association for Applied Linguistics Conference, Stamford, CT, March.

Duff, P. and Hornberger, N.H. (eds) (2008) *Encyclopedia of Language and Education, Volume 8: Language Socialization* (2nd edn). Heidelberg: Springer.

Duff, P., Wong, P. and Early, M. (2000) Learning language for work and life: The linguistic socialization of immigrant Canadians seeking careers in healthcare. *Canadian Modern Language Review* 57 (1), 9–57.

DuFon, M. (1999) The acquisition of linguistic politeness in Indonesian by sojourners in naturalistic interactions. Unpublished doctoral dissertation, University of Hawaii, Honolulu.

DuFon, M. (2006) The socialization of taste during study abroad in Indonesia. In M. Dufon and E. Churchill (eds) *Language Learners in Study Abroad Contexts* (pp. 114–151). Clevedon: Multilingual Matters.

DuFon, M. and Churchill, E. (eds) (2006) *Language Learners in Study Abroad Contexts*. Clevedon: Multilingual Matters.

Dunn, C. (1999) Public and private voices: Japanese style shifting and the display of affective intensity. In G. Palmer and D. Occhi (eds) *Languages of Sentiment: Cultural Constructions of Emotional Substrates* (pp. 107–127). Amsterdam: John Benjamins.

Duranti, A. (1984) *Intentions, Self and Local Theories of Meaning: Words and Social Action in a Samoan Context*. La Jolla: Center for Human Information Processing: University of California San Diego.

Duranti, A. (2006) Agency in language. In A. Duranti (ed.) *A Companion to Linguistic Anthropology* (pp. 451–473). Malden, MA: Blackwell Publishing.

Duranti, A. and Goodwin, C. (1992) *Rethinking Context: Language as an Interactive Phenomenon*. Cambridge: Cambridge University Press.

Eckert, P. and Rickford, J. (2001) *Style and Sociolinguistic Variation*. Cambridge: Cambridge University Press.

Eisenberg, A. (1986) Teasing: Verbal play in two Mexicano homes. In B. Schieffelin and E. Ochs (eds) *Language Socialization across Cultures* (pp. 182–198). Cambridge: Cambridge University Press.

Ervin-Tripp, S. (1972) On sociolinguistic rules: Alternation and co-occurrence. In J. Gumperz and D. Hymes (eds) *Directions in Sociolinguistics: The Ethnography of Communication* (pp. 213–250). New York: Holt, Rinehart and Winston.

Ferguson, C. (1975) Toward a characterization of English foreigner talk. *Anthropological Linguistics* 17, 1–14.

Ferguson, C. (1981) 'Foreigner talk' as the name of a simplified register. In M. Clyne (ed.) *International Journal of the Sociology of Language* (Vol. 28). The Hague: Mouton.

Fillmore, C. (1971) *Toward a theory of deixis*. The PCCLLU papers.

Fillmore, C. (1975) *Santa Cruz lectures on deixis*. Mimeo, Indiana University Linguistic Club.

Fillmore, C. (1998) Deixis and context. In K. Malmkjear and J. Williams (eds) *Context in Language Learning and Language Understanding*. New York: Cambridge University Press.

Fox, B. (2001) Evidentiality: Authority, responsibility, and entitlement in English conversation. *Journal of Linguistic Anthropology* 11, 167–192.

Freed, B. (1981) Foreigner talk, baby talk, native talk. In M. Clyne (ed.) *International Journal of the Sociology of Language* (Vol. 28). The Hague: Mouton.

Frommer, J.G. (1992) Languages for career and support. In W. Rivers (ed.) *Teaching Languages in College: Curriculum and Content* (pp. 91–116). Lincolnwood, IL: National Textbook Company.

Fukuda, C. (2005) Children's use of the *masu* form in play scenes. *Journal of Pragmatics* 37, 1037–1058.

Garfinkel, H. (1972) Remarks on ethnomethodology. In J. Gumperz and D. Hymes (eds) *Directions in Sociolinguistics: The Ethnography of Communication* (pp. 301–324). New York: Holt, Rinehart and Winston.

Gass, S. and Varonis, E.M. (1985) Variation in native speaker speech modification to non-native speakers. *Studies in Second Language Acquisition* 7, 37–58.

Giddens, A. (1979) *Central Problem in Social Theory: Action, Structure and Contradiction in Social Analysis*. Berkeley and Los Angeles: University of California Press.

Goffman, E. (1959) *The Presentation of Self in Everyday Life*. Garden City, NY: Doubleday Anchor Books.

Goffman, E. (1974) *Frame Analysis: An Essay on the Organization of Experience*. New York: Harper and Row.

Goffman, E. (1981) *Forms of Talk*. Philadelphia: University of Pennsylvania Press.

Goodwin, C. (1981) *Conversational Organization: Interaction Between Speakers and Hearers*. New York: Academic Press.

Goodwin, C. (1986) Between and within: Alternative sequential treatments of continuers and assessments. *Human Studies* 9, 205–217.

Grice, P.H. (1975) Logic and conversation. In P. Cole and J. Morgan (eds) *Syntax and Semantics 3: Speech Acts* (pp. 41–58). New York: Academic Press.

Gumperz, J. (1982) *Discourse Strategies*. Cambridge: Cambridge University Press.

Gumperz, J. (1986) Contextualization and understanding. Paper presented at the American Association for Applied Linguistics meeting.

Gumperz, J. (1996) The linguistic and cultural relativity of inference. In J. Gumperz and S. Levinson (eds) *Rethinking Linguistic Relativity* (pp. 374–406). Cambridge: Cambridge University Press.

Gumperz, J. and Levinson, S. (1996) Introduction to part III. In J. Gumperz and S. Levinson (eds) *Rethinking Linguistic Relativity* (pp. 225–231). Cambridge: Cambridge University Press.

Hanks, W. (1990) *Referential Practice: Language and Lived Space among the Maya*. Chicago: University of Chicago Press.

Hanks, W. (1992) The indexical ground of deictic reference. In A. Duranti and C. Goodwin (eds) *Rethinking Context* (pp. 43–76). Cambridge: Cambridge University Press.

Hanks, W. (1996) Language form and communicative practice. In J. Gumperz and S. Levinson (eds) *Rethinking Linguistic Relativity* (pp. 232–270). Cambridge: Cambridge University Press.

Hanks, W. (2000) *Intertexts: Writing on Language, Utterance, and Context*. Lanham, MD: Roman and Littlefield.

Harada, S-I. (1976) Honorifics. In M. Shibatani (ed.) *Syntax and Semantics 5: Japanese Generative Grammar* (pp. 499–561). New York: Academic Press.

Harmer, J. (1983) *The Practice of Teaching English*. London: Longman.

He, A.W. (1995) Co-constructing institutional identities: The case of student counselees. *Research on Language and Social Interaction* 28 (3), 213–231.

He, A.W. (2000) Grammatical and sequential organization of teacher's directives. *Linguistics and Education* 11 (2), 119–140.

He, A.W. (2003) Novices and their speech roles in Chinese heritage language classes. In R. Bayley and S. Schecter (eds) *Language Socialization in Bilingual and Multilingual Societies* (pp. 128–146). Clevedon: Multilingual Matters.

He, A.W. (2004) Identity construction in Chinese heritage language classes. *Pragmatics* 14 (2/3), 199–216.

Heath, S.B. (1986) What no bedtime story means: Narrative skills at home and school. In B. Schieffelin and E. Ochs (eds) *Language Socialization across Cultures* (pp. 97–124). Cambridge: Cambridge University Press.

Heritage, J. (1984) *Garfinkel and Ethnomethodology*. Cambridge: Polity Press.

Herron, C.A. and Seay, I. (1991) The effect of authentic oral texts on student listening comprehension in the foreign language classroom. *Foreign Language Annals* 24 (6), 487–495.

Hill, J. and Irvine, J. (eds) (1993) *Responsibility and Evidence in Oral Discourse*. Cambridge: Cambridge University Press.

Hinds, J. (1978) Conversational structure: An investigation based on Japanese interview discourse. In J. Hinds and I. Howard (eds) *Problems in Japanese Syntax and Semantics* (pp. 79–121). Tokyo: Kaitakusha.

Hiraike-Okawara, M. and Sakamoto, T. (1990) Japanese foreigner register in the use of vocabulary. In O. Kamada and W. Jacobsen (eds) *On Japanese and How to Teach It* (pp. 211–223). Tokyo: The Japan Times.

Hoffman-Hicks, S.D. (1999) The longitudinal development of French foreign language pragmatic competence: Evidence from study abroad. Unpublished doctoral dissertation, Indiana University.

Holms, J. and Myerhoff, M. (1999) The community of practice: Theories and methodology in language and gender research. *Language in Society* 28, 173–183.

Hymes, D. (1964) *Language in Culture and Society*. New York: Harper and Row.

Hymes, D. (1971) Competence and performance in linguistic theory. In R. Huxley and E. Ingram (eds) *Language Acquisition: Models and Methods* (pp. 3–28). London: Academic Press.

Hymes, D. (1972) Models of the interaction of language and social life. In J. Gumperz and D. Hymes (eds) *Directions in Sociolinguistics: The Ethnography of Communication* (pp. 35–71). New York: Holt, Rinehart and Winston.

Hymes, D. (1974) *Foundations in Sociolinguistics: An Ethnographic Approach.* Philadelphia: University of Pennsylvania Press.

Ide, S. (1982) Japanese sociolinguistics: Politeness and women's language. *Lingua* 57, 357–385.

Ide, S. (1989) Formal forms and discernment: Two neglected aspects of universals of linguistic politeness. *Multilingua* 8 (2/3), 223–248.

Ide, S. (1992) On the notion of wakimae: Toward an integrated framework of linguistic politeness. *Kotoba no Mozaiku, Mejiro Linguistics Society* 4, 298–305.

Ide, S. and Yoshida, M. (1999) Sociolinguistics: Honorifics and gender differences. In N. Tsujimura (ed.) *The Handbook of Japanese Linguistics* (pp. 444–478). Malden, MA: Blackwell.

Iino, M. (1996) "Excellent foreigner!": Gaijinization of Japanese language and culture in contact situations. PhD dissertation, University of Pennsylvania.

Iino, M. (2006) Norms of interaction in a Japanese homestay setting: Toward two-way flow of linguistic and cultural resources. In M. Dufon and E. Churchill (eds) *Language Learners in Study Abroad Contexts* (pp. 194–223). Clevedon: Multilingual Matters.

Ikuta, S. (1983) Speech level shift and conversational strategy in Japanese discourse. *Language Science* 5, 37–53.

Ikuta, S. (2002) Speech style shift as an interactional discourse strategy: A study of the shift between the use and non-use of des/mas in Japanese conversation interviews. Paper presented in the Japanese Speech Style Shift Symposium. University of Arizona, Tuscon, AZ, 8–10 March.

Irvine, J. (1979) Formality and informality in communicative events. *American Anthropologist* 81, 773–790.

Ishida, K. (2001) Learning the pragmatic functions of the Japanese "masu" and plain forms. Paper presented at the Annual Meeting of the Pacific Second Language Research Forum, Honolulu, HI.

Iwasaki, N. (2005) A year abroad in Japan: Participants' perspectives. *Occasional Papers, Association of Teachers of Japanese* 12–24.

Jorden, E. and Noda, M. (1987) *Japanese: The Spoken Language.* New Haven: Yale University Press.

Kamio, A. (1991) The theory of territory of information: The case of Japanese. *Journal of Pragmatics* 21, 67–100.

Kanagy, R. (1999) Interactional routines as a mechanism for L2 acquisition and socialization in an immersion context. *Journal of Pragmatics* 31, 1467–1492.

Kasper, G. (1997) The role of pragmatics in language teacher education. In K. Bardovi-Harlig and B. Hartford (eds) *Beyond Methods: Components of Second Language Teacher Education* (pp. 113–136). New York: McGraw-Hill.

Kasper, G. (2001) Four perspectives on L2 pragmatic development. *Applied Linguistics* 22, 502–530.

Kasper, G. and Rose, K. (2002) *Pragmatic Development in a Second Language.* Malden, MA: Blackwell.

Keane, W. (2001) Voice. In A. Duranti (ed.) *Key Terms in Language and Culture* (pp. 268–271). Malden, MA: Blackwell.

Kindaichi, H. (1982) *Nihongo Seminar* (Vol. 1). Tokyo: Chikuma Shoboo.

Kitano, H. (1999) On the interaction and grammar: Evidence form one use of the Japanese demonstrative *are. Pragmatics* 9, 383–400.

Klein, W., Dietrich, R. and Noyau, C. (1995) Conclusions. In R. Dietrich, W. Klein and C. Noyau (eds) *The Acquisition of Temporality in a Second Language* (pp. 261–280). Amsterdam: John Benjamins.

Knight, S. and Schmidt-Rinehart, B. (2002) Enhancing the homestay: Study abroad from the host family's perspective. *Foreign Language Annals* 35 (2), 190–201.

Kondo, S. (1997) The development of pragmatic competence by Japanese learners of English: Longitudinal study on interlanguage apologies. *Sophia Linguistica* 41, 265–284.

Kroskrity, P. (2001) Identity. In A. Duranti (ed.) *Key Terms in Language and Culture* (pp. 106–109). Malden, MA: Blackwell.

Labov, W. (1972) *Sociolinguistic Patterns*. Philadelphia: University of Pennsylvania Press.

Labov, W. (1984) Intensity. In D. Schiffrin (ed.) *Meaning, Form, and Use in Context: Linguistic Applications. Georgetown University Round Table on Language and Linguistics* (pp. 43–70). Washington D.C.: Georgetown University Press.

Lakoff, R. (1975) *Language and Women's Place*. New York: Harper and Row.

Lave, J. (1988) *Cognition in Practice: Mind, Mathematics, and Culture in Everyday Life*. Cambridge: Cambridge University Press.

Lave, J. and Wenger, E. (1991) *Situated Learning: Legitimate Peripheral Participation* (pp. 26–58). Cambridge: Cambridge University Press.

Lebra, T. (1976) *Japanese Patterns of Behavior*. Honolulu: University of Hawaii Press.

Leontyev, A.N. (1981a) *Problems of the Development of the Mind*. Moscow: Progress Publishers.

Leontyev, A.N. (1981b) The problem of activity in psychology. In J. Wertsch (ed.) *The Concept of Activity in Soviet Psychology*. Armonk, NY: M.E. Sharpe.

Levinson, S. (1983) *Pragmatics*. Cambridge: Cambridge University Press.

Levy, R. (1984) Emotion, knowing and culture. In R. Shweder and R. Levine (eds) *Culture Theory: Essays on Mind, Self, and Emotion* (pp. 214–237). Cambridge: Cambridge University Press.

Li, D. (2000) The pragmatics of making requests in the L2 workplace: A case study of language socialization. *Canadian Modern Language Review* 57 (1), 58–87.

Lo, A. (2004) Evidentiality and morality in a Korean heritage language school. *Pragmatics* 14 (2/3), 235–256.

Long, M. (1996) The role of linguistic environment in second language acquisition. In W. Ritchie and T. Bhatia (eds) *The Handbook of Second Language Acquisition* (pp. 413–468). San Diego: Academic Press.

Lucid, D.P. (1977) Introduction. In D.P. Lucid (ed.) *Soviet Semiotics*. Baltimore: John Hopkins University Press.

Lyons, J. (1977) *Semantics* (Vols. 1 and 2). Cambridge: Cambridge University Press.

MacWhinney, B. and Oshima-Takane, Y. (eds) (1998) *CHILDS Manual for Japanese*. Montreal: McGill University.

Makino, S. (1996) *Uchi to Soto no Gengo-Bunkagaku-Bunpoo o Bunka de Kiru* [*Culturo-Linguistics of Inside and Outside-Intersection between Language and Culture*]. Tokyo: ALC.

Makino, S. (2002) When does communication turn mentally inward?: A case study of Japanese formal-to-informal switching. In N. Akatsuka and S. Strauss (eds) *Japanese/Korean Linguistics* (Vol. 10, pp. 121–135). Stanford, CA: CSLI Publications.

Makino, S., Hatasa, Y. and Hatasa, K. (1998) *Nakama: Japanese Communication, Culture, and Context*. Boston and New York: Houghton Mifflin.

Marriott, H. (1993) Acquiring sociolinguistic competence: Australian secondary students in Japan. *Journal of Asian Pacific Communication* 4, 167–192.

Marriott, H. (1995) The acquisition of politeness patterns by exchange students in Japan. In B. Freed (ed.) *Second Language Acquisition in a Study Abroad Context* (pp. 197–224). Amsterdam: John Benjamins.

Martin, S. (1964) Speech levels in Japan and Korea. In D. Hymes (ed.) *Language in Culture and Society* (pp. 407–415). New York: Harper and Row.

Martin, S. (2004) *A Reference Grammar of Japanese*. Honolulu: University of Hawaii Press.

Matsumoto, Y. (2002) Gender identity and the presentation of self in Japanese. In S. Benor, M. Rose, D. Sharma, J. Sweetland and Q. Zhang (eds) *Gendered Practice in Language* (pp. 339–354). Stanford: CSLI.

Matsumoto, Y. and Okamoto, S. (2003) The construction of the Japanese language and culture in teaching Japanese as a foreign language. *Japanese Language and Literature* 37, 27–48.

Maynard, S. (1991) Pragmatics of discourse modality: A case of *da* and *desu/masu* forms in Japanese. *Journal of Pragmatics* 15, 551–582.

Maynard, S. (1993) *Discourse Modality: Subjectivity, Emotion and Voice in the Japanese Language*. Amsterdam: John Benjamins.

McGloin, N. (1990) Sex difference and sentence-final particles. In S. Ide and N. McGloin (eds) *Aspects of Japanese Women's Language* (pp. 23–41). Tokyo: Kuroshio Shuppan.

McMeekin, A.L. (2003) NS-NNS negotiation and communication strategy use in the host family versus the study abroad classroom. Unpublished doctoral dissertation, University of Hawaii-Manoa.

McMeekin, A.L. (2006) Negotiation in a Japanese study abroad setting. In M. Dufon and E. Churchill (eds) *Language Learners in Study Abroad Contexts* (pp. 225–255). Clevedon: Multilingual Matters.

McMeekin, A.L. (2007) Learners of Japanese and socialization through expert-novice negotiation in a study abroad setting. Paper presented at the 17th Conference on Pragmatics and Language Learning. Honolulu, Hawaii.

Megumi, M. (2002) The switching between *desu/masu* form and plain form: From the perspective of turn construction. In N. Akatsuka and S. Strauss (eds) *Japanese/Korean Linguistics* (Vol. 10, pp. 206–219). Stanford, CA: CSLI Publications.

Miller, P. (1986) Teasing as language socialization and verbal play in a white-working class community. In B. Schieffelin and E. Ochs (eds) *Language Socialization across Cultures* (pp. 199–211). New York: Cambridge: Cambridge University Press.

Mizutani, O. and Mizutani, N. (1995) *An Introduction to Modern Japanese*. Tokyo: The Japan Times.

Moeran, B. (1988) Japanese language and society: An anthropological approach. *Journal of Pragmatics* 12, 427–443.

Mushin, I. (2001) *Evidentiality and Epistemological Stance: Narrative Retelling*. Amsterdam: John Benjamins.

Myers-Scotton, C. (1993) *Social Motivations for Codeswitching: Evidence from Africa*. Oxford: Clarendon Press.

Myers-Scotton, C. and Bernsten, J. (1998) Natural conversation as a model for textbook dialogue. *Applied Linguistics* 9, 372–384.

Nakamura, K. (1996) Developmental pragmatics: A look at Japanese children's phone conversations. Paper presented at the 5th International Pragmatics Conference, Mexico City, Mexico.

Nakamura, K. (2002) Pragmatic development in Japanese monolingual children. In Y. Shirai, H. Kobayashi, S. Miyata, K. Nakamura, T. Ogura and H. Sirai (eds) *Studies in Language Sciences* (Vol. 2, pp. 23–41). Tokyo: Kuroshio Shuppan.

Nazikian, F. (2007) Shift of speech style and perspective in interview talk: Representing the other speaker and engaging audience. Paper presented at the 17th Conference on Pragmatics and Language Learning, Honolulu, Hawaii.

Neustupny, J.V. (1978) *Post-structural Approaches to Language: Language Theory in Japanese Context*. Tokyo: University of Tokyo Press.

Niyekawa, A.M. (1991) *Minimum Essential Politeness: A Guide to the Japanese Honorific Language*. Tokyo: Kodansha International.

Nostrand, H.L. (1989) Authentic texts and cultural authenticity: An editorial. *Modern Language Review* 73, 49–52.

Ochs, E. (1988) *Culture and Language Development*. Cambridge: Cambridge University Press.

Ochs, E. (1990) Indexicality and socialization. In G. Herdt, R. Shweder and J. Stigler (eds) *Cultural Psychology: Essays on Comparative Human Development* (pp. 287–307). Cambridge: Cambridge University Press.

Ochs, E. (1993) Constructing social identity: A language socialization perspective. *Research on Language and Social Interaction* 26 (3), 287–306.

Ochs, E. (1996) Linguistic resources for socializing humanity. In J. Gumperz and S. Levinson (eds) *Rethinking Linguistic Relativity* (pp. 407–437). Cambridge: Cambridge University Press.

Ochs, E. (2002) Becoming a speaker of culture. In C. Kramsch (ed.) *Language Socialization and Language Acquisition: Ecological Perspectives* (pp. 99–120). London and New York: Continuum Press.

Ochs, E. and Schieffelin, B. (1984) Language acquisition and socialization: Three developmental stories. In R. Shweder and R. LeVine (eds) *Culture Theory: Essays in Mind, Self, and Emotion* (pp. 276–320). Cambridge: Cambridge University Press.

Ochs, E. and Schieffelin, B. (1995) The impact of language socialization on grammatical development. In P. Fletcher and B. MacWhinney (eds) *Handbook of Child Language* (pp. 73–94). Malden, MA: Blackwell.

Ochs, E., Smith, R. and Taylor, C. (1989) Dinner narratives as detective stories. *Cultural Dynamics* 2, 238–257.

Ochs, E., Taylor, C., Rudolph, D. and Smith, R. (1992) Storytelling as a theory-building activity. *Discourse Processes* 15 (1), 37–72.

Ohta, A. (1993) The foreign language learner in Japanese society: Successful learners of Japanese respond to Miller's law of inverse returns. *Journal of the Association of Teachers of Japanese* 27, 205–228.

Ohta, A. (1999) Interactional routines and the socialization of interactional style in adult learners of Japanese. *Journal of Pragmatics* 31, 1493–1512.

Okamoto, S. (1995) 'Tasteless' Japanese: Less feminine speech among young Japanese women. In K. Hall and M. Bucholtz (eds) *Gender Articulated: Language and the Socially Constructed Self* (pp. 297–325). New York: Routledge.

Okamoto, S. (1998) The use and non-use of honorifics in sales talk in Kyoto and Osaka: Are they rude or friendly? In N. Akatsuka, H. Hoji, S. Iwasaki, S.-O.

Sohn and S. Strauss (eds) *Japanese/Korean Linguistics* (Vol. 7, pp. 141–157). Stanford, CA: Center for the Study of Language Information.

Okamoto, S. (1999) Situated politeness: Manipulating honorific and non-honorific expressions in Japanese conversation. *Pragmatics* 9, 51–74.

Okamoto, S. and Smith, J.S. (2004) *Japanese Language, Gender, and Ideology.* Oxford: Oxford University Press.

Ono, T. and Jones, K. (2005) Discourse-centered approaches to Japanese language pedagogy. *Japanese Language and Literature* 39, 237–254.

Peirce, C.S. (1955) *Philosophical Writings of Peirce.* New York: Dover Publishers.

Pomerantz, A. (1984) Agreeing and disagreeing with assessments: Some features of preferred/dispreferred turn shapes. In J.M. Atkinson and J. Heritage (eds) *Structures of Social Action: Studies in Conversation Analysis* (pp. 75–101). Cambridge: Cambridge University Press.

Poole, D. (1992) Language socialization in the second language classroom. *Language Learning* 42, 593–616.

Quinn, C. (1994a) *Uchi/soto*: Tip of a semiotic iceberg? 'Inside' and 'outside' knowledge in the grammar of Japanese. In J. Bachnik and C. Quinn (eds) *Situated Meaning: Inside and Outside in Japanese Self, Society, and Language* (pp. 247–294). New Jersey: Princeton University Press.

Quinn, C. (1994b) The terms *uchi* and *soto* as windows on a world. In J. Bachnik and C. Quinn (eds) *Situated Meaning: Inside and Outside in Japanese Self, Society, and Language* (pp. 38–72). New Jersey: Princeton University Press.

Richardson, C. (1997) A study of Japanese "foreigner talk". Unpublished MA thesis, University of Hawaii-Manoa.

Rogoff, B. (1990) *Apprenticeship in Thinking: Cognitive Development in Social Context.* New York: Oxford University Press.

Rose, K and Ng Kwai-fun, C. (2001) Inductive and deductive teaching of compliments and compliment responses. In K. Rose and G. Kasper (eds) *Pragmatics in Language Teaching* (pp. 145–170). Cambridge: Cambridge University Press.

Rounds, P., Falsgraf, C. and Seya, R. (1997) Acquisition of sociolinguistic competence in a Japanese immersion school. *Journal of the Association of Teachers of Japanese* 31, 25–51.

Sacks, H., Schegloff, E. and Jefferson, G. (1974) A simplest systematics for the organization of turn-taking for conversation. *Language* 50, 696–735.

Sacks, H., Schegloff, E. and Jefferson, G. (1977) The preference for self-correction in the organization of repair in conversation. *Language* 53, 361–382.

Sawyer, M. (1992) The development of pragmatics in Japanese as a second language: The particle *ne*. In G. Kasper (ed.) *Pragmatics of Japanese as a Native and Target Language* (Technical Report #3, pp. 83–125). Honolulu: University of Hawaii, Second Language Teaching and Curriculum Center.

Schegloff, E. (1968) Sequencing in conversational openings. *American Anthropologist* 70, 1075–1095

Schegloff, E. (1980) Preliminaries to preliminaries: "Can I ask you a question?" *Sociological Inquiry* 50, 104–152.

Schieffelin, B. (1990) *The Give and Take of Everyday Life: Language Socialization of Kaluli Children.* Cambridge: Cambridge University Press.

Schieffelin, B. and Ochs, E. (1986) Language socialization. *Annual Review of Anthropology* 15, 163–191.

Schieffelin, B. and Ochs, E. (1996) The microgenesis of competence: Methodology in language socialization. In D. Slobin, J. Gerhardt, A. Kyratzis and J.S. Guo (eds) *Social Interaction Social Context, and Language: Essays in Honor of Susan Ervin-Trip* (pp. 251–263). Lawrence Erlbaum.

Schmidt, R. (1993) Consciousness, learning and interlanguage pragmatics. In G. Kasper and S. Blum-Kulka (eds) *Interlanguage Pragmatics* (pp. 21–42). Oxford: Oxford University Press.

Schmidt, R. (1995) *Attention and Awareness in Foreign Language Learning* (Technical Report No.9). Hawaii: University of Hawaii Second Language Teaching and Curriculum Center.

Schmidt, R. (2001) Attention. In P. Robinson (ed.) *Cognition and Second Language Instruction* (pp. 3–33). New York: Cambridge University Press.

Searle, J. (1969) *Speech Acts*. Cambridge: Cambridge University Press.

Searle, J. (1975) Indirect speech acts. In P. Cole and J.L. Morgan (eds) *Syntax and Semantics 3: Speech Acts* (pp. 59–82). New York: Academic Press.

Searle, J. (1979) *Expression and Meaning*. Cambridge: Cambridge University Press.

Shibatani, M. (1990) *The Languages of Japan*. Cambridge: Cambridge University Press.

Siegal, M. (1994) Looking East: Identity construction and white women learning Japanese. Unpublished doctoral dissertation, University of California at Berkeley.

Siegal, M. (1995) Individual differences and study abroad: Women learning Japanese in Japan. In B. Freed (ed.) *Second Language Acquisition in a Study Abroad Context* (pp. 225–244). Amsterdam: John Benjamins.

Siegal, M. (1996) The role of learner subjectivity in second language socio-linguistic competency: Western women learning Japanese. *Applied Linguistics* 17, 356–382.

Siegal, M. and Okamoto, S. (2003) Toward reconceptualizing the teaching and learning of gendered speech styles in Japanese as a foreign language. *Japanese Language and Literature* 37, 49–66.

Silverstein, M. (1976) Shifters, linguistic categories and cultural description. In K. Basso and H. Selby (eds) *Meaning in Anthropology* (pp. 11–55). Albuquerque: University of New Mexico.

Silverstein, M. (2001) The limits of awareness. In A. Duranti (ed.) *Linguistic Anthropology: A Reader* (pp. 328–401). Malden, MA: Blackwell.

Skoutarides, A. (1980) Nihongo ni okeru foorinaa tooku ['Foreigner talk' in Japanese]. *Nihongo Kyooiku* 45, 53–62.

Snow, C., Perlmann, R., Gleason, J. and Hooshyar, N. (1990) Developmental perspectives on politeness: Sources of children's knowledge. *Journal of Pragmatics* 14, 27–305.

Snow, C., van Eeden, R. and Muysken, P. (1981) The interactional origins of foreigner talk: Municipal employees and foreign workers. *International Journal of the Sociology of Language* 28, 81–92.

Strauss, S. (1995) Assessments as a window to socio-linguistic research: The case of Japanese, Korean, and (American) English. In M. Tokunaga (ed.) *Gengo-henyoo ni kansuru taikeiteki kenkyuu oyobi sono Nihongo kyoiku e no ooyoo. [Systematic Study of Language Variation with Applications for Japanese Foreign Language Education]* (pp. 177–191). Tokyo: Kanda University of Foreign Studies.

Sukle, R. (1994) *Uchi/soto*: Choices in directive speech acts in Japanese. In J. Bachnik and C. Quinn (eds) *Situated Meaning: Inside and Outside in Japanese Self, Society, and Language* (pp. 113–142). New Jersey: Princeton University Press.

Suzuki, T. (1984) *Words in Context* (A. Miura, trans.) Tokyo: Kodansha International.

Takagi, T. (2002) Data. Presented at the Japanese Speech Style Shift Symposium, University of Arizona, Tuscon, AZ, 9 March.

Takahashi, E., Harrington, M. and Yoda, N. (1995) Lexical composition of spoken JL2 textbooks: A comparison of textbook and authentic conversations. Paper presented at the Annual Meeting of the American Association of Applied Linguistics Long Beach, CA.

Takahashi, S. (2001) The role of input enhancement in developing pragmatic competence. In K. Rose and G. Kasper (eds) *Pragmatics in Language Teaching* (pp. 171–199). Cambridge: Cambridge University Press.

Tannen, D. (1989) *Talking Voices*. Cambridge: Cambridge University Press.

Tannen, D. (1993) *Framing in Discourse*. New York and Oxford: Oxford University Press.

Tannen, D. (2005) Abduction as indirectness: Borrowing identities in family. Paper presented at the 104th Annual Meeting of the American Anthropological Association, Washington, DC.

Tateyama, Y. (2001) Explicit and implicit teaching of pragmatic routines: Japanese *sumimasen*. In K. Rose and G. Kasper (eds) *Pragmatics in Language Teaching* (pp. 200–222). New York: Cambridge University Press.

Ten Have, P. (1999) *Doing Conversation Analysis*. London: Sage Publications.

Tohsaku, Y-H. (1994) *Yokoso: An Invitation to Contemporary Japanese*. Boston: McGraw-Hill.

Tohsaku, Y-H. (2006) Presentation at the HATJ Pre-Workshop, Honolulu, HI, 3 November.

Tsukuba Language Group (1992) *Situational Functional Japanese* (Vol. 1). Tokyo: Bonjinsha Co. Ltd.

Voloshinov, V.N. [Bakhtin] (1973/1929) *Marxism and the Philosophy of Language* (L. Matejka and I.R. Titunik, trans.) New York: Seminar Press.

Voloshinov, V.N. [Bakhtin] (1978/1929) Reported speech. In L. Matejka and K. Pomorska (eds) *Reading in Russian Poetics: Formalist and Structuralist Views* (pp. 176–196). Ann Arbor, MI: Michigan Slavic Publications.

Vygotsky, L.S. (1962) *Thought and Language* (E. Hanfmann and G. Vaker, trans.) Cambridge, MA: Harvard University Press.

Vygotsky, L.S. (1978) *Mind in Society*. Cambridge, MA: Harvard University Press.

Wade, J. (2003) Searching for "place" in the Japanese language classroom: Linguistic realizations of social identity in discourse and the acquisition of sociopragmatics. Unpublished doctoral dissertation, University of California-Berkeley.

Watson-Gegeo, K.A. (2001) Mind, language, and epistemology: Toward a language socialization paradigm for SLA. Plenary address presented at PacSLRF, Honolulu, October.

Watson-Gegeo, K.A. and Gegeo, D. (1986) Calling out and repeating routines in Kwara'ae children's language socialization. In B. Schieffelin and E. Ochs (eds) *Language Socialization across Cultures* (pp. 17–50). Cambridge: Cambridge University Press.

Watson-Gegeo, K.A. and Nielsen, S. (2003) Language socialization in SLA. In C. Doughty and M. Long (eds) *Handbook of Second Language Acquisition* (pp. 155–177). Oxford: Blackwell.

Wetzel, P.J. (1985) In-group/out-group deixis: Situational variation in the verbs of giving and receiving in Japanese. In J. Forgas (ed.) *Language and Social Situation* (pp. 141–157). New York: Springer-Verlag.

Wetzel, P.J. (1994) A movable self: The linguistic indexing of *uchi* and *soto*. In J. Bachnik and C. Quinn (eds) *Situated Meaning: Inside and Outside in Japanese Self, Society, and Language* (pp. 73–87). New Jersey: Princeton University Press.

Wetzel, P.J. (1995) Japanese social deixis and the pragmatic of politeness. *Japanese Discourse* 1, 85–105.

Wong, J. (2002) "Applying conversation analysis" in applied linguistics: Evaluating dialogue in English as a second language textbooks. *International Review of Applied Linguistics in Language Teaching* 40, 37–60.

Yamashita, S. (1996) Formal-informal style shifting in university JSL teacher talk. *Research Studies in TESOL* 4, 23–54. Tokyo: Temple University, Japan.

Yoshimi, D. (1999) L1 language socialization as a variable in the use of *ne* by L2 learners of Japanese. *Journal of Pragmatics* 31, 1513–1525.

Young, R. and He, A.W. (eds) (1998) *Talking and Testing: Discourse Approaches to the Assessment of Oral Proficiency.* Amsterdam: John Benjamins.

Zimmerman, D. (1998) Discourse, identities and social identities. In C. Antaki and S. Widdicomb (eds) *Identities in Talk* (pp. 87–106). London and New York: Academic Press.

Zuengler, J. and Cole, K. (2005) Language socialization and L2 learning. In E. Hinkel (ed.) *Handbook of Research in Second Language Teaching and Learning* (pp. 301–316). Mahwah, NJ: Lawrence Erlbaum.

# Index

addressee honorific(s) 1, 2, 8, 18, 35, 37, 199
affective stance 28-32, 46, 51, 64, 103, 104, 199
agency 3, 85, 177, 181, 185, 196
awareness 42, 43, 46, 49, 65, 67, 142, 147,
    160, 177, 194, 197, 202

Bachnik, J. 43, 65, 193
Bakhtin, M. 4, 20, 21, 26, 33, 34, 51, 62, 92, 102
Bourdieu, P. 25
Brown, P. 22, 37, 42, 64, 137, 138, 146, 201

Churchill, E. 6, 148, 204
Clancy, P. 2, 50, 54, 61, 65, 108, 142, 150, 151,
    166, 200
contextualization cue 20, 23, 24, 178
Cook, H.M. 1, 2, 4, 8, 10, 30-32, 34, 37, 38, 40,
    41, 45, 48, 51-54, 56, 57, 59-65, 67, 68, 80,
    105, 108, 145, 147, 151, 160, 161, 166,
    174-176, 178, 192, 195, 200, 204

deictic 2, 22-24, 34, 92, 93
deixis 2, 22-24
dinnertime 1, 2, 7, 8, 9, 10, 12-18, 35, 46, 50,
    64, 66, 70, 72-76, 80, 81, 85, 102, 104, 145,
    148, 155, 175, 178, 191, 200, 202
direct index 17, 28, 30, 31, 45, 48, 64, 76, 103,
    104, 149, 163, 192, 193, 195, 199, 200
direct quotation 21, 92, 93, 95, 96, 98, 99,
    102, 112, 123, 200
direct speech 92, 93, 103
Duff, P. 6, 203,
Dufon, M. 6, 10, 166, 178, 204
Duranti, A. 2, 3, 19, 26

epistemic stance 27-29
evidential 29, 203
explicit language socialization 18, 150, 151,
    153, 155, 157, 159, 161, 163, 165, 167, 169,
    171, 173, 175, 202

Fillmore, C. 22, 24
foreigner talk 19, 138, 139, 146, 197, 201
formality 1, 7, 8, 37, 44, 47-51, 66, 104, 148,
    193, 196, 199, 200

Goodwin, C. 2, 3, 19, 26, 128
Gumperz, J. 2, 9, 19, 20, 23, 24, 32, 178

Hanks, W. 2, 3, 22, 23, 32

He, A.W. 6, 7, 27-30
homestay 9, 17, 18, 69, 76, 103, 104, 107, 108,
    110, 112, 116, 149, 159, 166, 177-179, 181,
    196, 200-202, 204, 205
honorific form(s) 8, 19, 39, 158, 176
honorifics 1, 2, 7, 19, 24, 26, 30, 35, 37-40,
    106, 150, 155, 160, 166, 167, 174-176, 185,
    202
host family/families 1, 7, 8, 9, 10-18, 66, 69,
    70, 72-77, 81, 85, 94, 99, 103-105, 107, 108,
    112-114, 117-119, 121, 123-125, 129, 132,
    133, 137-139, 142, 145, 146, 148-151, 155,
    159-161, 163, 166, 174, 175, 177-183, 191,
    192, 197, 199-205

Ide, S. 8, 27, 30, 37-39
identity construction 5, 6, 66, 69, 71, 73, 75,
    77, 79, 81, 83, 85, 87, 89, 91, 93, 95, 97, 99,
    101, 103, 105, 200
Iino, M. 9, 10, 108, 138, 142, 166, 178, 191,
    204
indexical approach 1, 2, 4, 8, 17, 177,
    192-195, 199, 203
indexical relation 6, 17, 27, 28, 30, 31, 45,
    103, 163, 193, 200, 203
indexicality v, 1-4, 9, 17, 19, 21, 23-27, 29, 31,
    33, 45, 203
indirect index 28, 30, 103
indirect speech 25, 32, 92, 93
implicit language socialization 4, 7, 12, 202
interactional style 124, 137, 142, 145, 146,
    201, 205

Kasper, G. 1, 9, 10, 123, 177, 179, 181

language socialization 1-7, 9, 18, 33, 65, 66,
    142, 150-153, 155, 157, 159, 161, 163, 165,
    167, 169, 171, 173, 175, 180, 181, 193, 199,
    202-205
Leontyev, A.N. 4, 22, 33
Levinson, S. 2, 19, 22, 37, 42, 64, 137, 146,
    201

marked 3, 17, 18, 33, 58, 63, 68, 90, 104,
    107-115, 117-121, 123-125, 127, 129-133,
    135, 137-139, 141-147, 149
Marriott, H. 2, 8, 68, 179, 204
Matsumoto, Y. 27, 41, 44, 180, 186-188, 192
Maynard, S. 41-43, 46, 65, 105, 174, 194, 195

McMeekin, A. 10, 142, 178, 179, 205
metalinguistic 167, 172, 173, 175, 202
metapragmatic 160
modeling 4, 18, 150, 151, 153, 155, 159, 160, 175, 202
Myers-Scotton, C. 3, 17, 32, 33, 185

native speaker(s) 6, 7, 9, 11, 12, 15, 16, 17, 26, 47, 63-65, 67, 68, 70, 76, 105, 107, 108, 112, 113, 115, 116, 118, 119, 121, 123, 139, 145-148, 175, 177-181, 189, 191, 195-197, 204, 206
non-native speaker(s) 8, 105, 148, 191, 197, 214
non-referential index 24, 26, 29, 30

Ochs, E. 2-7, 10, 17, 18, 20, 25-30, 32, 33, 34, 45, 65, 66, 142, 150, 176, 199, 200, 202, 203
off-stage 160, 161, 163, 165, 166, 175, 194
Okamoto, S. 27, 37, 40, 41, 44, 63, 102, 105, 106, 166, 168, 173, 180, 186-188, 192, 195
on-stage vi, 45, 46, 63, 160, 161, 163, 165, 166, 175

politeness 1, 7, 8, 19, 20, 35, 37-39, 41, 42, 44, 47-49, 51, 53, 64, 66, 70, 95, 104, 106, 107, 110, 112, 115, 137, 138, 146, 148, 159, 172, 189, 191, 193, 194, 196, 199, 200, 201
pragmatic meaning 34
pre-sequence 127, 128, 135-137
proficiency 11, 13, 18, 68-70, 73, 74, 102, 108, 115, 119, 120, 121, 139, 146, 148, 159, 176, 178, 182, 185, 204

Quinn, C. 43, 65, 193

referent honorific form 158, 176
referent honorifics 38, 106, 150, 155, 160, 175, 202
referential index 23

Schieffelin, B. 2, 4-6, 20, 29, 66, 142, 150, 199, 202
Schmidt, R. 10, 67, 195, 204
self-presentational stance 8, 17, 46, 47, 49, 51, 56, 62, 65, 76, 85, 90, 92, 97, 102-104, 107, 160, 162, 163, 172, 175, 178, 192-196, 199, 200
set formula 51, 52, 63, 64, 76, 121, 122, 133, 148, 158, 175, 176
*shisei o tadasu* 46, 47, 62, 64, 173, 193, 199

Silverstein, M. 2, 4, 23, 24, 26, 47, 65, 195, 202
social meaning 7, 9, 17, 18, 19, 21, 23, 25, 27, 29, 30-37, 44, 47-49, 51, 65, 67, 105, 106, 147, 178, 193, 194, 199
sociocultural knowledge 3, 4, 6, 10, 61, 93, 196
sociolinguistic rules 166, 175, 176, 202
sociolinguistics 8, 23, 26
*soto* 1, 35, 42-44, 47-49, 51, 63-65, 93, 102, 103, 107, 108, 110, 112, 114-119, 127, 129-132, 145, 147-149, 151, 160, 161, 167, 176, 181, 191, 193, 196, 199, 200, 204
speech style 33, 37, 38, 65, 67-70, 73, 99, 104, 119, 121, 137, 138, 142, 146, 147, 153, 159, 160, 167, 175, 177, 179-181, 185, 186, 189, 191-193, 196, 197, 202-205
study abroad 6, 9, 10, 12, 18, 69, 123, 177-179, 181, 182, 196, 197, 203, 205
study abroad experience 12, 18, 123, 177, 178, 181, 196, 203
style shift(s) 8, 9, 15, 17, 18, 33, 35, 41, 62, 64-67, 69, 145, 161, 174, 177, 179, 181, 182, 185, 192, 195-197, 202, 204

Tannen, D. 92, 160
teaching voice 124, 132, 133, 135, 137, 138, 142, 143, 145, 146, 148, 166, 201, 202
textbook(s) 142, 177, 185-189, 193, 196-198
two-step indexical model 199
two-step model 6, 17, 28, 29, 203

*uchi* 2, 35, 43, 44, 47, 49, 50, 51, 62-65, 70, 76, 103, 107, 110, 112, 113, 118, 119, 121, 123, 127, 131, 132, 142, 145, 148, 149, 151, 176, 191, 193, 194, 196, 199, 200, 202
unmarked 3, 33, 103, 104, 107-109, 111-114, 118, 119, 121-125, 127, 129, 131-133, 135, 137, 139, 141, 143, 145-147, 149, 193, 201-204

voice 16, 19, 20, 21, 25, 34, 45, 47, 51, 56, 59, 60, 62, 64, 66, 75, 88, 93-98, 100, 101, 102, 124, 127, 129, 132, 133, 135, 137, 138, 139, 142-146, 148, 151, 153, 155, 162, 166, 178, 181, 194, 195, 201, 202
Voloshinov, V. N. 4, 20
Vygotsky, L. 4, 22, 33, 34

Watson-Gegeo, K. A. 6, 150
Wetzel, P. 34, 37, 43